the **BUSH ★ JUNTA**

Cartoonists on the Mayberry Machiavelli and the Abuse of Power

Edited by
Mack White & Gary Groth

Edited by *Mack White & Gary Groth*

Art Direction & Design by *Jacob Covey*

Promotion by *Eric Reynolds*

Published by *Gary Groth & Kim Thompson*

FANTAGRAPHICS BOOKS

7563 Lake City Way · Seattle, Wash. 98115 USA

Distributed in the USA by
WW Norton
tel: 212.354.5500

Distributed in Canada by
Raincoast
tel: 800.663.5714

Distributed in the UK by
Turnaround
tel: 011.44.208.829.3009

FIRST FANTAGRAPHICS BOOKS EDITION: SEPTEMBER, 2004 • ISBN 1-56097-612-8 • PRINTED IN CANADA

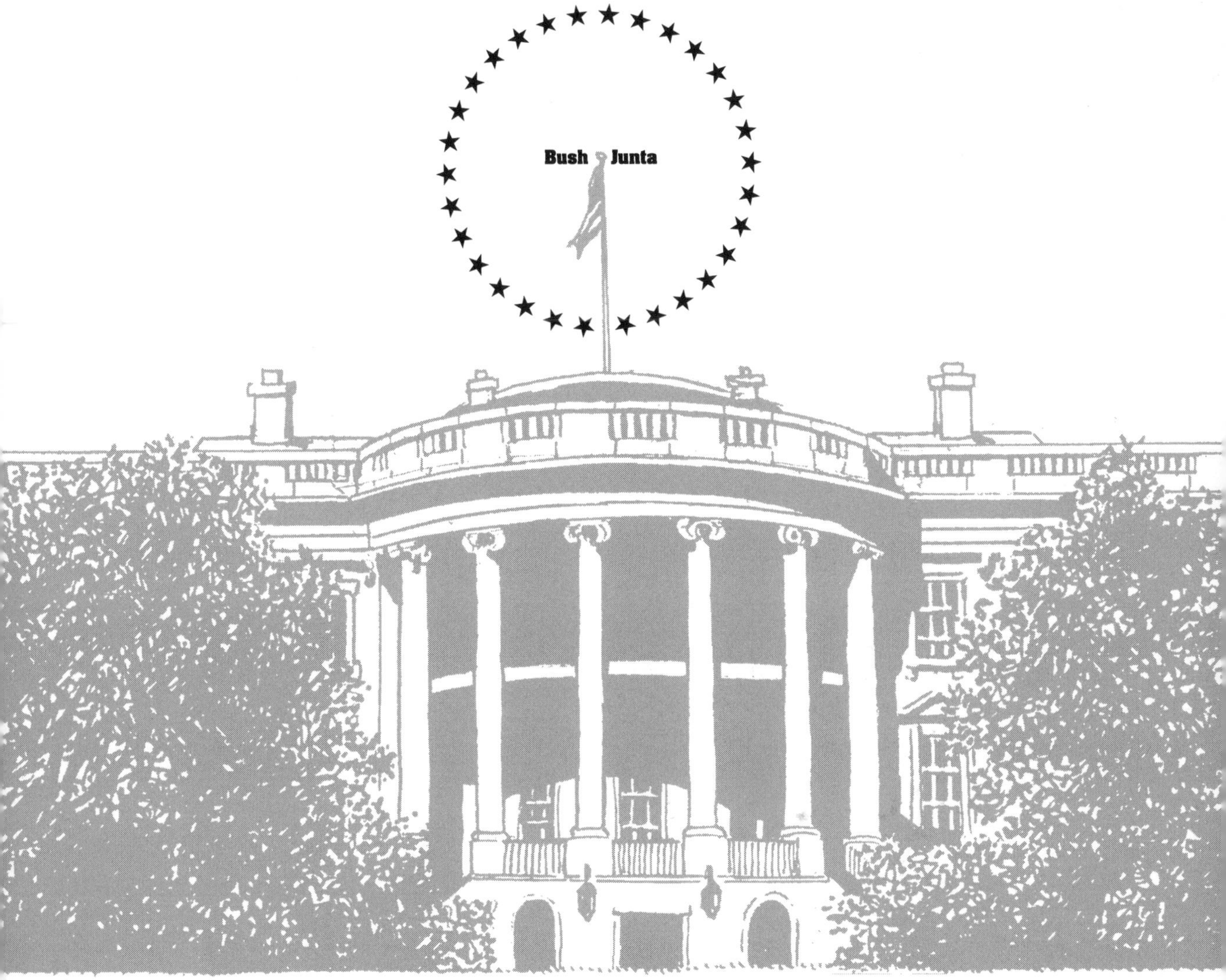
Bush Junta

Contents **Bush Junta** Contents

✓	Alex Jones	INTRODUCTION	vii
✓	Uri Dowbenko	FOREWORD	viii

★ ★ ★ ★ ★

SECTION I : THE FAMILY

✓	Marcel Ruijters	THE BUSH-NAZI CONNECTION	002
✓	Jaime Crespo	BAD TO THE BONE	011
✓	Albo Helm	SUPER SPOOK	020
✓	Larry Rodman	IRAN-CONTRA	027
✓	David Paleo & Mack White	THE BUSH-HINCKLEY CONNECTION	033
✓	Aleksandar Zograf & Mack White	OPERATION JUST CAUSE	038
✓	Jem Eaton	POPPY THE PRESIDENT	041
✓	Kenneth R. Smith	BUSH FAMILY VALUES	052

★ ★ ★ ★ ★

SECTION II : THE SON

✓	Scott Gilbert	THE SKIES OF TEXAS	072
✓	Penny Van Horn & Mack White	THE COMPASSIONATE CONSERVATIVE	077
✓	Carol Swain	FLORIDA 11/7/00	079
✓	Seth Tobocman	THE CARLYLE GROUP	089
✓	Ted Rail	CHECKLIST FOR THE NEO-FASCISTS	095
✓	Mack White	SEPTEMBER 11TH	099
✓	Steve Brodner	ENVIRONMENTAL PLUNDER ADMINISTRATION	108
✓	Alejandro Alvarez	CAMP X-RAY GUANTANAMO	110
✓	Spain Rodriguez	THE WAR	126
✓	Ethan Persoff & Jasun Huerta	YOUR VERY OWN INFORMATION CAMPAIGN	129

★ ★ ★ ★ ★

SECTION III : THE KEY PLAYERS

✓	Scott Marshall	SNOWFLAKE	140
✓	Lloyd Dangle	TURD BLOSSOM	155
✓	Ted Jouflas	WITH SWEETNESS	159
✓	Ethan Persoff	BLACKS, BABIES, AND BATTERED WOMEN	175
✓	Mark Landman	THE MAN IN THE SHADOWS	184
✓	Peter Kuper	CECI N'EST PAS UNE COMIC	194

★ ★ ★ ★ ★

✓	Adam Gorightly	AFTERWORD	198
		SOURCES	201
		ARTIST BIOGRAPHIES	215

Edited by Mack White and Gary Groth. Results published by Fantagraphics Books, Incorporated.
Not valid in Florida.

INTRODUCTION

★ ★ ★ ★ ★ ★ ★ ★ by Alex Jones

YOU are about to enter the real world. The book you hold in your hand is an amazing assemblage of world-class cartoonists exposing the Bush crime family. But this work is a lot bigger than just the Bushes. By focusing in on "W" and his handlers we get the big picture of corporations becoming the state and declaring themselves God and the people their slaves.

I have researched the overlords of this planet for many years and have exhaustively chronicled their crimes. Each of the works in this rich compilation gives the reader a look through a forbidden window into the sinister world of the New World Order. Mack White's incredible documentation blows wide open the events of September 11th. Marcel Ruijter's bombshell exposé of the Bush-Nazi connection will leave no doubt in your mind concerning the bloodthirsty nature of these creatures. The explosive pages tear away the façade of kingpins like Dick Cheney. John Ashcroft's fascist PATRIOT Act I and II is torn apart piece by piece by Ethan Persoff and Jasun Huerta. Witness the systematic dismantling of America and the Free World as a whole by an infinitely corrupt gaggle of control freaks and murderers.

The pages of this work are in reality a beautifully illustrated history of the Bush Syndicate as told by some of the world's most renowned cartoonists. The claims of this book are meticulously backed up by scholarly documentation. If you

IT'S THE FIRST COMIC BOOK IN HISTORY TO HAVE A BIBLIOGRAPHY

want a crash course in reality this is the book for you. And yes, it's terrifying because it's real. But at the same time you may be in danger of busting a gut or suffocating as you roll on the floor in uncontrolled laughter.

There is a massive awakening taking place. Not just in America but across the world. This is happening because millions of people have had the courage to get out of their denial, and to face the facts of the geo-political scene. We've got twenty-first century robber barons with legions of PR men spewing space age propaganda. But the truth explodes with the power of a thousand hydrogen bombs blasting away their mountain range of lies. Simply put, this book is an information warfare bomb and I suggest you use it to wake up your friends, your family and the people in your community. For some of you it's only confirmation of what you already knew. For others it will start your journey of discovery through the looking glass and down the rabbit hole. Buy this book, read it, research it, and confirm for yourself that it's true. It's up to **YOU**

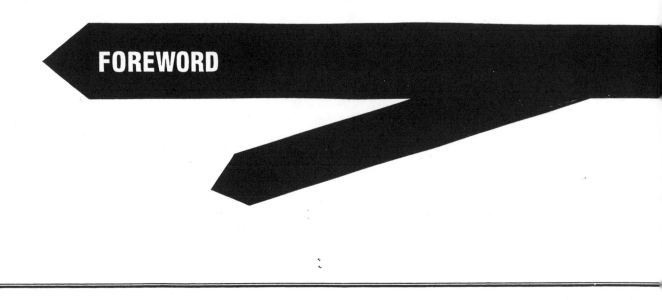

FOREWORD

Bush Junta. Bush Cabal. Bush Crime Family. Whatever you want to call it, this is the White-Collar Crime Syndicate that took over America. In no uncertain terms, the United States is now officially "One Nation Under Fraud."

OR AS SENATOR BOB DOLE ONCE SAID, "Ah... America, Land of the Naïve and Home of the Provincial. Thank God."

The Bush Junta by Mack White and his Merry Band of World Class Illustrators is a valuable contribution to art and literature, since it graphically connects the dots between history and current events. It is a treasure trove of true crime and sordid characters, a real world noir that is scarcely believable even though it's all true. Well documented and completely referenced, this book uses so many quotations from so many annotated sources that even the most anal-retentive academic will be happy.

The Bush Family has it all. Deviant elites. Aberrant psychology. High crimes and treason. Corporate/ government fraud. Even crimes against humanity. All weird. All true. And all censored by the mainstream media cartel.

This book could be subtitled "Weird! Bizarre! True! Tales from the Bush Family Closet."

You'll find suppressed and arcane facts that still read like heresy, when compared to the sanitized history books that pretend to tell the history of this planet.

"The Bush-Nazi Connection" illustrates how the Bush Family helped bankroll the Nazi War Machine during World War II, proving that no conflict of interest is too big for this family of blackguards. (Read *Rule by Secrecy* (Harper Collins) by Jim Marrs for a complete history of wickedness in high places.)

"The Bush-Hinckley Connection" illustrates the absolutely weird, but true story of how President Ronald Reagan's Vice President George H.W. Bush was connected with would-be Reagan assassin John Hinckley.

"Bad to the Bone: The Bush Family and Yale's Skull and Bone Society" covers the favorite secret society of America's Ruling Class (The Order), which counts as its members George Bush Sr., George Bush Jr., William F. Buckley and his son Christopher Buckley, among others. (For more information, read the ground-breaking classic by the late Professor Antony Sutton, America's Secret Establishment: An Introduction to the Order of Skull and Bones (TrineDay)).

Today's Bush Cabal is full of unsavory characters with sordid stories to match. "John Ashcroft: Missouri Years" is the wild and wooly

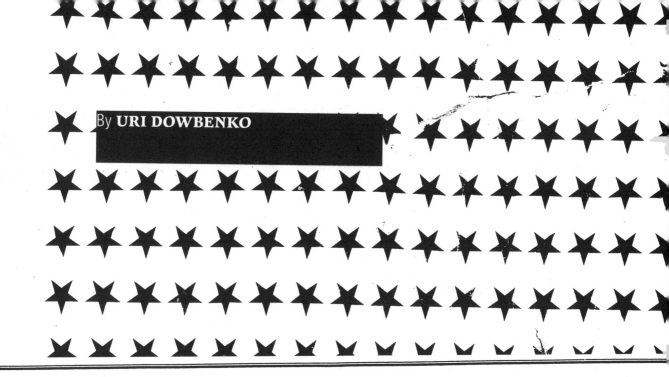

By **URI DOWBENKO**

history of Attorney General John Ashcroft, whose previous claim to fame was losing an election to a dead guy in Missouri – Mel Carnahan. Likewise "The Man in the Shadows" tells the story of Big Dick Cheney, Bush Sr.'s Secretary of Defense and Bush Jr.'s Vice President. Cheney is also the former Chairman and CEO of the fraud-driven Halliburton Corporation, which has gotten numerous no-bid no-fault contracts from the Pentagon and the Department of Justice for the War on Iraq and the War on Terrorism Scam.

"Iran Contra" tells the story of Bush Family involvement in the US Shadow Government during the mid-1980s, when government-sanctioned narcotics trafficking, illicit arms dealing and wholesale corporate-government fraud reached unprecedented levels. (For more details, read the uncensored memoir of Al Martin called The Conspirators: Secrets of an Iran Contra Insider (National Liberty Press; www.almartinraw.com). Martin, who calls himself a "Recovering Republican Scamscateer," has written The Conspirators as a true crime expose' of the Bush Cabal.)

"September 11" illustrates the confluence of events that led to the destruction of the World Trade Center in New York City on September 11, 2001. This traumatic shock against the nation's psyche was then used as a rationale for the USA Patriot Act, which brought the United States one step closer to a full-blown militarized police state. Like the Murder of President John F. Kennedy, "9/11" will be debated endlessly. It was after all the "New Pearl Harbor" for the 21st Century, which boosted spending for the Pentagon and the Homeland Security Scam, a brand new boondoggle for corporate-government insiders. As America's own "Reichstag Fire," an event which created a faux nouveau enemy, "9/11" remains a spectacular success in simultaneously paralyzing Americans with fear, while accelerating increasingly unsupportable budget deficits.

So what's missing in The Bush Junta? Nothing really. OK, there's no R. Crumb illustration of the apocryphal story of aging party animal brothers George and Jeb Bush landing at Florida's Tamiami Airport to pick up a couple of kilos of coke -- then inadvertently stumbling into a DEA sting. That's in a chapter called "Secrets of the Bush Crime Family" in my book Bushwhacked: Inside Stories of True Conspiracy (Conspiracy Digest; www.conspiracydigest.com).

The Bush Junta is as good as it gets. Interesting. Informative. Very entertaining. It's the perfect antidote to mainstream media, and the perfect artifact for the post-literate generation. Read it now. While we still have the First Amendment... Yuck. Yuck.

1

The Family

IT MAY BE TRITE TO COMPARE POLITICIANS TO HITLER, JUST BECAUSE ONE DOES NOT LIKE THEM. IN GEORGE W. BUSH'S CASE, IT IS SOMEWHAT LESS INAPPROPRIATE THAN IN OTHER'S—AND NOT ONLY BECAUSE OF HIS DESTRUCTIVE POLITICS. THERE'S ALSO THE...

BUSH-NAZI CONNECTION

©MARCEL RUIJTERS 2004

MUCH HAS BEEN SAID ABOUT HITLER'S AFFINITY FOR THE OCCULT (ALONG WITH SOME OF HIS CRONIES LIKE HESS OR HIMMLER).

WHILE HITLER'S CHARISMATIC SPELL OVER THE GERMAN CROWDS DURING HIS SPEECHES WAS UNCANNY AND CAN BE EASILY LABELLED AS DEMONIC, HIS METEORIC RISE TO POWER HAS LITTLE TO DO WITH HIS ASTRAL SIGN OR THE LEGENDARY SPEAR OF LONGINUS.
BAH! HUMBUG!

LIKE ANY ASPIRING POLITICIAN HITLER NEEDED MONEY, LOTS OF MONEY. AND CORPORATE BUSINESS WAS EAGER TO PROVIDE IT.

THE LIST OF NAZI SPONSORS IS FAIRLY WELL-KNOWN TODAY: I.G. FARBEN, KRUPP, BOSCH, SIEMENS, ITT, FORD, DUPONT, GENERAL ELECTRIC, STANDARD OIL, AND SO ON. WITHOUT A DOUBT, THE MOST GENEROUS SUPPORTER WAS FRITZ THYSSEN, THEN HEAD OF THE ALMIGHTY THYSSEN CORPORATION.

OF COURSE, MANY CORPORATIONS FINANCED THE NAZIS FOR OPPORTUNISTIC REASONS, BUT THYSSEN'S RELATIONSHIP WITH HITLER IS REPORTED AS A CORDIAL ONE.

THE N.S.D.A.P. WAS ABLE TO BUY THE PRESTIGIOUS "BRAUNE HAUS" IN MUNICH AND MAKE IT THEIR HEADQUARTERS, THANKS TO A GIFT OF 100.000 GOLD MARKS FROM THYSSEN IN 1923.

WE ARE TALKING OLD MONEY HERE, BUT IT WAS THE GREAT PATRIARCH AUGUST THYSSEN (1842-1926) WHO HAD MADE THE COMPANY INTO ONE OF GERMANY'S LEADING INDUSTRIES BY THE BEGINNING OF THE 20TH CENTURY. WITHOUT ITS GUNS AND CANNONS, GERMANY COULD NOT HAVE STARTED WORLD WAR I. A WAR THAT LEFT THE COUNTRY IN RUINS AND THE THYSSENS WITH EVEN GREATER RICHES. AUGUST DIVIDED THE CAPITAL BETWEEN HIS TWO SONS FRITZ AND HEINRICH. ONE HAD TO SIDE WITH THE NAZIS, THE OTHER TO OPPOSE THEM. AT LEAST, TO THE PUBLIC EYE...

SINCE THE MID 19TH CENTURY, THE THYSSENS HAD BEEN POWER-FUL ENOUGH TO ESTABLISH THEIR OWN BANKS WITH RESPECT-ABLE-SOUNDING NAMES. FRITZ THYSSEN WOULD PROVE HIMSELF WORTHY OF CARRYING ON THIS FAMILY TRADITION AND WAS EVEN SKILLFUL ENOUGH TO HIDE THEIR ASSETS FROM THE ALLIED FORCES AFTER WW2!

BHS

ROTTER-DAM

HOLLAND

HAMBURG

BERLIN

POLAND

SILESIA

RUHR REGION

FRANCE

GERMANY

SWITZER-LAND

AUSTRIA

MUCH OF THEIR MONEY-LAUND-ERING WENT THROUGH THE BANK VOOR HANDEL EN SCHEEP-VAART (BANK FOR COMMERCE AND SHIPPING), CLEVERLY ESTABLISHED IN HOLLAND IN 1926.

IN HIS APOLOGETIC, GHOST-WRITTEN AUTOBIOGRAPHY "I PAID HITLER", THYSSEN CLAIMED THAT HE QUIT SUPPORTING THE NAZI PARTY IN 1939 AFTER HE REALIZED WHAT THEY WERE PLANNING FOR THE JEWS. HE FURTHER CLAIMED THAT HE HIMSELF WAS PERSEC-UTED BY THE NAZIS, FLED TO SWITZERLAND AND WAS FINALLY CAPTURED IN 1942 IN VICHY-FRANCE. HOWEVER, OFFICIAL DOCUMENTS PROVE THAT HE WAS ABLE TO TRAVEL FREELY UNTIL THEN.

ANYWAY, MUCH OF THE MONEY THAT WAS BEING MADE WENT TO AMERICA VIA THE BHS-OWNED UNION BANKING CORPORATION, LOCATED AT 39 BROADWAY.

IT'S HERE WHERE WE MEET PRESCOTT SHELDON BUSH.

BROADWAY

PRESCOTT BUSH WAS MADE VICE-PRESIDENT OF THE U.B.C. BY HIS FATHER-IN-LAW, GEORGE HERBERT WALKER IN 1926 AFTER MARRYING WALKER'S DAUGHTER DOROTHY.
TOGETHER WITH HIS PARTNERS HARRIMAN AND BROWN BROTHERS, HE IS AT THIS POINT AN EMPLOYEE OF THE THYSSEN FIRM.
HE IS ALSO INVOLVED WITH THE NEWLY FORMED GERMAN STEEL TRUST, THANKS TO DILLON READ, A FRIEND OF HIS FATHER SAMUEL BUSH.

AH... ANOTHER GOOD DAY'S WORK!

MANY WALL STREET PLAYERS OF THE ERA WERE ENDORSING TOTALITARIANISM: THE BUSHES, WALKERS, HARRIMANS, LOVETTS, BROWN BROTHERS (WHO HAD BECOME RICH FROM SHIPPING SLAVE COTTON) THE ROCKEFELLERS, MONTAGU COLLET NORMAN OF THE BANK OF ENGLAND. EVEN THE WARBURGS, WHO STAYED IN GERMANY UNTIL 1938, WHEN LIFE HAD ALREADY BECOME UNBEARABLE FOR COMMON JEWS.

FASCISM = POLITICS X CORPORATE BUSINESS

IN 1927, AVERELL HARRIMAN REPORTED TO THE UBC ABOUT HIS FRUITFUL MEETING WITH MUSSOLINI.

HARRIMAN AND WALKER HAD TAKEN CONTROL OF THE STEAMSHIP COMPANY HAMBURG-AMERIKA LINE, BACK IN 1920. IN THE YEARS PRIOR TO HITLER'S ELECTION AS CHANCELLOR IN 1933, THE FIRM HAD BEEN CRUCIAL FOR THE ARMAMENT OF THE S.S. AND S.A. TONS OF REVOLVERS AND MACHINE GUNS WERE SMUGGLED INTO THE COUNTRY VIA HOLLANDS RIVER DELTA TO OBSTRUCT AND TERRORIZE THE OPPOSITION. THE GUNS WERE MADE IN THE UNITED STATES BY REMINGTON AND THOMSON.

MAX WARBURG OF HAMBURG, THEIR REPRESENTATIVE AT THE TIME, PROTECTED THE BUSH-WALKER CLAN FROM ALLEGATIONS OF SUPPORT TO ANTI-SEMITIC FORCES IN EUROPE. WITH THIS FAMOUS JEWISH BANKER AS THEIR ASSOCIATE, THEIR BUSINESS SEEMED ALL KOSHER TO THE AMERICAN SPONSORS.

WALKER, HARRIMAN AND BUSH WERE NOT TOO BOTHERED BY BEING PARTNERS TO TOP NAZI FRIEDRICH FLICK, EITHER, WHO, TOGETHER WITH THYSSEN, OWNED THE COAL AND ZINC MINES AND STEEL WORKS OF THE CONSOLIDATED SILESIAN STEEL CORPORATION, SITUATED IN SOUTHERN POLAND.

1934, PROBLEMS AROSE WITH POLISH ACCUSATIONS OF MISMANAGEMENT AND EMBEZZLEMENT. FLICK RETALIATED BY REPLACING THE POLISH WORKERS WITH GERMANS TO CONTINUE HIS CONTRIBUTION TO THE BUILD-UP OF HITLER'S WAR MACHINE. THE DISPUTE WAS ENDED BY THE BLITZKRIEG.

FOR MOST PEOPLE, THE START OF THE SECOND WORLD WAR FELT PRETTY MUCH LIKE THE END OF THE WORLD, BUT NOT FOR THE WALKER-BUSH DYNASTY AND THEIR FRIENDS.

HARRIMAN INTERNATIONAL CO, LED BY AVERELL HARRIMAN'S COUSIN OLIVER, HAD BEEN RESPONSIBLE FOR GERMAN EXPORTS TO THE U.S. SINCE 1933, AS WAS AGREED BETWEEN HJALMAR SCHACHT AND JOHN FOSTER DULLES.

WHILE MILLIONS WERE SLAUGHTERED, BUSINESS WENT ON AS USUAL. THAT IS, UNTIL OCTOBER 20 1942. UNDER THE 'TRADING WITH THE ENEMY' ACT, THE GOVERNMENT SEIZED THE STOCK SHARES OF THE UNION BANKING CORP. (OF WHICH THE BULK WAS OWNED BY E. ROLAND HARRIMAN) ON THE 28TH OF OCTOBER. ALSO THE HOLLAND-AMERICAN TRADING CORP AND SEAMLESS STEEL EQUIPMENT CORP, RUN BY THE UBC, FOLLOWED. NOVEMBER 17, INTERESTS IN THE SILESIAN-AMERICAN CORP WERE SEIZED.
BUT THAT WAS ABOUT ALL THE ROOSEVELT ADMINISTRATION DID AGAINST THESE BLATANT ACTS OF TREACHERY. WAS IT BECAUSE THE SCANDAL WOULD BE TOO DEMORALIZING FOR THE TROOPS WHO HAD BEEN SENT INTO WAR A YEAR BEFORE?

NONE OF THESE TRAITORS WAS BROUGHT TO JUSTICE. THE ONLY 'VICTIM' WAS BUSH'S OIL PARTNER WILLIAM FARISH I, WHO DIED OF A HEART ATTACK AFTER THE HEARINGS.

WILL FARISH III, THE SOLE HEIR, IS STILL A FRIEND OF THE BUSH'S.

IN A MOVE TO CLEAR THE FAMILY'S NAME, GEORGE H.W. BUSH, WHO HAD TURNED 18, WAS SENT TO JOIN THE AIR FORCE. GEORGE BUSH WAS SHOT DOWN IN A BATTLE OVER THE PACIFIC AND GIVEN A MEDAL OF HONOR. HOWEVER, RUMOR HAS IT THAT HE BAILED OUT TOO SOON AND LEFT HIS TWO CO-PILOTS TO DIE IN THE PLANE, JUST TO SAVE HIS OWN HIDE.

ANYWAY, HE DID BETTER THAN HIS FATHER. PRESCOTT BUSH HAD BEEN EXPOSED AS A FRAUDULENT WAR HERO IN WW1 IN FRANCE, MUCH TO HIS EMBARRASSMENT.

1945. HITLER COMMITTED SUICIDE. THE NIGHTMARE OF W.W.2 WAS FINALLY OVER. OR WAS IT?

THEN THERE WAS, AMONG OTHER THINGS, THE MATTER OF THE NAZI LOOT, WHICH WAS BEING RAPIDLY RELOCATED OVER THE GLOBE.

CONSIDERING THE FACT THAT SUCH POWERFUL AMERICANS HAD BEEN IN LEAGUE WITH THE NAZIS, IT COMES AS NO SURPRISE THAT SO MANY GOT AWAY. FOR INSTANCE, FRIEDRICH FLICK ONLY SERVED THREE YEARS IN JAIL, THEN GOT HIS MONEY BACK AND DIED A BILLIONAIRE IN 1972. THE MAN WHO PARDONED FLICK IN 1951 WAS JOHN JAY MCCLOY, THE LEGAL COUNSELLOR FOR I.G. FARBEN IN THE U.S. THIS WAS THE FIRM THAT OPERATED THE CONCENTRATION CAMPS. MCCLOY WAS ONE OF THE MEN THAT OBSTRUCTED THE BOMBING OF THE RAILWAYS TO THOSE CAMPS. HE WENT ON TO WORK FOR THE FORD FOUNDATION (THE BIGGEST AMERICAN NAZI SPONSOR), THE MANHATTAN CHASE BANK AND EVENTUALLY BECAME PRESIDENT OF THE WORLD BANK. HE ALSO PARDONED THYSSEN, SCHACHT AND KRUPP.

JUST DON'T DO IT AGAIN!

tap

GENERAL WILLIAM H. DRAPER JR, WHO HAD BEEN WORKING WITH BUSH FOR THE THYSSENS AND FINANCED THE INTERNATIONAL EUGENETICS CONGRESS IN NEW YORK IN 1932, WAS APPOINTED TO "DE-NAZIFY" GERMAN CORPORATE BUSINESS.

ALSO ALLEN DULLES WORKED WITH BUSH AS A LEGAL COUNSELLOR (SPY) FOR I.G. FARBEN AND STANDARD OIL, WHICH WERE CONTROLLED BY THE ROCKEFELLERS BEFORE, DURING AND AFTER THE WAR.

TOGETHER WITH GERMAN MASTER-SPY GERHARD GEHLEN, DULLES ARRANGED THE SECRET IMMIGRATION OF 760 SCIENTISTS WHO WERE HARD-CORE NAZIS INTO THE U.S. THIS IS NOW KNOWN AS "PROJECT PAPERCLIP".

IN 1951, FRITZ THYSSEN DIED IN ARGENTINA. PRESCOTT BUSH AND HIS FATHER-IN-LAW RECLAIMED THE UNION BANK FROM THE U.S. ALIEN PROPERTY CUSTODIAN AND WERE ABLE TO CASH IN THEIR SHARES FOR A COOL $1.500.000 EACH.

ALL THAT TROUBLE FOR NOTHING! ACH!

IN SHORT, IT TOOK QUITE SOME CLEVER SCHEMING TO CONCEAL THE ORIGIN OF THE BUSH FORTUNE AND CHANGE THEIR PUBLIC IMAGE FROM THIS...

New York Herald Tribune

THYSSEN HAD 3 MILLION CASH IN NY VAULTS

OH SHIT!

...TO THIS: IN 1952, PRESCOTT BUSH WAS ELECTED AS SENATOR. AND HIS OFFSPRING? PRESIDENTIAL MATERIAL!

THANK YOU AND GOD BLESS AMERICA!

THE END

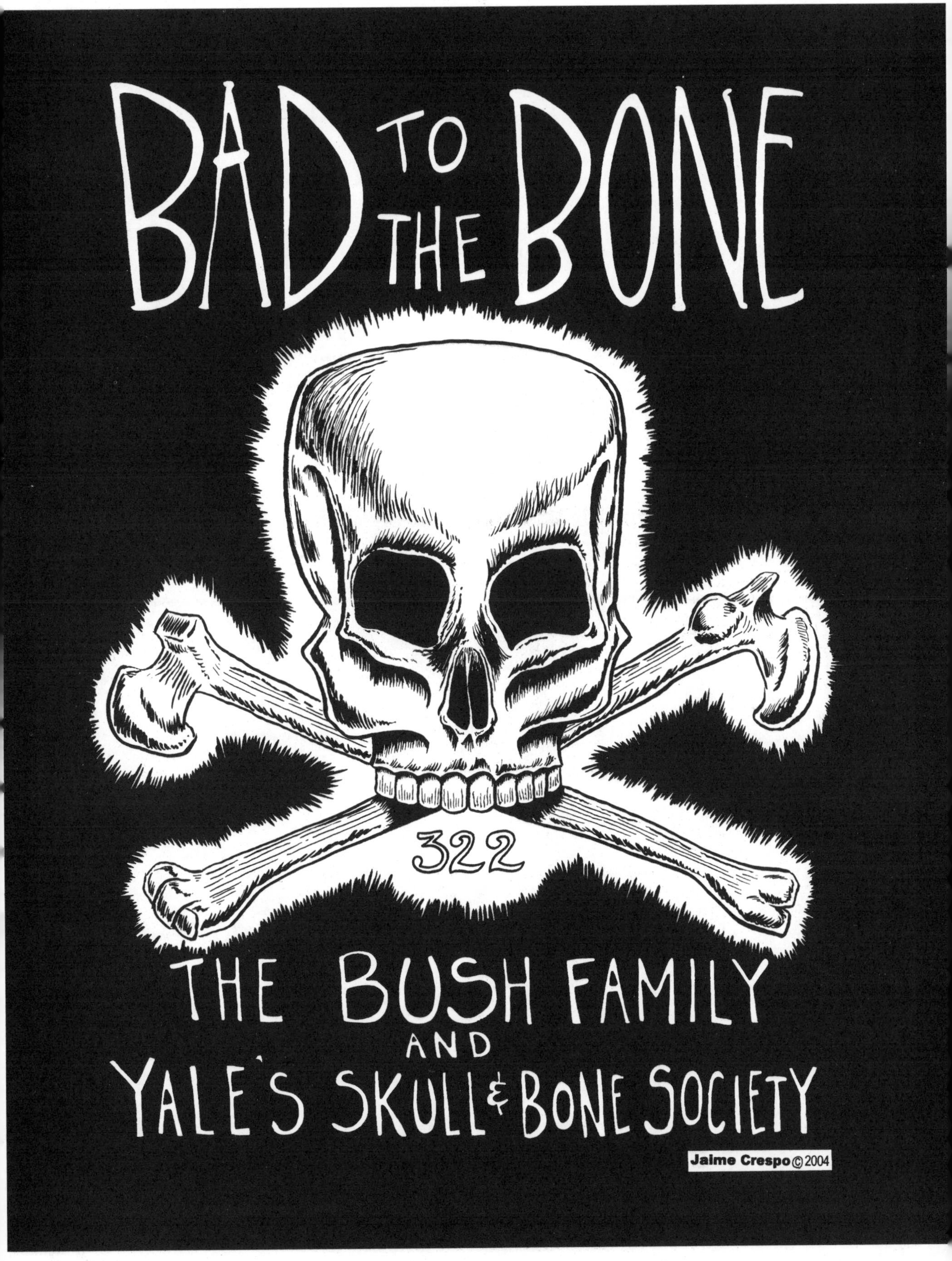
BAD TO THE BONE
322
THE BUSH FAMILY
AND
YALE'S SKULL & BONE SOCIETY
Jaime Crespo © 2004

The irony is not far from the surface.
A symbol that has traditionally been used by pirates and on poisons.

The Order of Skull and Bones began at Yale by one William Huntington Russell. His cousin was Samuel Russell, whose family operated as America's largest opium smugglers.

ʕʕʕ

Many families of the New England region as well as the south who were involved in the "China trade" sent their sons to Yale where many were tapped into the Skull and Bones.

The roll call of Skull and Bones is a proverbial "who's who" of America's most powerful families:

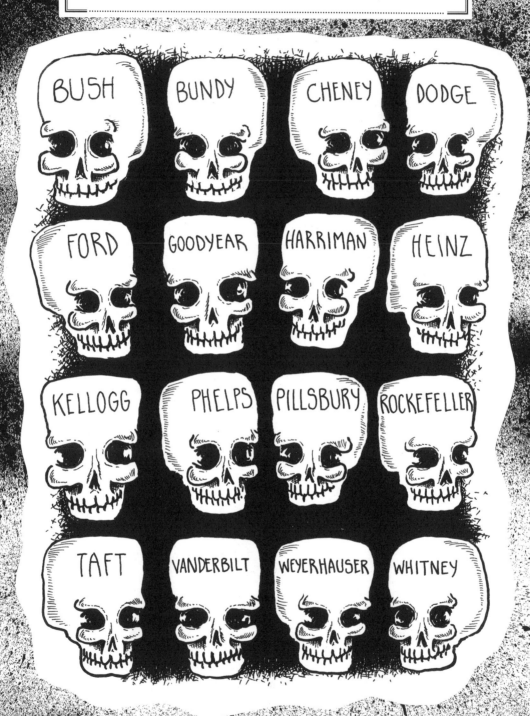

These are but a few.

Richard M. Bissell, Jr., though not in Skull and Bones, was the younger brother of William Truesdale Bissell, a Bonesman from the Class of 1925. Their father, Connecticut insurance executive Richard M. Bissell Sr., was a powerful Yale alumnus and the director of the Neuro-Psychiatric Institute of the Hartford Retreat for the Insane. There, in 1904, Yale graduate Clifford Beers underwent mind-destroying treatment which led to the founding of the Mental Hygiene Society, a Yale-based Skull and Bones project.

ℰℰℰ

This would evolve into the CIA's cultural engineering effort of the 1950's, the drugs and brainwashing adventure known as "*MK Ultra.*"

The Bush Family tradition started with Prescott Bush who, during his tenure at Yale as a Bonesman, dug up the bones of the great Native-American leader Geronimo with three other Bonesmen and took the remains back to the Yale campus, placing them inside the "Tomb," the house of the secret Skull and Bones Society where they are said to still be.

ɞ ɞ ɞ

Just before the outbreak of WWII as well as during the war, Prescott Bush and his father-in-law, George Herbert Walker, along with German industrialist Fritz Thyssen, financed Adolf Hitler and made considerable profits off of Auschwitz slave labor.

In fact, *President George W. Bush* is an heir to these profits from the Holocaust which was placed in a blind trust in 1980 by his father, George H.W. Bush.

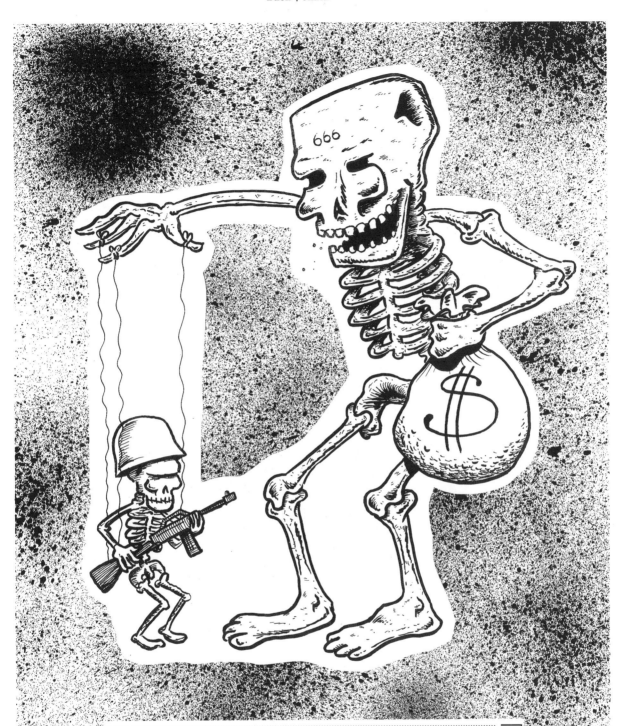

Today we see our government being operated like a secret society as we continue through present actions in the Middle East and elsewhere.

ℭ ℭ ℭ

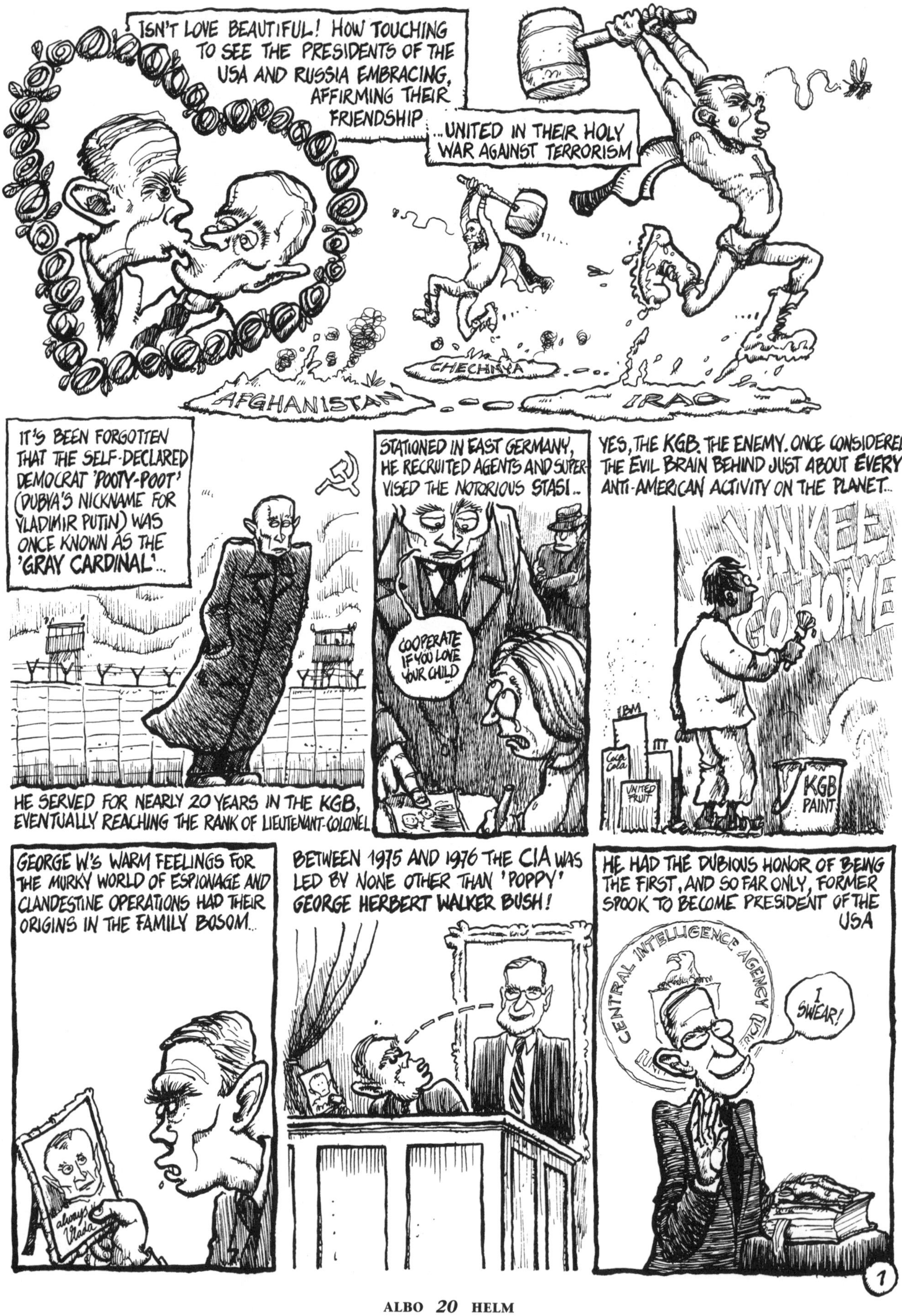
ISN'T LOVE BEAUTIFUL! HOW TOUCHING TO SEE THE PRESIDENTS OF THE USA AND RUSSIA EMBRACING, AFFIRMING THEIR FRIENDSHIP
...UNITED IN THEIR HOLY WAR AGAINST TERRORISM
AFGHANISTAN
CHECHNYA
IRAQ
IT'S BEEN FORGOTTEN THAT THE SELF-DECLARED DEMOCRAT 'POOTY-POOT' (DUBYA'S NICKNAME FOR VLADIMIR PUTIN) WAS ONCE KNOWN AS THE 'GRAY CARDINAL'...
HE SERVED FOR NEARLY 20 YEARS IN THE KGB, EVENTUALLY REACHING THE RANK OF LIEUTENANT-COLONEL
STATIONED IN EAST GERMANY, HE RECRUITED AGENTS AND SUPERVISED THE NOTORIOUS STASI...
COOPERATE IF YOU LOVE YOUR CHILD
YES, THE KGB. THE ENEMY. ONCE CONSIDERED THE EVIL BRAIN BEHIND JUST ABOUT EVERY ANTI-AMERICAN ACTIVITY ON THE PLANET...
YANKEE GO HOME
IBM
ITT
Coca Cola
UNITED FRUIT
KGB PAINT
GEORGE W.'S WARM FEELINGS FOR THE MURKY WORLD OF ESPIONAGE AND CLANDESTINE OPERATIONS HAD THEIR ORIGINS IN THE FAMILY BOSOM...
always Vlada
BETWEEN 1975 AND 1976 THE CIA WAS LED BY NONE OTHER THAN 'POPPY' GEORGE HERBERT WALKER BUSH!
HE HAD THE DUBIOUS HONOR OF BEING THE FIRST, AND SO FAR ONLY, FORMER SPOOK TO BECOME PRESIDENT OF THE USA
CENTRAL INTELLIGENCE AGENCY
I SWEAR!
7

FORMER SPOOK? YOU MUST BE JOKING! GHW's WORK FOR THE AGENCY NEVER ENDED..

SUPERSPOOK

THE CAREER OF THE MAN WHO CLAIMED TO BE AN OUTSIDER WHEN HE WAS APPOINTED CHIEF SPOOK BEGINS IN MIAMI 1960

CIA AGENT GHW USES HIS ZAPATA OIL COMPANY AS A SMOKESCREEN..

..TO RECRUIT CUBAN EMIGRANTS FOR ANTI-CASTRO OPERATIONS

②

USING THE CODE NAME JM/WAVE, AN UNDERCOVER ARMY IS FORMED OF CUBANS TRAINED TO CARRY OUT POLITICAL AND TERRORIST ATTACKS

GHW IS ALSO INVOLVED IN TRANSFORMING THREE FORMER NAVAL VESSELS INTO THE FREIGHTERS 'ZAPATA', 'HOUSTON' AND 'BARBARA'

THAT'S MY GAL

CHE'S WATCH

ONE OF THE EMIGRANTS, FELIX RODRIGUEZ, BECOMES A PERSONAL FRIEND OF GHW. RODRIGUEZ WAS POLICE COMMANDER DURING THE BATISTA DICTATORSHIP. HE BECAME 'FAMOUS' FOR KILLING CHE GUEVARA

...THESE ARE USED IN THE CIA'S DISASTROUS BAY OF PIGS INVASION

CUBA APRIL 1961

THE CUBAN ARMY AND NATIONAL GUARD KILL 114 ANTI-CASTRISTS..

...AND CAPTURE 1189...

CIA AGENTS BLAME THE DISASTER ON PRESIDENT KENNEDY, WHOM THEY ACCUSE OF FAILING TO SUPPORT THEM...

DALLAS TEXAS NOVEMBER 1963

BANG BANG

③

THE NAMES RODRIGUEZ AND BUSH APPEAR AGAIN DURING THE INVESTIGATION INTO THE ASSASSINATION OF JFK.

VOILÀ!

?

AN FBI-DOCUMENT POINTS TO ANTI-CASTRO EMIGRANTS IN FLORIDA. THE CIA AT FIRST VEHEMENTLY DENIES ANY KNOWLEDGE, BUT THEN - UNUSUALLY FOR AN INTELLIGENCE AGENCY - REVEALS THE BUSH MENTIONED IS A GEORGE WILLIAM BUSH, AN INSIGNIFICANT CIA CLERK. THIS MAN, TOO, KNOWS NOTHING

GHW BUSH'S NAME ALSO APPEARS IN THE ADDRESS BOOK OF GEORGE DE MOHRENSCHILDT, A CIA FREE-LANCER AND FRIEND OF KENNEDY'S ALLEGED KILLER LEE HARVEY OSWALD

SAY CHEESE!

POPPY? THAT YOU?

AFTERWARDS, GHW EXCHANGES HIS OIL RIGS FOR POLITICS

ZAPATA

REPUBLICAN PARTY

HE CLIMBS UPWARDS: FIRST CONGRESS, THEN U.S. AMBASSADOR TO THE U.N., NEW YORK 1971-1973

DURING THIS PERIOD A NUMBER OF UNSOLVED BREAK-INS ARE COMMITTED IN THE NEW YORK AREA. THE MAJOR TARGETS ARE CHILEAN POLITICIANS AND THE CHILEAN EMBASSY. THEY OCCUR WHEN THE SOCIALIST ALLENDE IS PRESIDENT OF CHILE (HE IS ASSASSINATED ON SEPTEMBER 11, 1973 DURING A CIA-BACKED MILITARY COUP)...

HOWEVER, THOSE WHO BREAK INTO THE HEADQUARTERS OF THE DEMOCRATS AT THE WATERGATE BUILDING ARE ARRESTED

WASHINGTON 1973

④

THIS GROUP OF CIA AGENTS ARE KNOWN AS THE WHITE HOUSE PLUMBERS, AND INCLUDE CUBANS INVOLVED WITH THE BAY OF PIGS INVASION

FIX YOUR SINK, MISTER?

THEY ARE FINANCED BY GHW'S ZAPATA BUSINESS PARTNER **WILLIAM LIEDTKE**, WHO COLLECTS THE FUNDS FROM THEIR MUTUAL BUSINESS ASSOCIATES (THROUGH THE COMMITTEE TO RE-ELECT THE PRESIDENT- CREEP)

AS REPUBLICAN PARTY CHAIRMAN, GHW PLAYS A CRUCIAL ROLE IN ENSURING NO EMBARRASSING DETAILS COME TO LIGHT AND LATER THAT NIXON STEP DOWN AS PRESIDENT

ET TU..?

THE WHOLE AFFAIR IS CONSIDERED AN ATTEMPT BY THE MILITARY-INDUSTRIAL COMPLEX TO TIGHTEN ITS GRIP ON AMERICAN POLITICS...

IN ORDER TO PROTECT BUSH FROM WATERGATE'S FALL-OUT, HE IS SENT TO BEIJING AS LIAISON OFFICER IN 1974... SUCCEEDING FORMER OSS COMMANDER DAVID BRUCE...

USA

CHINA

...HERE HE ENJOYS EXCEPTIONALLY GOOD TIES WITH FOREIGN MINISTER QIAO GUANHA (WHO IS OUSTED FROM POWER AFTER MAO'S DEATH BECAUSE OF HIS SUPPORT OF THE GANG OF FOUR)

IN THE SAME YEAR THE U.S. GIVES CAMBODIA TO CHINA. CAMBODIA, WHICH HAS SUFFERED BETWEEN 30.000 AND 500.000 DEATHS BECAUSE OF THE U.S. BOMBING CAMPAIGN 'ARCLIGHT,' IS CAPTURED BY THE MAOIST KHMER ROUGE

KISSINGER

MAO ZEDONG

...THIS LEADS TO THE SLAUGHTER OF MORE THAN 2 MILLION CAMBODIANS

5

GHW IS SWORN IN AS CIA DIRECTOR AT THE START OF 1976.

HIS 'OUTSIDER' IMAGE IS INSTRUMENTAL IN SECURING HIS APPOINTMENT. AT THE TIME, THE AGENCY IS UNDER FIRE BECAUSE OF THE PIKE COMMITTEE INVESTIGATIONS

LOOK MAMA

CLEAN HANDS!

BUSH SAYS THE AGENCY COULD AGAIN BECOME...

AN INSTRUMENT OF PEACE AND AN OBJECT OF PRIDE!

UNDER GHW THIS FOR THE MOST PART MEANS DENIAL AND COVER-UP, AMONGST WHICH:

THE CIA ORGANIZES ILLEGAL ARMS SHIPMENTS TO SAVIMBI'S UNITA FACTION DURING THE CIVIL WAR IN OIL-RICH ANGOLA

BOMB ATTACKS AGAINST CUBA'S U.N. MISSION IN NEW YORK

WHAM

KEEPING DOUBLE AGENT AND COCAINE SMUGGLER MANUEL NORIEGA ON THE CIA PAYROLL

AS PRESIDENT, BUSH DEPOSES THE DICTATOR NORIEGA DURING THE US-INVASION OF PANAMA IN 1989...

THE CIA AND GENERAL PINOCHET'S INTELLIGENCE AGENCY DINA HELP CUBAN TERRORISTS CARRY OUT A DEADLY BOMB ATTACK IN WASHINGTON AGAINST FORMER CHILEAN MINISTER LETELLIER

CIA-TRAINED CUBANS LUIS POSADA **CARRILES** AND ORLANDO BOSCH ARE RESPONSIBLE FOR THE BOMBING OF A **CUBANA DC-8** AIRLINER, CAUSING 73 DEATHS. BECAUSE OF BUSH'S PRESIDENTIAL PARDON BOSCH CAN RETIRE COMFORTABLY IN **FLORIDA** 20 YEARS LATER ....

WEAPONS SMUGGLING AND ATTEMPTS BY GANGSTERS TO DESTABILIZE THE COUNTRY IN ORDER TO PREVENT THE RE-ELECTION OF **JAMAICAN** PRESIDENT MICHAEL MANLEY.

ELECTRONIC SURVEILLANCE OF **MICRONESIAN** POLITICIANS TO LEARN ABOUT THEIR NEGOTIATING STRATEGY ON THE GAINING OF INDEPENDENCE FROM THE USA...

AS CIA DIRECTOR GHW GIVES A NUMBER OF EXCLUSIVE BRIEFINGS TO COMMERCIAL BANKS SUCH AS BROWN BROTHERS HARRIMAN AND CHASE MANHATTAN

BECAUSE OF HIS EARLIER AND LATER BUSINESS DEALINGS THIS POINTS TO A CLEAR-CUT CONFLICT OF INTEREST

6

SINCE HE DOESN'T GET ALONG WITH THE INCOMING PRESIDENT JIMMY CARTER, GHW STEPS DOWN IN JANUARY 1977 AND RETURNS TO THE WORLD OF BIG BUSINESS

WELCOME, GEORGE!

Texas Gulf Inc.

PUROLATOR OIL CO.

First National Bank

ELI LILLY & Co.

..BUT STILL PAYS WORKING VISITS TO OTHER FORMER CIA DIRECTORS

OFF AGAIN FOR SOME 'PERSONAL TIME', JEN!

ENJOY, MR BUSH!

MARCH 1980

AT LEAST 25 FORMER MEMBERS OF THE CIA AND OTHER INTELLIGENCE AGENCIES WORK DIRECTLY FOR BUSH'S CAMPAIGN DURING THE REPUBLICAN PRIMARIES...

OCTOBER. DURING MEETINGS IN PARIS BUSH MAKES A SECRET DEAL WITH THE IRANIAN MULLAHS.

..IN WHICH THEY PROMISE NOT TO RELEASE THE 52 AMERICAN HOSTAGES - WHO WERE CARTER'S GREATEST EMBARRASSMENT- UNTIL AFTER THE ELECTIONS OF NOVEMBER 4...

DOWN with U.S.A The Great DEVI

IN EXCHANGE, THE US WILL DELIVER MILITARY EQUIPMENT TO IRAN VIA ISRAEL...

REMEMBER: SADDAM HUSSEIN'S IRAQ -ALSO SUPPORTED BY THE US -JUST LAUNCHED A FULL SCALE OFFENSIVE AGAINST IRAN. THE WAR LASTS 8 YEARS, LEAVING ONE MILLION MILITARY DEAD IN ITS WAKE...

IRAN PUTS THE HOSTAGES ON A PLANE HOME ON JANUARY 20, 1981, THE DAY RONALD REAGAN AND GHW BUSH TAKE THEIR PRESIDENTIAL OATHS

LATER, MUCH LATER, GHW IS AN ADVISOR FOR THE MULTIBILLION CARLYLE INVESTMENT COMPANY. AS FORMER PRESIDENT HE RECEIVES WEEKLY CIA-BRIEFINGS...

CARLYLE

...INTERESTING INFORMATION FOR A BUSINESSMAN WHOSE SON SUCCEEDS HIM TO THE PRESIDENCY...

George Bush Center For Intelligence CIA NEXT RIGHT

AUTHORIZED VEHICLES ONLY

7

Iran-Contra

"Secrecy was imperative... As part of the plan, there would be no change in the schedule of the top man. President Reagan would travel to Augusta, GA, for a golf weekend. Secretary of State Shultz would go too."

– NSC Operative Constantine Menges

Reagan was called "The Great Communicator," but according to Peter Wallison, former White House Council, he was the Great Delegator.

CIA Dir. William Casey

John Poindexter

Robert McFarlane

Vice President George Bush...

...is barely mentioned in several major studies of the Reagan administration, even a few that specifically address Iran-Contra. His media style contrasted intensely with Reagan's. Bush was hyper-aware that greater visibility meant greater accountability. He was the exemplar of the quiet, but deadly effective VP, the veiled operative. The Mole.

1/20/81: Ronald Reagan inaugurated.	**3/25/81:** VP Bush named head of U.S. crisis management staff, a component of the National Security Council (N.S.C.).	**5/14/82:** Bush's position as chief of all covert action & de facto head of U.S. intel formalized in secret memo.	**8/82:** Retired C.I.A. Donald P. Gregg, C.I.A. "Assassinations Manager" Felix I. Rodriguez, and Lt. Colonel Oliver North (N.S.C.) join Bush team.

Timeline info quoted from or based on Tarpley and Chaitkin, George Bush: The Unauthorized Biography.

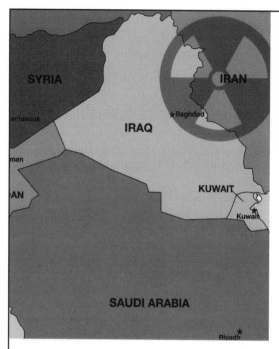

"What's a thousand square miles and glows in the dark in the Persian Gulf? Iran, five minutes after Reagan takes office." The 1979 hostage crisis, involving the takeover of the American embassy in Tehran—lasting 444 days—had unseated Jimmy Carter. It was the era of paranoid, Cold War control freak overkill. Iraq (an American ally) was at war with Iran. Consequently, Hezbollah, in association with Iran, took American hostages in Lebanon. The U.S. retaliated by giving its full support to Saddam Hussein's regime.

The stability of official U.S. interests was also at stake in Central America. Having overthrown Nicaraguan dictator Somoza, Sandinista party leader Daniel Ortega came into popular power.

Reagan and his foreign policy advisors considered the Sandinistas a threat. They saw the guerrilla anti-Sandinista group the Contras as "the only hope for bringing the communist-leaning government of Nicaragua into the diplomatic framework of Central America, and for stopping the flow of weapons from Cuba to El Salvador. At (Reagan's) urging, Congress supported covert activity by the C.I.A. to aid the military and paramilitary...Contras." [1]

1981:
U.S.-funded and-trained insurgents put 30,000 Nicaraguans to death.*

12/21/82:
Congress enacts first Boland Amendment, to keep defense appropriation funds from use against Nicaraguan government.

2/13/83:
Fawn Hall joins Oliver North as assistant, would later be forced to testify against him.

3/17/83:
Bush aide Gregg, and assassinations mgr. Rodriguez, meet at White House, submit Nicaragua attack plan to N.S.C. advisor Robert "Bud" McFarlane.

*I almost wrote "Nicaraguans died" instead, in the passive voice—as if they weren't, in fact, killed as a byproduct of a C.I.A. initiative. The Spanish language allows for statements in the passive voice... as does the language of coversion.

1 - Walsh

The Contras were an extremely corrupt group, even if they were glorified by the U.S. as 'freedom fighters.' They'd have the American flag next to the Nicaraguan flag when meeting the C.I.A., but were also in collusion with the people from Fidel Castro.

In 1984, President Reagan was completing his first term in office. In a reelection campaign stump speech, he denounced Democratic rival Walter Mondale as a commie symp.

"After the Sandinista revolution, (Mondale) said that the 'winds of democracy were stirring where they had long been stifled.' This was right before the Sandinistas slaughtered the Miskito Indians, abused and deported church leaders, slandered the Holy Father, and moved to kill freedom of speech." [1]

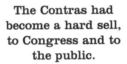

The Contras had become a hard sell, to Congress and to the public.

Reagan was rebuffed on funding for the 'freedom fighters.' Congress cut off all forms of aid late in 1984.

The president moved to evade the ban. He and National Security Council advisor Robert C. McFarlane obtained funding of over a million dollars a month from Saudi Arabia. McFarlane selected Lieutenant Colonel Oliver North to facilitate Contra affairs. "North was no run-of-the-mill NSC staffer. He had a well-deserved reputation as something of a swashbuckler." [2]

5/25/83: Secretary of State Shultz writes a memo for President to undercut Bush authority in Central American ops., to no avail.

10/20/83: Meta-Governmental meeting convened under Bush, re: invasion of Caribbean island Grenada.

10/4/84: Congress attempts to curb admin secret war ops with 2nd Boland Amendment.

1 - Noonan, 2 - Wallison

Fawn Hall's Shredables

The importance of the Iran-Contra affair is that its functions were conducted via a supranational governmental corporation—an entity set up by Reagan administration staff and Iranian businessmen, in order to sell guns to Iran. "North and his colleagues ultimately organized a supply network with funds in Swiss banks, arms sources in Portugal, and a small fleet of aircraft for transporting weapons to Nicaragua." [1]

North, and a cadre of retired U.S. military officers, directly advised Contra leaders on military strategy and tactics.

Acting against the advice of his principal foreign policy advisors—Secretary of State Shultz and Secretary of Defense Caspar W. Weinberger—the president agreed to deal with the kidnappers.

This directly contradicted U.S. stated policy against negotiation with terrorists. "At the time, the U.S. vigorously urged its allies not to traffic with, and refrain from, shipping arms to either Iran or Iraq." [2]

North was too effective for his own good. He was possessed of the "undimmed confidence of a man who lacks insight into his own weaknesses." [3] Success only increased the visibility of the covert operation, bringing with it unwelcome Congressional oversight. Administration suits stonewalled, big time.

11/1/84: Rodriguez associate arrested by F.B.I. for cocaine smuggling as part of plot to assassinate Honduran President Cordova.

1/12/85: Rodriguez seeks $10 mil from Medellin cocaine cartel money launderer for Contras, in exchange for direct access to Bush.

2/7/85: Bush subcommittee meets to circumvent effect of Boland Amendment ban.

1,2 - Walsh, 3 - Noonan

The 'arms for hostages' arrangement essentially used Israel as a fence, to front the weaponry, in defiance of the Arms Control Export Act. [North notebooks (12/1/85): 600 TOWs = 1 release. 2,000 TOWs = 3 releases.] [1]

[Tube-launched, Optically tracked, Wire-guided missiles]

"It seems likely that North saw the operation as another exciting adventure–this time to free the hostages in Lebanon–rather than some high-falutin' strategic initiative." [2] "As foreign funding for the Contras ran out, North's team inflated the price of the weapons sold to Iran and... diverted the excess proceeds...to private Swiss bank accounts," [3] and then to Contra support.

Nicaraguan Revolutionary Mural

The administration vetoed a World Bank loan to the Sandinistas, forcing Daniel Ortega to openly seek Kremlin aid. The massing of this communist front caused Congress' financial interests to whipsaw back in favor of the Contras. After the veto, however, Ortega was given a conciliatory meeting with Secretary Shultz.

```
3/15-16/85 - Bush
and Rodriguez in
Central America met
with Honduran
President Cordova
to offer $110 mil
in aid to his
government as a
bribe to use main
Honduran base to
run Contra
supplies.

8/8/85 - Bush group
met "in the
residence section
of the White House.
The officials
discussed shipment
of US made arms to
Iran through
Israel-to replenish
stocks of TOW
missiles and to
permit Israel to
sell arms to Iran."

12/18/85 - "CIA
official Charles E.
Allen, a member of
...Bush's Terrorism
Task Force, wrote
an update on the
arms-for-hostages
dealings with Iran.
Allen wrote:
'[Speaker of the
Iranian Parliament
Hashemi]
Rafsanjani...
believes VP Bush is

orchestrating the
US initiative with
Iran. Rafsanjani
believes that Bush
is the most
powerful man in the
US because in
addition to being
VP, he was once
Director of
the CIA.'"
```

1,3 - Virga, 2 - Wallison

On October 5, 1986, Eugene Hasenfus' plane, bearing arms for the Contras, was shot down by Nicaraguan soldiers.

The great, convoluted plot began to unravel. The Iranian/American 'dialogue'– arms sales included–was exposed in Lebanese and Iranian periodicals. North's network faced imminent collapse. In a White House-based talk with an Iranian attaché, he pressed for total release of the hostages. But they were dispersed between feuding factions. One group of captors would only cooperate once its own prisoners were released by Kuwait.

North, ever the multi-tasker, bragged to the Iranian rep that he'd "already started" on the plan to release the Kuwaiti detainees, claiming he'd "met with the Kuwaiti foreign minister, secretly, in my spare time between blowing up Nicaragua." [1]

Investigators uncovered a North memo. "$12 million in profits from the Iranian sales (will) be used to 'bridge' the gap until 'Congressionally approved lethal assistance can be delivered.'" [2] The public phase of Iran-Contra began, with administration officials furiously dissembling to protect Reagan from disgrace.

Bush refuted all charges:

"That out of the Vice President's office, we were running this war in Nicaragua, that Hasenfus was involved in it, it's absolutely, totally untrue."

Dan Webb, attorney: "You were unaware of North's activities?"

Reagan: "Well, I'm not sure I'm understanding this. My major was in economics, not law."

Once the scandal broke, its magnitude demanded some sort of narrative structure. North acquired symbolic authority—the guy who ignored the fumblings of Congress and just did his damn job. "Ollie, standing ramrod straight in his uniform in the hearing room... that moment will be 'the truth' forever." [3] Upon Bush's ascendance to the presidency, North and his fellow conspirators were pardoned.

1,2 - Hewitt, 3 Noonan

THE HISTORY OF THE BUSH FAMILY IS REPLETE WITH STRANGE CONNECTIONS. AMONG THE BETTER KNOWN ARE THE NAZI CONNECTION, AND THE BIN LADEN CONNECTION. LESS KNOWN, BUT EQUALLY STRANGE IS...

THE BUSH-HINCKLEY CONNECTION

Script: Mack White

Art: David Paleo

ON MARCH 30, 1981, NEWLY ELECTED PRESIDENT (AND FORMER MOVIE STAR) RONALD REAGAN WAS SHOT AS HE LEFT THE WASHINGTON HILTON HOTEL AFTER GIVING A SPEECH...

REAGAN WAS SERIOUSLY WOUNDED.

ALSO WOUNDED WERE PRESS SECRETARY JAMES BRADY AND A SECRET SERVICE AGENT...

A 25-YEAR OLD MAN NAMED JOHN HINCKLEY JR. WAS ARRESTED FOR THE SHOOTING...

HINCKLEY'S ATTEMPT TO KILL THE MOVIE STAR PRESIDENT WAS LATER EXPLAINED AS AN ATTEMPT TO IMPRESS A MOVIE STAR, JODIE FOSTER, WHO HAD STARRED IN "TAXI DRIVER", A MOVIE IN WHICH THE MAIN CHARACTER TRAVIS BICKLE PLOTS TO ASSASSINATE A PRESIDENTIAL CANDIDATE

IT WAS AN INTERESTING EXPLANATION BUT NOT HALF AS INTERESTING AS THE TRUE PICTURE OF HINCKLEY WHICH EMERGED...

ON MARCH 31, 1981, THE HOUSTON POST REPORTED THAT SCOTT HINCKLEY, THE BROTHER OF JOHN HINCKLEY JR., WAS TO HAVE BEEN A DINNER GUEST THE DAY AFTER THE SHOOTINGS AT THE DENVER HOME OF NEIL BUSH, SON OF VICE PRESIDENT GEORGE BUSH. NEIL BUSH READILY ACKNOWLEDGED TO REPORTERS THAT HE WAS A FRIEND OF SCOTT HINCKLEY. BUT WHEN ASKED IF HE HAD EVER MET JOHN HINCKLEY JR., HE SAID...

I HAVE NO IDEA...

I DON'T RECOGNIZE ANY PICTURES OF HIM...

I JUST WISH I COULD SEE A BETTER PICTURE OF HIM

NEIL'S BROTHER, GEORGE W. BUSH, WAS ASKED THE SAME QUESTION:

ON APRIL 1, THE ASSOCIATED PRESS REPORTED THAT JOHN HINCKLEY SR., FATHER OF THE WOULD-BE ASSASSIN, WAS CHAIRMAN OF THE DENVER BASED VANDERBILT ENERGY CORPORATION. THE AP ALSO REPORTED THAT AUDITORS FROM THE DEPARTMENT OF ENERGY HAD MET WITH SCOTT HINCKLEY, VICE PRESIDENT OF OPERATIONS, ON THE DAY OF THE SHOOTINGS...

IT'S CERTAINLY CONCEIVABLE THAT I MET HIM OR MIGHT HAVE BEEN INTRODUCED TO HIM. I DON'T RECOGNIZE HIS FACE FROM THE BRIEF, KIND OF DISTORTED THING THEY HAD ON TV AND THE NAME DOESN'T RING ANY BELLS

MR. HINCKLEY, WE HAVE FOUND THAT YOUR COMPANY OVERCHARGED PURCHASERS OF CRUDE OIL BY TWO MILLION DOLLARS. SURELY YOU WERE AWARE OF THE PRICE CONTROLS?

YES, OF COURSE I WAS. I CAN'T ACCOUNT FOR THE DISCREPANCIES IN THE BOOKS. BUT, IF YOU'LL GIVE ME A FEW HOURS, I'LL LOOK INTO THE MATTER AND FIND OUT

THE MEETING ENDED. AN HOUR LATER HINCKLEY'S BROTHER JOHN SHOT PRESIDENT REAGAN...

NEIL BUSH, A LAND MAN FOR STANDARD OIL OF INDIANA, CLAIMED THAT IT HAD BEEN THROUGH HIS INVOLVEMENT IN THE OIL BUSINESS THAT HE GOT TO KNOW SCOTT HINCKLEY. HOWEVER, THE HOUSTON POST REPORTED THAT THE SOCIAL AND FINANCIAL CONNECTIONS BETWEEN THE BUSH AND HINCKLEY FAMILIES WENT BACK MUCH FURTHER. IN FACT, JOHN HINCKLEY SR., HAD FOR YEARS BEEN A MAJOR CONTRIBUTOR TO GEORGE BUSH'S POLITICAL CAMPAIGNS...

ALSO, WHEN JOHN HINCKLEY SR.'S COMPANY BEGAN TO FAIL IN THE 1960'S, GEORGE BUSH'S COMPANY, ZAPATA OIL, BAILED OUT THE COMPANY. IT WENT FROM BEING A COMPANY WHICH OWNED SIX DEAD OIL WELLS TO A COMPANY THAT MADE MILLIONS OF DOLLARS A YEAR...

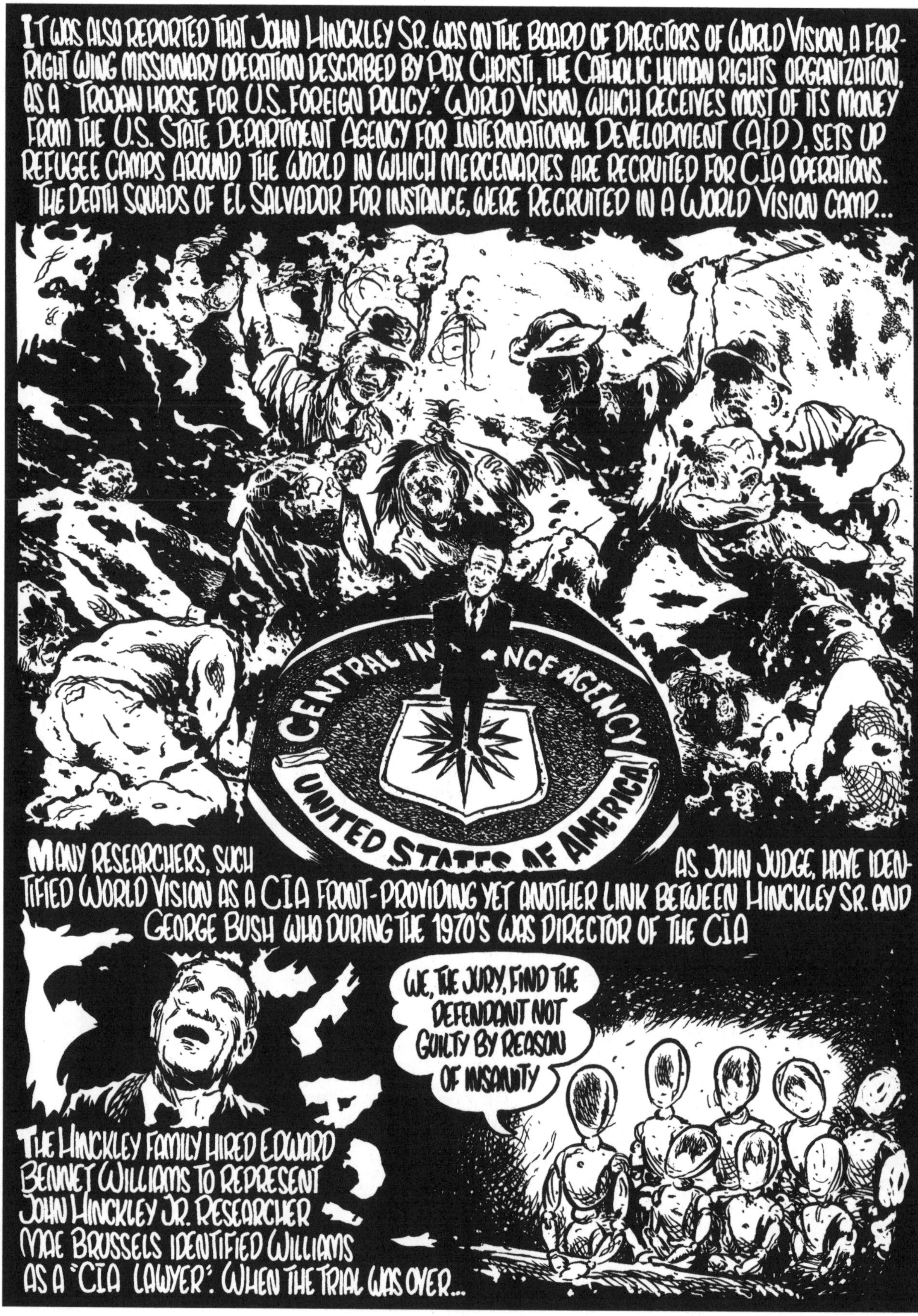
IT WAS ALSO REPORTED THAT JOHN HINCKLEY SR. WAS ON THE BOARD OF DIRECTORS OF WORLD VISION, A FAR-RIGHT WING MISSIONARY OPERATION DESCRIBED BY PAX CHRISTI, THE CATHOLIC HUMAN RIGHTS ORGANIZATION, AS A "TROJAN HORSE FOR U.S. FOREIGN POLICY." WORLD VISION, WHICH RECEIVES MOST OF ITS MONEY FROM THE U.S. STATE DEPARTMENT AGENCY FOR INTERNATIONAL DEVELOPMENT (AID), SETS UP REFUGEE CAMPS AROUND THE WORLD IN WHICH MERCENARIES ARE RECRUITED FOR CIA OPERATIONS. THE DEATH SQUADS OF EL SALVADOR FOR INSTANCE, WERE RECRUITED IN A WORLD VISION CAMP...
CENTRAL IN NCE AGENCY
UNITED STATES OF AMERICA
MANY RESEARCHERS, SUCH AS JOHN JUDGE, HAVE IDENTIFIED WORLD VISION AS A CIA FRONT- PROVIDING YET ANOTHER LINK BETWEEN HINCKLEY SR. AND GEORGE BUSH WHO DURING THE 1970'S WAS DIRECTOR OF THE CIA
WE, THE JURY, FIND THE DEFENDANT NOT GUILTY BY REASON OF INSANITY
THE HINCKLEY FAMILY HIRED EDWARD BENNET WILLIAMS TO REPRESENT JOHN HINCKLEY JR. RESEARCHER MAE BRUSSELS IDENTIFIED WILLIAMS AS A "CIA LAWYER". WHEN THE TRIAL WAS OVER...

Meanwhile the government's audit of Vanderbilt Energy continued. Had Reagan been killed, Bush of course would have become president, and, as president, Bush might have ended the audit of his long time friend John Hinckley Sr. But, alas, Reagan was not killed, and the audit not only continued, it grew worse. On July 13, the Denver Post asked an unidentified source if the audit had been protracted out of retaliation for the assassination attempt and the not guilty verdict; the source said that "that could be one inference that could be drawn from the facts."

The Bush-Hinckley connection raises a number of troubling questions which various authors have tried to answer. Most suspect that the shooting of Reagan was an attempted coup by Bush and his cronies in the CIA and Big Oil, and they point to the FBI's continued refusal to release documents concerning John Hinckley Jr.'s "associates and organizations" as well as other information. Thus, the Bush-Hinckley connection will remain a mystery for a long time...

END

OPERATION JUST CAUSE

SCRIPT: **MACK WHITE**
ART: **ALEKSANDAR ZOGRAF**

SHORTLY AFTER MIDNIGHT ON DECEMBER 20, 1989, THE *U.S.* INVADED THE CENTRAL AMERICAN COUNTRY OF PANAMA...

PRESIDENT **GEORGE H.W. BUSH** ORDERED THE INVASION OSTENSIBLY TO ARREST PANAMA'S LEADER, GENERAL **MANUEL NORIEGA**, FOR DRUG RUNNING.

YET, FOR YEARS, THE **U.S.** GOVERNMENT HAD NOT ONLY KNOWN ABOUT **NORIEGA'S** ACTIVITIES, IT HAD ACTIVELY ENCOURAGED THEM.

NORIEGA HAD BEEN ON THE **CIA'S** PAYROLL WHILE BUSH WAS DIRECTOR, AND LATER WAS INVOLVED IN THE **IRAN-CONTRA** AFFAIR, THE **REAGAN-BUSH** ADMINISTRATION'S PLOT TO SHIP ARMS TO NICARAGUA IN EXCHANGE FOR COCAINE.

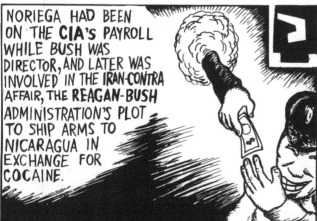

HOWEVER, LIKE MANY **U.**S.-BACKED DICTATORS, NORIEGA WAS UNPOPULAR AT HOME. SO, IN ORDER TO GAIN SUPPORT FROM THE PANAMANIAN PEOPLE, HE BEGAN CRITICIZING U.S. POLICY IN CENTRAL AMERICA...

SUDDENLY HE LOST THE SUPPORT OF THE **U.S.**

IN THE INVASION, WHICH WAS CALLED "**OPERATION JUST CAUSE**," BOMBS DESTROYED FACTORIES, OFFICES, AND HOMES. THE POOREST AREAS, WHERE NORIEGA'S SUPPORT WAS STRONGEST, WERE HIT HARDEST. ENTIRE BLOCKS OF APARTMENTS COLLAPSED, BURYING THE RESIDENTS ALIVE.

THE MOST SOPHISTICATED WEAPONS AT THE PENTAGON'S DISPOSAL WERE USED IN THE INVASION: STEALTH BOMBERS, APACHE HELICOPTERS, AND LASER-GUIDED MISSILES.

A YEAR LATER THESE WEAPONS WOULD BE USED IN THE **PERSIAN GULF WAR**, PROMPTING FORMER U.S. ATTORNEY GENERAL **RAMSEY CLARK** TO SAY ABOUT THE PANAMA INVASION: "IT WAS HIGHLY PROBABLE THEY USED SOPHISTICATED WEAPONS MERELY TO TEST THEM..."

IN THE GROUND FIGHTING, U.S. TROOPS INDISCRIMINATELY KILLED HUGE NUMBERS OF CIVILIANS.

ONE EYEWITNESS SAID, "I SAW TANKS RUN OVER AND CRUSH OUR DEAD. I SAW A GREAT NUMBER OF CIVILIAN CARS WITH WHOLE FAMILIES INSIDE - WOMEN, KIDS AND DRIVERS TORN TO PIECES AND CRUSHED".

THE DEAD WERE BURIED SECRETLY IN MASS GRAVES. LATER, WHEN HUMAN RIGHTS GROUPS UNCOVERED THESE GRAVES, THEY FOUND PEOPLE AS YOUNG AS 15 AND AS OLD AS 70, MANY SHOT IN THE BACK OF THE HEAD WITH THEIR HANDS TIED BEHIND THEM.

THE U.S. STATED THAT THE OFFICIAL DEATH TOLL OF CIVILIANS WAS 250. HOWEVER, THE UNITED NATIONS LATER ESTIMATED THAT OVER 2000 WERE KILLED. THE PANAMA NATIONAL HUMAN RIGHTS COMMISSION PUT THE FIGURE EVEN HIGHER: OVER 4000.

ALL THESE PEOPLE WERE KILLED IN ORDER TO ARREST ONE MAN. NORIEGA WAS BROUGHT BACK TO THE U.S. WHERE HE STOOD TRIAL AND WAS SENTENCED TO 40 YEARS IN PRISON.

MEANWHILE, A REGIME WAS INSTALLED THAT WOULD BE MORE SUPPORTIVE OF U.S. INTERESTS IN THIS STRATEGICALLY IMPORTANT COUNTRY, WHICH IS HOME TO **PANAMA CANAL**.

AND THE DRUG-RUNNING CONTINUES...

HOW I LEARNED TO LOVE THE WIMP'S WAR
An Appreciation of Hack Smith's Poppy the President

HACK SMITH

To all of us who sensed something rotten on the wind during the latter months of 1990, as President George Herbert Walker Bush began making his moves towards attacking Iraq, I offer this contribution to Fantagraphic's *Bush Junta* anthology. Though the artist is an unknown amateur of limited talent, his acute awareness, as to the danger of Bush's blustering and its present sad legacy, is hard to overlook. I hope it speaks as loudly to our present situation as it must have to the few who saw it when his work was initially published.

When I was first invited to create a cartoon for this book, I envisioned any number of approaches to take, from a barn-burning evisceration of the Bush politic to a more sober delineation of the damning facts. It wasn't until I was actually offered the chapter focusing on the 1991 Persian Gulf War that I recalled the treasure I had stuffed away in my art studio files and knew that here was a cartoon of far more import than anything I could come up with myself.

What I had were ten pages of original art for a thirty-installment strip by Hector "Hack" Smith, an amateur cartoonist from Occidental, California, who died in 1997 at the young age of 48. This strip, *The Wimp's War*, originally crafted in 1992 and styled as a daily, starred Poppy the President, a none-too-veiled caricature of then-President Bush, who took his nominee from the president's actual nickname. It was quite irreverent, a true personal "surgical strike" at the persona of the 41st leader of the United States, and yet it was also a nostalgic throwback to a simpler time when slapstick ruled the funny pages, especially in the realm of political commentary.

This was no *Doonesbury*.

It had more in common with the corny yet brilliant vaudevillian staging of classics like E. C. Segar's early *Thimble Theater* strip. And Poppy the President was clearly an allusion to that strip's Popeye the Sailor, not to mention the obvious appropriation of Segar's Eugene the Jeep character as Bush's "wimp factor" gremlin (referred to as "yellabelly" in Smith's prodigious notes).

Though it would be less than honest of me to claim this to be a feat of cartooning virtuosity (it is, at best, a rough example of journeyman strip work, varying greatly in its proficiency), I will offer it as a uniquely insightful example of political/social commentary. At a time in recent American history, when the ugly voice of jingoism bellowed freely and the press still cowered, here was a proponent for a clear revealing of the facts, an artist not afraid to hold Presidential character and action up to scrutiny, in that most American of forms, the cartoon strip. *The Wimp's War* is the cartoon I wish I could have made in those days following the Persian Gulf War, in spirit, if not form.

I became aware of Hack Smith about the time that President Bush was huffing and puffing and threatening to blow down Saddam Hussein's "new house in Kuwait." The first letter I received from him arrived on November 2, 1990. This was in response to the September 13th installment of my own strip, *A Sleepyhead Tale*, which was then running in the *San Diego Reader*. Entitled "*Offensive*," it was an angry response to the warmongering brewing in the country and touched upon the evident oil

interests that were sparking President Bush's drive for conflict. That it was my first foray into direct political commentary only shows how sensitive Hack was to these issues. We soon began a lively and often engaging volley of letter-writing and I learned that Hack had been a budding cartoonist throughout his university days in Berkeley and had created a short-lived student strip called "*Trickarious Dickarious*," during Nixon's infamous tenure. He also claims to have been a one-time assistant on the venerable *Alley Oop* daily strip (this I have not been able to confirm).

We certainly had a mutual affection for the clean line work and shading of *Alley Oop*'s creator, V.T. Hamlin. And, Smith, by association, soon influenced my own work.

Hack was a notorious political and social muckraker. He was once arrested, wearing only a rubber Bush mask, as he attempted to climb one of the towering palm trees on the grounds of the state capitol in Sacramento, ready to unfurl a banner that read: BROC-COLI IS NOT HEALTHY FOR CHILDREN AND OTHER LIVING THINGS, a keen satirical reference to Bush's public distaste for the protein-rich vegetable. He, in fact, met his wife, Graciela, while attending a peace rally in 1972 and it was she who mailed me the package containing the *Poppy the President* originals in 1996, when Hack, sick with complications from the pneumonia that eventually killed him, had instructed her to see that I have

them. Before he was too weak to do so, he had updated the original 1992 strip, adding incisive bits, like the reference to Timothy McVeigh in the Desert Humor installment. He also, I feel to its detriment, re-lettered the originals with the then-novel comic sans computer font. But it was his keen attention to detail and factual accuracy that, for me, makes his work so rewarding. Don't let the goofy, big-nose artwork and often awkward narrative mislead you, for *The Wimp's War* is literally stuffed with documented quotes and incidents, from major sources and more obscure ones. In keeping in line with this book's journalistic directive, I've gone through Hack's work and have key-numbered all of these quotes and facts. Hack's own extensive notes helped me a great deal in my research.

It is saddening to realize that Hack's initial attempt at having his strip published only ever resulted in it running in one newspaper, the now-defunct Madison, Wisconsin weekly *Social Sense*. His satirical insight was sadly overlooked and his art outright ignored. But, in all fairness, what was even the editor of a socialist paper to make of Hack's ability to foresee the role of George Walker Bush in our current lives? And how can one explain Hack's visionary characterization of his manchild "W" as a language-shattering idiot? To say nothing of his villainous portrayal of Dick Cheney and the inclusion of his ominous "...far better to deal with Saddam now than...five or ten years from now" quote? I can only conclude that Hector "Hack" Smith was as in-tune with the country's political zeitgeist as he was with the great cartoonists of the past who he so revered. It's as if he saw the dreaded punchline of the 2000 elections coming and was already reacting, showing his boot soles in a dramatic slapstick response.

Let us all hope that Hack's commitment and foresight, regardless of his questionable place in cartooning history, might somehow help

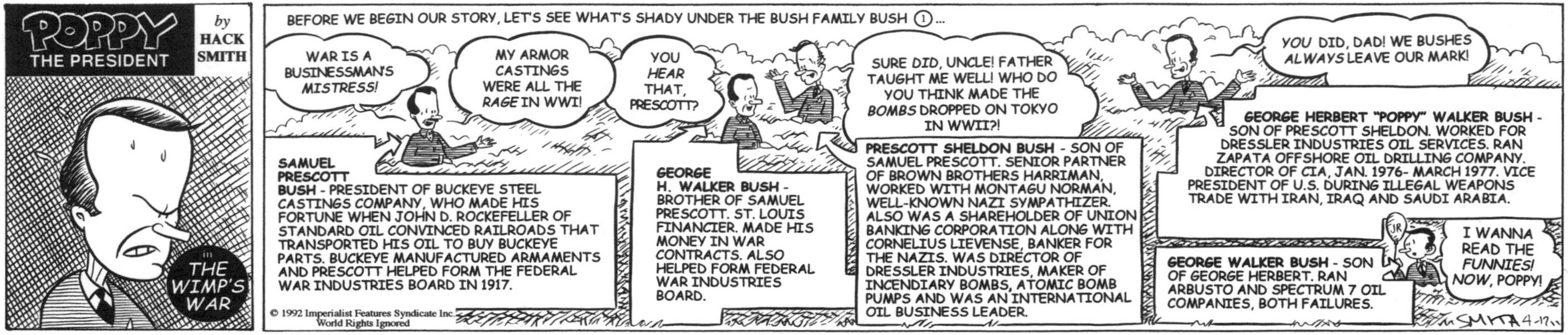
POPPY THE PRESIDENT
by HACK SMITH
"THE WIMP'S WAR"
BEFORE WE BEGIN OUR STORY, LET'S SEE WHAT'S SHADY UNDER THE BUSH FAMILY BUSH (1)...
WAR IS A BUSINESSMAN'S MISTRESS!
MY ARMOR CASTINGS WERE ALL THE RAGE IN WWI!
YOU HEAR THAT, PRESCOTT?
SURE DID, UNCLE! FATHER TAUGHT ME WELL! WHO DO YOU THINK MADE THE BOMBS DROPPED ON TOKYO IN WWII?!
YOU DID, DAD! WE BUSHES ALWAYS LEAVE OUR MARK!
SAMUEL PRESCOTT BUSH - PRESIDENT OF BUCKEYE STEEL CASTINGS COMPANY, WHO MADE HIS FORTUNE WHEN JOHN D. ROCKEFELLER OF STANDARD OIL CONVINCED RAILROADS THAT TRANSPORTED HIS OIL TO BUY BUCKEYE PARTS. BUCKEYE MANUFACTURED ARMAMENTS AND PRESCOTT HELPED FORM THE FEDERAL WAR INDUSTRIES BOARD IN 1917.
GEORGE H. WALKER BUSH - BROTHER OF SAMUEL PRESCOTT. ST. LOUIS FINANCIER. MADE HIS MONEY IN WAR CONTRACTS. ALSO HELPED FORM FEDERAL WAR INDUSTRIES BOARD.
PRESCOTT SHELDON BUSH - SON OF SAMUEL PRESCOTT. SENIOR PARTNER OF BROWN BROTHERS HARRIMAN, WORKED WITH MONTAGU NORMAN, WELL-KNOWN NAZI SYMPATHIZER. ALSO WAS A SHAREHOLDER OF UNION BANKING CORPORATION ALONG WITH CORNELIUS LIEVENSE, BANKER FOR THE NAZIS. WAS DIRECTOR OF DRESSLER INDUSTRIES, MAKER OF INCENDIARY BOMBS, ATOMIC BOMB PUMPS AND WAS AN INTERNATIONAL OIL BUSINESS LEADER.
GEORGE HERBERT "POPPY" WALKER BUSH - SON OF PRESCOTT SHELDON. WORKED FOR DRESSLER INDUSTRIES OIL SERVICES. RAN ZAPATA OFFSHORE OIL DRILLING COMPANY. DIRECTOR OF CIA, JAN. 1976- MARCH 1977. VICE PRESIDENT OF U.S. DURING ILLEGAL WEAPONS TRADE WITH IRAN, IRAQ AND SAUDI ARABIA.
GEORGE WALKER BUSH - SON OF GEORGE HERBERT. RAN ARBUSTO AND SPECTRUM 7 OIL COMPANIES, BOTH FAILURES.
I WANNA READ THE FUNNIES! NOW, POPPY!
JR
© 1992 Imperialist Features Syndicate Inc. World Rights Ignored
SMITH 4-17

POPPY THE PRESIDENT starring in **THE WIMP FACTOR** by HACK SMITH

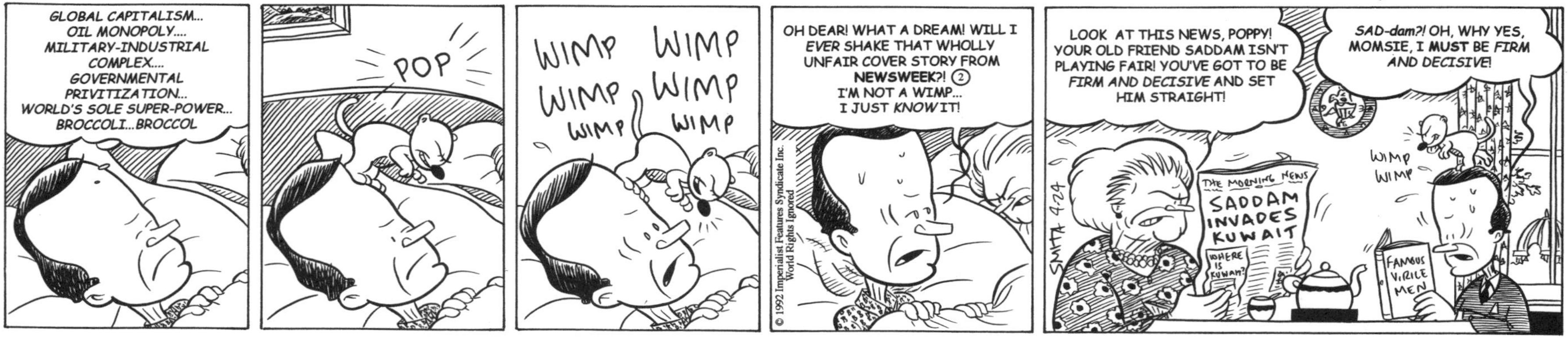
GLOBAL CAPITALISM... OIL MONOPOLY.... MILITARY-INDUSTRIAL COMPLEX.... GOVERNMENTAL PRIVITIZATION... WORLD'S SOLE SUPER-POWER... BROCCOLI...BROCCOL
POP
WIMP WIMP WIMP WIMP WIMP WIMP
OH DEAR! WHAT A DREAM! WILL I EVER SHAKE THAT WHOLLY UNFAIR COVER STORY FROM NEWSWEEK?! (2) I'M NOT A WIMP... I JUST KNOW IT!
© 1992 Imperialist Features Syndicate Inc. World Rights Ignored
LOOK AT THIS NEWS, POPPY! YOUR OLD FRIEND SADDAM ISN'T PLAYING FAIR! YOU'VE GOT TO BE FIRM AND DECISIVE AND SET HIM STRAIGHT!
SAD-dam?! OH, WHY YES, MOMSIE, I MUST BE FIRM AND DECISIVE!
THE MORNING NEWS
SADDAM INVADES KUWAIT
WHERE IS KUWAIT?
WIMP WIMP
FAMOUS VIRILE MEN
SMITH 4-24

POPPY THE PRESIDENT starring in **INVASION EVASION** by HACK SMITH

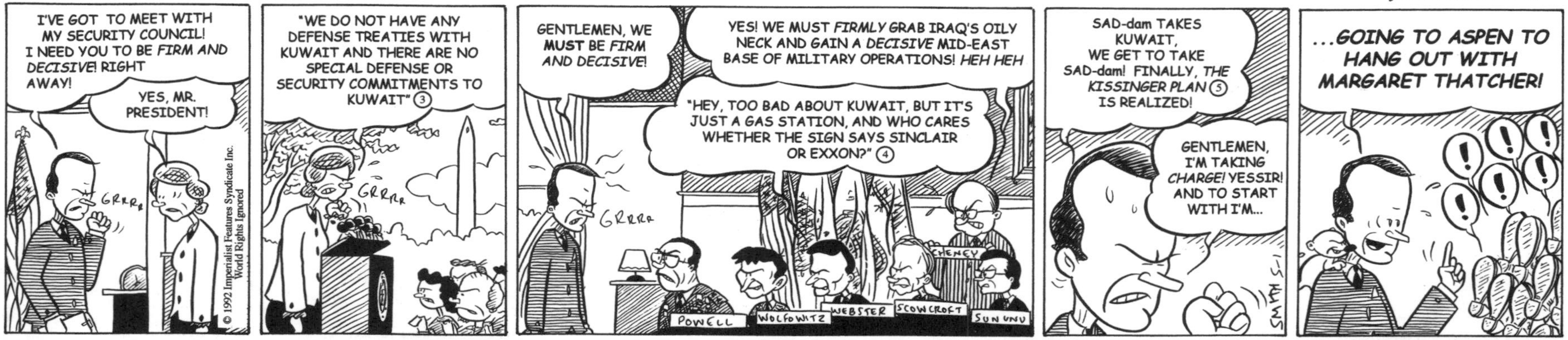
I'VE GOT TO MEET WITH MY SECURITY COUNCIL! I NEED YOU TO BE FIRM AND DECISIVE! RIGHT AWAY!
YES, MR. PRESIDENT!
GRRRR
© 1992 Imperialist Features Syndicate Inc. World Rights Ignored
"WE DO NOT HAVE ANY DEFENSE TREATIES WITH KUWAIT AND THERE ARE NO SPECIAL DEFENSE OR SECURITY COMMITMENTS TO KUWAIT" (3)
GRRRR
GENTLEMEN, WE MUST BE FIRM AND DECISIVE!
YES! WE MUST FIRMLY GRAB IRAQ'S OILY NECK AND GAIN A DECISIVE MID-EAST BASE OF MILITARY OPERATIONS! HEH HEH
"HEY, TOO BAD ABOUT KUWAIT, BUT IT'S JUST A GAS STATION, AND WHO CARES WHETHER THE SIGN SAYS SINCLAIR OR EXXON?" (4)
GRRRR
POWELL
WOLFOWITZ
WEBSTER
SCOWCROFT
CHENEY
SUNUNU
SAD-dam TAKES KUWAIT, WE GET TO TAKE SAD-dam! FINALLY, THE KISSINGER PLAN (5) IS REALIZED!
GENTLEMEN, I'M TAKING CHARGE! YESSIR! AND TO START WITH I'M...
SMITH 5-1
...GOING TO ASPEN TO HANG OUT WITH MARGARET THATCHER!

POPPY THE PRESIDENT *starring in* **THE FINK TANK** by HACK SMITH

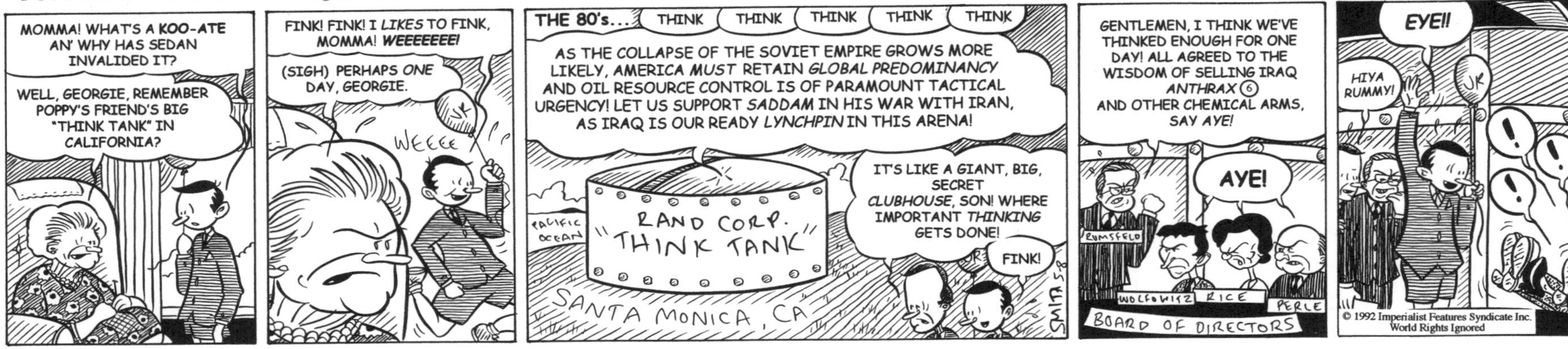
MOMMA! WHAT'S A KOO-ATE AN' WHY HAS SEDAN INVALIDED IT?
WELL, GEORGIE, REMEMBER POPPY'S FRIEND'S BIG "THINK TANK" IN CALIFORNIA?
FINK! FINK! I LIKES TO FINK, MOMMA! WEEEEEEE!
(SIGH) PERHAPS ONE DAY, GEORGIE.
WEEEE
JK
THE 80's...
THINK THINK THINK THINK THINK
AS THE COLLAPSE OF THE SOVIET EMPIRE GROWS MORE LIKELY, AMERICA MUST RETAIN GLOBAL PREDOMINANCY AND OIL RESOURCE CONTROL IS OF PARAMOUNT TACTICAL URGENCY! LET US SUPPORT SADDAM IN HIS WAR WITH IRAN, AS IRAQ IS OUR READY LYNCHPIN IN THIS ARENA!
PACIFIC OCEAN
RAND CORP. "THINK TANK"
SANTA MONICA, CA
IT'S LIKE A GIANT, BIG, SECRET CLUBHOUSE, SON! WHERE IMPORTANT THINKING GETS DONE!
FINK!
SMITH 5-8
GENTLEMEN, I THINK WE'VE THINKED ENOUGH FOR ONE DAY! ALL AGREED TO THE WISDOM OF SELLING IRAQ ANTHRAX (6) AND OTHER CHEMICAL ARMS, SAY AYE!
AYE!
RUMSFELD
WOLFOWITZ
RICE
PERLE
BOARD OF DIRECTORS
EYE!!
HIYA RUMMY!
JK
!
!
!
© 1992 Imperialist Features Syndicate Inc. World Rights Ignored

POPPY THE PRESIDENT *starring in* **FRIENDLY AMBITIONS** by HACK SMITH

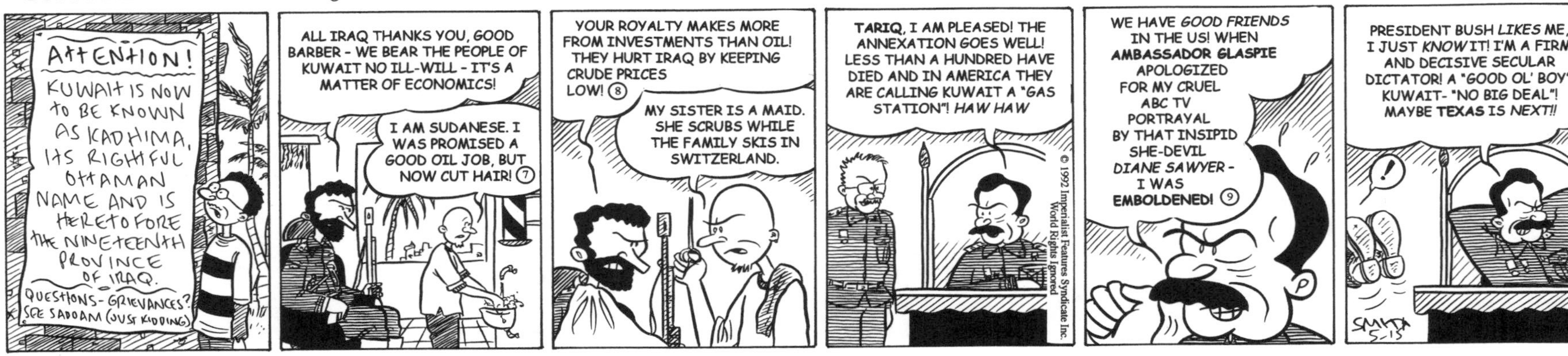
ATTENTION!
KUWAIT IS NOW TO BE KNOWN AS KADHIMA, ITS RIGHTFUL OTTAMAN NAME AND IS HERETOFORE THE NINETEENTH PROVINCE OF IRAQ.
QUESTIONS - GRIEVANCES? SEE SADDAM (JUST KIDDING)
ALL IRAQ THANKS YOU, GOOD BARBER - WE BEAR THE PEOPLE OF KUWAIT NO ILL-WILL - IT'S A MATTER OF ECONOMICS!
I AM SUDANESE. I WAS PROMISED A GOOD OIL JOB, BUT NOW CUT HAIR! (7)
YOUR ROYALTY MAKES MORE FROM INVESTMENTS THAN OIL! THEY HURT IRAQ BY KEEPING CRUDE PRICES LOW! (8)
MY SISTER IS A MAID. SHE SCRUBS WHILE THE FAMILY SKIS IN SWITZERLAND.
© 1992 Imperialist Features Syndicate Inc. World Rights Ignored
TARIQ, I AM PLEASED! THE ANNEXATION GOES WELL! LESS THAN A HUNDRED HAVE DIED AND IN AMERICA THEY ARE CALLING KUWAIT A "GAS STATION"! HAW HAW
WE HAVE GOOD FRIENDS IN THE US! WHEN AMBASSADOR GLASPIE APOLOGIZED FOR MY CRUEL ABC TV PORTRAYAL BY THAT INSIPID SHE-DEVIL DIANE SAWYER - I WAS EMBOLDENED! (9)
PRESIDENT BUSH LIKES ME, I JUST KNOW IT! I'M A FIRM AND DECISIVE SECULAR DICTATOR! A "GOOD OL' BOY"! KUWAIT- "NO BIG DEAL"! MAYBE TEXAS IS NEXT!!
!
SMITH 5-15

POPPY THE PRESIDENT *starring in* **KICK HIM IN THE ASPEN** by HACK SMITH

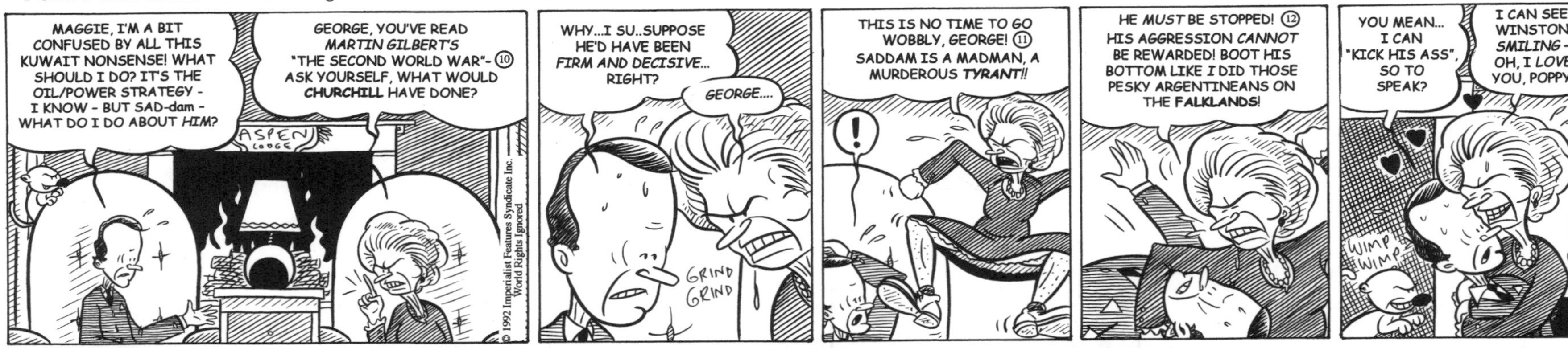
MAGGIE, I'M A BIT CONFUSED BY ALL THIS KUWAIT NONSENSE! WHAT SHOULD I DO? IT'S THE OIL/POWER STRATEGY - I KNOW - BUT SAD-dam - WHAT DO I DO ABOUT HIM?
GEORGE, YOU'VE READ MARTIN GILBERT'S "THE SECOND WORLD WAR" - (10) ASK YOURSELF, WHAT WOULD CHURCHILL HAVE DONE?
ASPEN LODGE
© 1992 Imperialist Features Syndicate Inc. World Rights Ignored
WHY...I SU..SUPPOSE HE'D HAVE BEEN FIRM AND DECISIVE... RIGHT?
GEORGE....
GRIND GRIND
THIS IS NO TIME TO GO WOBBLY, GEORGE! (11) SADDAM IS A MADMAN, A MURDEROUS TYRANT!!
!
HE MUST BE STOPPED! (12) HIS AGGRESSION CANNOT BE REWARDED! BOOT HIS BOTTOM LIKE I DID THOSE PESKY ARGENTINEANS ON THE FALKLANDS!
YOU MEAN... I CAN "KICK HIS ASS", SO TO SPEAK?
I CAN SEE WINSTON SMILING - OH, I LOVE YOU, POPPY!
WIMP WIMP
SMITH 5-22

POPPY THE PRESIDENT starring in **THE FIGHT HOUSE** *by* HACK SMITH

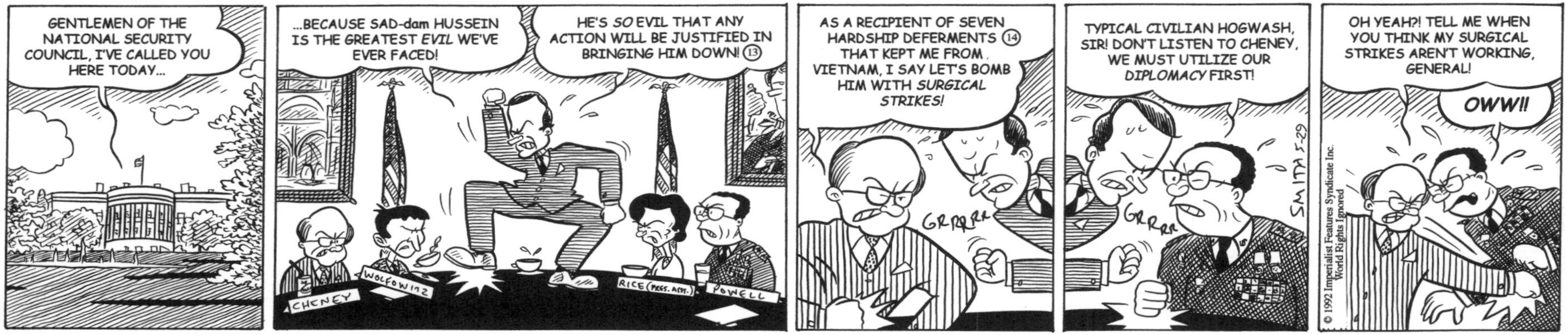
GENTLEMEN OF THE NATIONAL SECURITY COUNCIL, I'VE CALLED YOU HERE TODAY...
...BECAUSE SAD-dam HUSSEIN IS THE GREATEST EVIL WE'VE EVER FACED!
HE'S SO EVIL THAT ANY ACTION WILL BE JUSTIFIED IN BRINGING HIM DOWN! (13)
CHENEY
WOLFOWITZ
RICE (PRES. ASST.)
POWELL
AS A RECIPIENT OF SEVEN HARDSHIP DEFERMENTS (14) THAT KEPT ME FROM VIETNAM, I SAY LET'S BOMB HIM WITH SURGICAL STRIKES!
GRRRRR
TYPICAL CIVILIAN HOGWASH, SIR! DON'T LISTEN TO CHENEY, WE MUST UTILIZE OUR DIPLOMACY FIRST!
GRRRR
SMITH 5-29
OH YEAH?! TELL ME WHEN YOU THINK MY SURGICAL STRIKES AREN'T WORKING, GENERAL!
OWW!!
© 1992 Imperialist Features Syndicate Inc. World Rights Ignored

POPPY THE PRESIDENT starring in **A BLOODLESS LEADER** *by* HACK SMITH

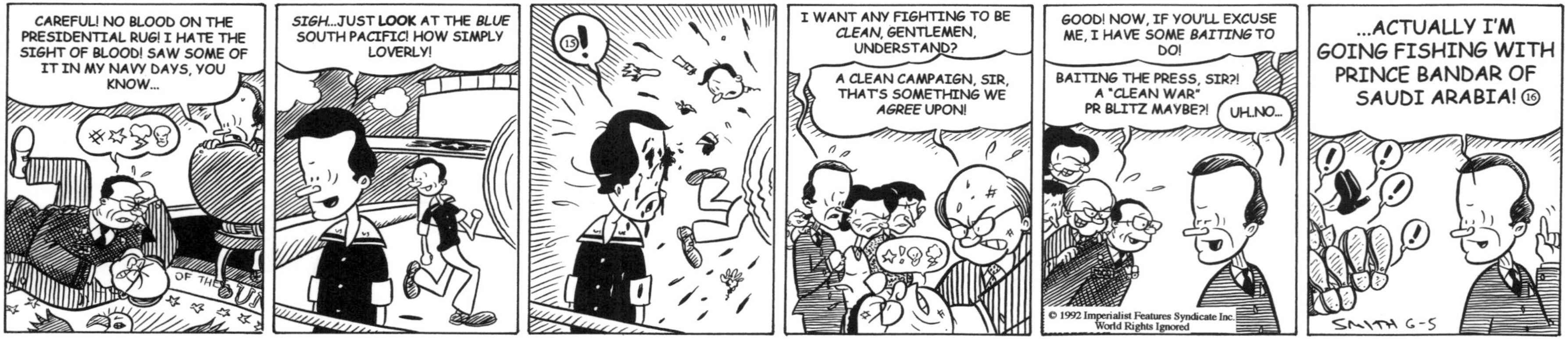
CAREFUL! NO BLOOD ON THE PRESIDENTIAL RUG! I HATE THE SIGHT OF BLOOD! SAW SOME OF IT IN MY NAVY DAYS, YOU KNOW...
OF THE U
SIGH...JUST LOOK AT THE BLUE SOUTH PACIFIC! HOW SIMPLY LOVERLY!
(15) !
I WANT ANY FIGHTING TO BE CLEAN, GENTLEMEN, UNDERSTAND?
A CLEAN CAMPAIGN, SIR, THAT'S SOMETHING WE AGREE UPON!
GOOD! NOW, IF YOU'LL EXCUSE ME, I HAVE SOME BAITING TO DO!
BAITING THE PRESS, SIR?! A "CLEAN WAR" PR BLITZ MAYBE?!
UH..NO...
© 1992 Imperialist Features Syndicate Inc. World Rights Ignored
...ACTUALLY I'M GOING FISHING WITH PRINCE BANDAR OF SAUDI ARABIA! (16)
SMITH 6-5

POPPY THE PRESIDENT starring in **CATCHING A POLITICAL PITCH** *by* HACK SMITH

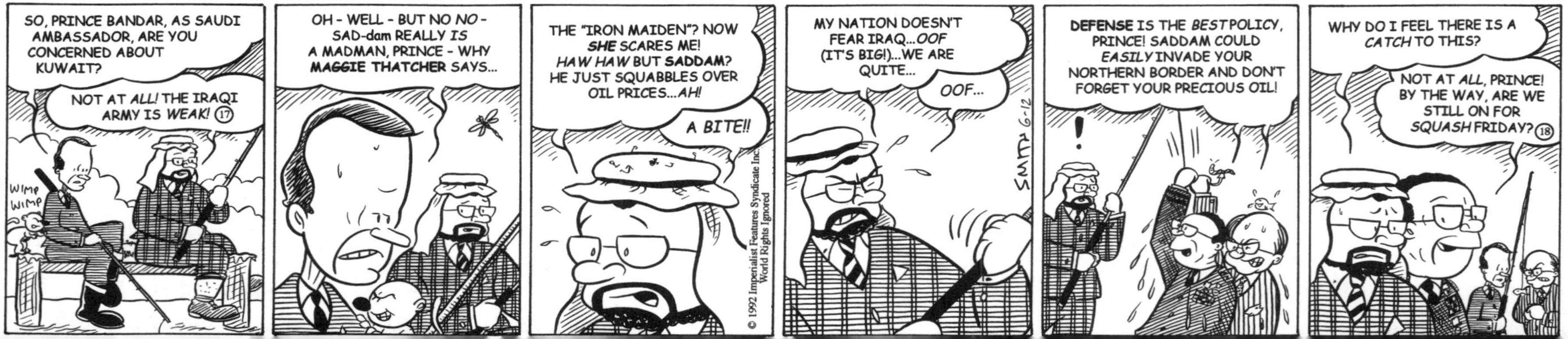
SO, PRINCE BANDAR, AS SAUDI AMBASSADOR, ARE YOU CONCERNED ABOUT KUWAIT?
NOT AT ALL! THE IRAQI ARMY IS WEAK! (17)
WIMP WIMP
OH - WELL - BUT NO NO - SAD-dam REALLY IS A MADMAN, PRINCE - WHY MAGGIE THATCHER SAYS...
THE "IRON MAIDEN"? NOW SHE SCARES ME! HAW HAW BUT SADDAM? HE JUST SQUABBLES OVER OIL PRICES...AH!
A BITE!!
© 1992 Imperialist Features Syndicate Inc. World Rights Ignored
MY NATION DOESN'T FEAR IRAQ...OOF (IT'S BIG!)...WE ARE QUITE...
OOF...
SMITH 6-12
DEFENSE IS THE BEST POLICY, PRINCE! SADDAM COULD EASILY INVADE YOUR NORTHERN BORDER AND DON'T FORGET YOUR PRECIOUS OIL!
!
WHY DO I FEEL THERE IS A CATCH TO THIS?
NOT AT ALL, PRINCE! BY THE WAY, ARE WE STILL ON FOR SQUASH FRIDAY? (18)

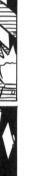

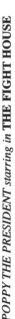

POPPY THE PRESIDENT *starring in* **THE TRUTH CAN KUWAIT**

by HACK SMITH

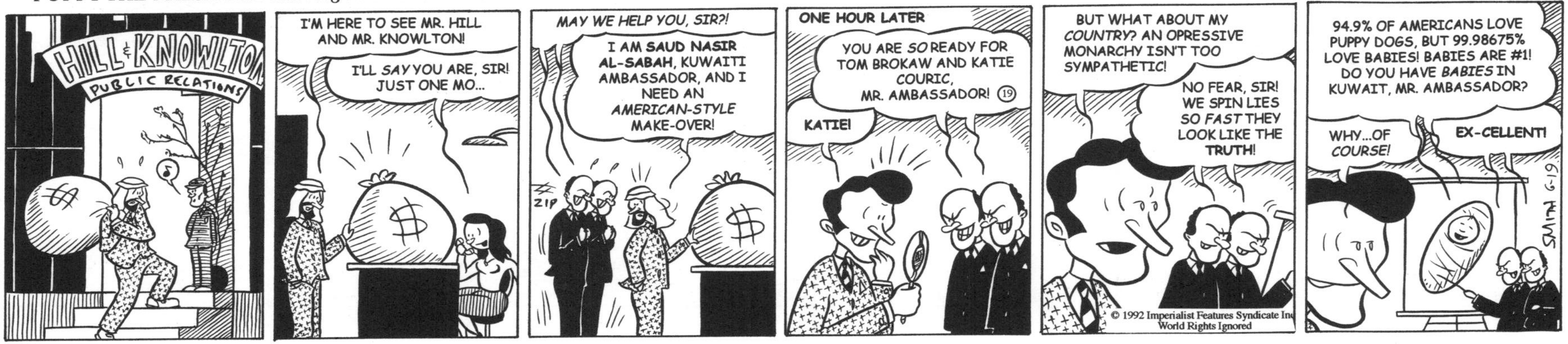
HILL & KNOWLTON PUBLIC RELATIONS
I'M HERE TO SEE MR. HILL AND MR. KNOWLTON!
I'LL SAY YOU ARE, SIR! JUST ONE MO...
ZIP
MAY WE HELP YOU, SIR?!
I AM SAUD NASIR AL-SABAH, KUWAITI AMBASSADOR, AND I NEED AN AMERICAN-STYLE MAKE-OVER!
ONE HOUR LATER
YOU ARE SO READY FOR TOM BROKAW AND KATIE COURIC, MR. AMBASSADOR! (19)
KATIE!
BUT WHAT ABOUT MY COUNTRY? AN OPRESSIVE MONARCHY ISN'T TOO SYMPATHETIC!
NO FEAR, SIR! WE SPIN LIES SO FAST THEY LOOK LIKE THE TRUTH!
© 1992 Imperialist Features Syndicate Inc. World Rights Ignored
94.9% OF AMERICANS LOVE PUPPY DOGS, BUT 99.98675% LOVE BABIES! BABIES ARE #1! DO YOU HAVE BABIES IN KUWAIT, MR. AMBASSADOR?
WHY...OF COURSE!
EX-CELLENT!
SMITH 6-19

POPPY THE PRESIDENT *starring in* **WELL-TRAINED TEARS**

by HACK SMITH

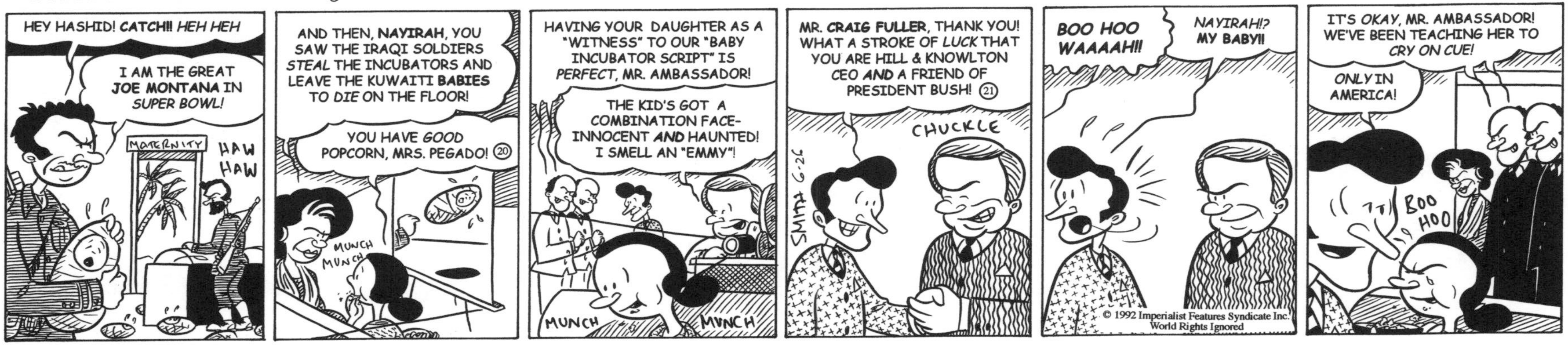
HEY HASHID! CATCH!! HEH HEH
I AM THE GREAT JOE MONTANA IN SUPER BOWL!
MATERNITY
HAW HAW
AND THEN, NAYIRAH, YOU SAW THE IRAQI SOLDIERS STEAL THE INCUBATORS AND LEAVE THE KUWAITI BABIES TO DIE ON THE FLOOR!
YOU HAVE GOOD POPCORN, MRS. PEGADO! (20)
MUNCH MUNCH
HAVING YOUR DAUGHTER AS A "WITNESS" TO OUR "BABY INCUBATOR SCRIPT" IS PERFECT, MR. AMBASSADOR!
THE KID'S GOT A COMBINATION FACE-INNOCENT AND HAUNTED! I SMELL AN "EMMY"!
MUNCH
MUNCH
MR. CRAIG FULLER, THANK YOU! WHAT A STROKE OF LUCK THAT YOU ARE HILL & KNOWLTON CEO AND A FRIEND OF PRESIDENT BUSH! (21)
CHUCKLE
SMITH 6-26
BOO HOO WAAAAH!!
NAYIRAH!? MY BABY!!
© 1992 Imperialist Features Syndicate Inc. World Rights Ignored
IT'S OKAY, MR. AMBASSADOR! WE'VE BEEN TEACHING HER TO CRY ON CUE!
ONLY IN AMERICA!
BOO HOO

POPPY THE PRESIDENT *starring in* **RING AROUND THE LEADER**

by HACK SMITH

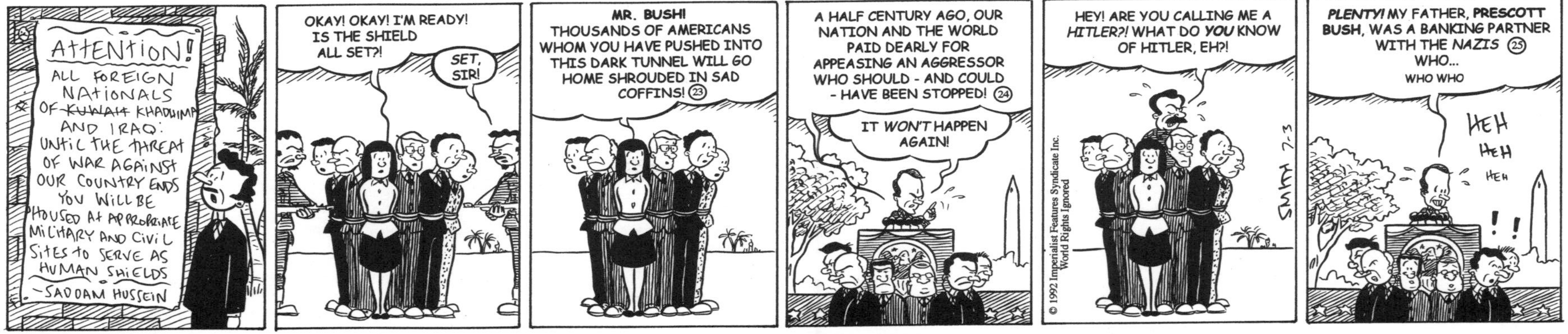
ATTENTION! ALL FOREIGN NATIONALS OF ~~KUWAIT~~ KHADUMA AND IRAQ: UNTIL THE THREAT OF WAR AGAINST OUR COUNTRY ENDS YOU WILL BE HOUSED AT APPROPRIATE MILITARY AND CIVIL SITES TO SERVE AS HUMAN SHIELDS —SADDAM HUSSEIN
OKAY! OKAY! I'M READY! IS THE SHIELD ALL SET?!
SET, SIR!
MR. BUSH! THOUSANDS OF AMERICANS WHOM YOU HAVE PUSHED INTO THIS DARK TUNNEL WILL GO HOME SHROUDED IN SAD COFFINS! (23)
A HALF CENTURY AGO, OUR NATION AND THE WORLD PAID DEARLY FOR APPEASING AN AGGRESSOR WHO SHOULD - AND COULD - HAVE BEEN STOPPED! (24)
IT WON'T HAPPEN AGAIN!
SMITH 7-3
© 1992 Imperialist Features Syndicate Inc. World Rights Ignored
HEY! ARE YOU CALLING ME A HITLER?! WHAT DO YOU KNOW OF HITLER, EH?!
PLENTY! MY FATHER, PRESCOTT BUSH, WAS A BANKING PARTNER WITH THE NAZIS (25) WHO...
WHO WHO
HEH HEH HEH
! !

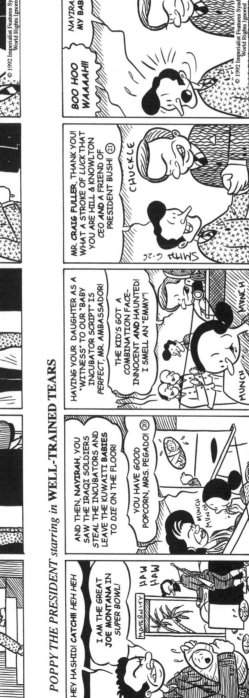

POPPY THE PRESIDENT starring in **HOT-BUTTERED TESTIMONY** — *by* HACK SMITH

POPPY THE PRESIDENT starring in **MASS MEDIA** — *by* HACK SMITH

POPPY THE PRESIDENT starring in **DICTORIAL TASTE BUDS** — *by* HACK SMITH

POPPY THE PRESIDENT starring in **A SQUASHED MEMORY** *by* HACK SMITH

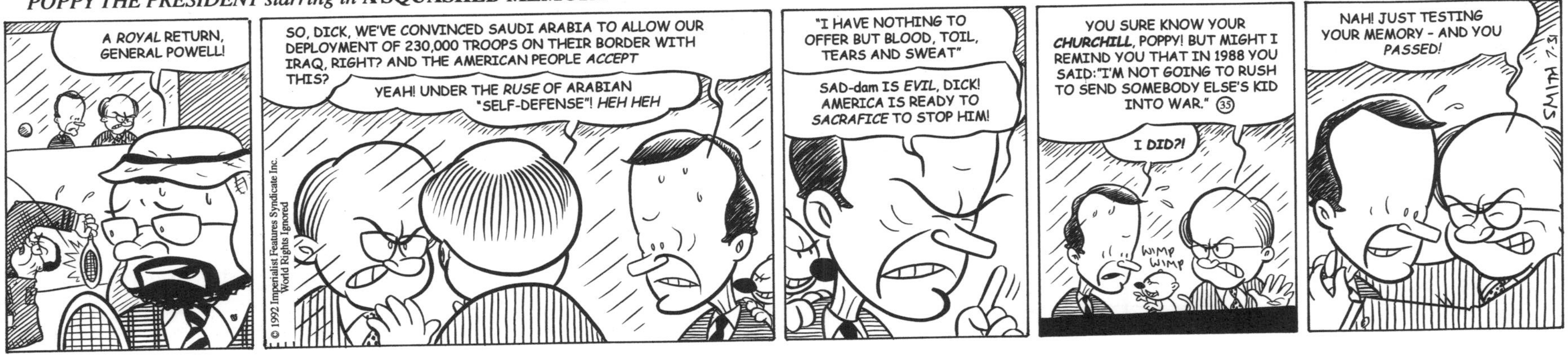
A *ROYAL* RETURN, GENERAL POWELL!
SO, DICK, WE'VE CONVINCED SAUDI ARABIA TO ALLOW OUR DEPLOYMENT OF 230,000 TROOPS ON THEIR BORDER WITH IRAQ, RIGHT? AND THE AMERICAN PEOPLE *ACCEPT* THIS?
YEAH! UNDER THE *RUSE* OF ARABIAN "SELF-DEFENSE"! *HEH HEH*
© 1992 Imperialist Features Syndicate Inc. World Rights Ignored
"I HAVE NOTHING TO OFFER BUT BLOOD, TOIL, TEARS AND SWEAT"
SAD-dam IS *EVIL*, DICK! AMERICA IS READY TO *SACRAFICE* TO STOP HIM!
YOU SURE KNOW YOUR ***CHURCHILL***, POPPY! BUT MIGHT I REMIND YOU THAT IN 1988 YOU SAID: "I'M NOT GOING TO RUSH TO SEND SOMEBODY ELSE'S KID INTO WAR." (35)
I *DID*?!
WIMP WIMP
NAH! JUST TESTING YOUR MEMORY - AND YOU *PASSED!*
SMITH 7-31

POPPY THE PRESIDENT starring in **SAND IN THE PAGES** *by* HACK SMITH

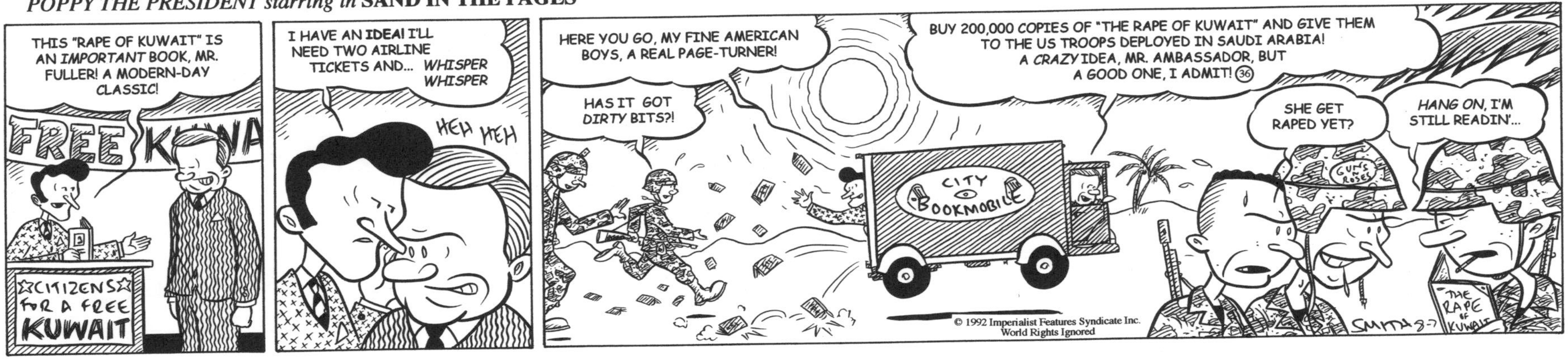
THIS "RAPE OF KUWAIT" IS AN *IMPORTANT* BOOK, MR. FULLER! A MODERN-DAY CLASSIC!
FREE KUWA
☆CITIZENS☆ FOR A FREE KUWAIT
I HAVE AN **IDEA!** I'LL NEED TWO AIRLINE TICKETS AND... *WHISPER WHISPER*
HEH HEH
HERE YOU GO, MY FINE AMERICAN BOYS, A REAL PAGE-TURNER!
BUY 200,000 COPIES OF "THE RAPE OF KUWAIT" AND GIVE THEM TO THE US TROOPS DEPLOYED IN SAUDI ARABIA! A *CRAZY* IDEA, MR. AMBASSADOR, BUT A GOOD ONE, I ADMIT! (36)
HAS IT GOT *DIRTY BITS*?!
CITY BOOKMOBILE
SHE GET RAPED YET?
GUNS N ROSES
HANG ON, I'M STILL READIN'...
THE RAPE OF KUWAIT
SMITH 8-7
© 1992 Imperialist Features Syndicate Inc. World Rights Ignored

POPPY THE PRESIDENT starring in **A LITTLE BIRD IN THE OFFICE** *by* HACK SMITH

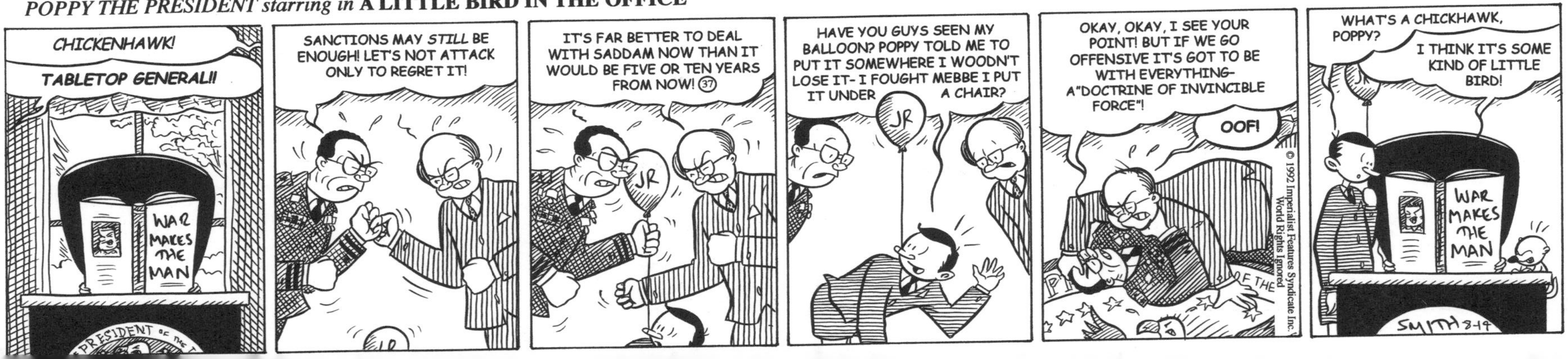
CHICKENHAWK!
TABLETOP GENERAL!!
WAR MAKES THE MAN
PRESIDENT OF THE
SANCTIONS MAY *STILL* BE ENOUGH! LET'S NOT ATTACK ONLY TO REGRET IT!
IT'S FAR BETTER TO DEAL WITH SADDAM NOW THAN IT WOULD BE FIVE OR TEN YEARS FROM NOW! (37)
JR
HAVE YOU GUYS SEEN MY BALLOON? POPPY TOLD ME TO PUT IT SOMEWHERE I WOODN'T LOSE IT- I FOUGHT MEBBE I PUT IT UNDER A CHAIR?
OKAY, OKAY, I SEE YOUR POINT! BUT IF WE *GO* OFFENSIVE IT'S *GOT* TO BE WITH EVERYTHING- A "DOCTRINE OF INVINCIBLE FORCE"!
OOF!
© 1992 Imperialist Features Syndicate Inc. World Rights Ignored
WHAT'S A CHICKHAWK, POPPY?
I THINK IT'S SOME KIND OF LITTLE BIRD!
WAR MAKES THE MAN
SMITH 8-14

POPPY THE PRESIDENT starring in **HEAVYWEIGHT CHUMPS**

by HACK SMITH

THERE WILL BE NO COMPROMISE. IRAQ WILL NEVER GIVE UP ONE INCH OF THIS LAND NOW CALLED PROVINCE NUMBER 19 38

NO CONCESSION. NO NEGOTIATION FOR ONE INCH OF TERRITORY. AND MR. SAD-dam HUSSEIN, SIMPLY DO WHAT THE WORLD IS CALLING UPON YOU TO DO: GET OUT! 39

PRESIDENT BUSH! WHAT IF SADDAM REFUSES?!

HE'S GOING TO GET HIS ASS KICKED! 40

STOP CALLING ME SAD-dam! IT'S SADDAM!

SAD-dam MEANS "LITTLE BOY WHO CLEANS THE SHOES OF OLD MEN"! THIS INSULT IS A DIRTY CIA TRICK! 41

SAD-dam! SAD-dam!

WIMP! WIMP!

BOY! I JUST LOVE THESE SATURDAY NIGHT FIGHTS!

HIC

JOE'S BAR

© 1992 Imperialist Features Syndicate Inc.
World Rights Ignored

KLIWS 12-8

POPPY THE PRESIDENT starring in **THE FIRST AND FOREMOST LADY**

by HACK SMITH

YES, THE UN SECURITY COUNCIL HAS JUST GIVEN APPROVAL OF USE OF FORCE AGAINST SAD-dam! 42

NO, I'M NOT WORRIED ABOUT SAM NUNN'S SENATE HEARINGS! WE'LL CLAMP DOWN ON THAT SILLINESS!

YES, WE NOW HAVE 33 COALITION COUNTRIES! THE SAUDI'S HANDS ARE TIED, "DESERT SHIELD" IS IN FULL EFFECT!

NO, NOT TO WORRY! GENERAL POWELL HAS BEEN SOFTENED! CHENEY'S BULLYING DID THE TRICK!

AND, YES, I'M SURE THIS GENERAL SCHWARZKOPF WILL DO THE JOB FOR US! ESPECIALLY NOW THAT I'VE JUST DECIDED TO DOUBLE HIS MEN TO 460,000! 43

GOOD, POPPY, AND I HOPE YOU REMEMBERED TO TAKE YOUR THYROID MEDICINE?! 44

YES, MOM,SIE!

WIMP WIMP

WIMP WIMP

© 1992 Imperialist Features Syndicate Inc.
World Rights Ignored

KLIWS 8-28

POPPY THE PRESIDENT starring in **THAT AIN'T NO DOVE!**

by HACK SMITH

HEY, JAMES! WHY AREN'T YOU PACKED FOR BAGHDAD?!

HAW HAW! 'CAUSE DOVES DON'T FLY TO BAGHDAD!

THE MORNING NEWS U.N. DEADLINE FOR IRAQI WITHDRAWAL FROM KUWAIT

BRILLIANT SCHEME, DICK, THIS WHOLE PHONEY "PEACE OFFER" TO SAD-dam 45 MAKES US LOOK GOOD! WE'VE SCORED A 90% APPROVAL RATING IN THE POLLS! 46

WE'RE CRUISING! NOW ALL WE NEED IS...

THE MORNING NEWS U.S. HOUSE VOTE APPROVES USE OF FORCE AGAINST SADDAM 250-183

THAT'S OUR PR GREEN LIGHT, POPPY! TIME TO "KICK SOME ASS"! 47

IT'S THAT BIG DICK! IT'S THAT IMPORTANT! NOTHING OF THIS MORAL IMPORTANCE SINCE WORLD WAR III 47

WAR IS A TERRIBLE THING WITH UNPREDICTABLE CONSEQUENCES—MANY, MANY PEOLE ARE GOING TO DIE 48

THE MORNING NEWS DEADLINE PASSES— SADDAM RESISTANT WAR?

© 1992 Imperialist Features Syndicate Inc.
World Rights Ignored

KLIWS 9-4

POPPY THE PRESIDENT starring in **A PARTING GESTURE** *by* HACK SMITH

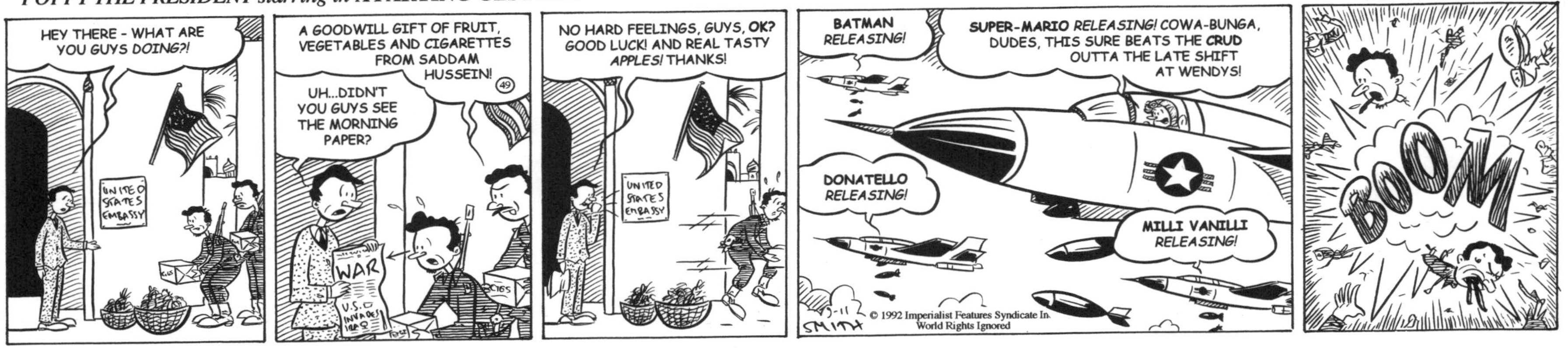
HEY THERE - WHAT ARE YOU GUYS DOING?!
UNITED STATES EMBASSY
A GOODWILL GIFT OF FRUIT, VEGETABLES AND CIGARETTES FROM SADDAM HUSSEIN! (49)
UH...DIDN'T YOU GUYS SEE THE MORNING PAPER?
WAR
U.S. INVADES IRAQ
NO HARD FEELINGS, GUYS, OK? GOOD LUCK! AND REAL TASTY APPLES! THANKS!
UNITED STATES EMBASSY
BATMAN RELEASING!
SUPER-MARIO RELEASING! COWA-BUNGA, DUDES, THIS SURE BEATS THE CRUD OUTTA THE LATE SHIFT AT WENDYS!
DONATELLO RELEASING!
MILLI VANILLI RELEASING!
9-11 SMITH
© 1992 Imperialist Features Syndicate In. World Rights Ignored
BOOM

POPPY THE PRESIDENT starring in **WE'RE THE BOMB!** *by* HACK SMITH

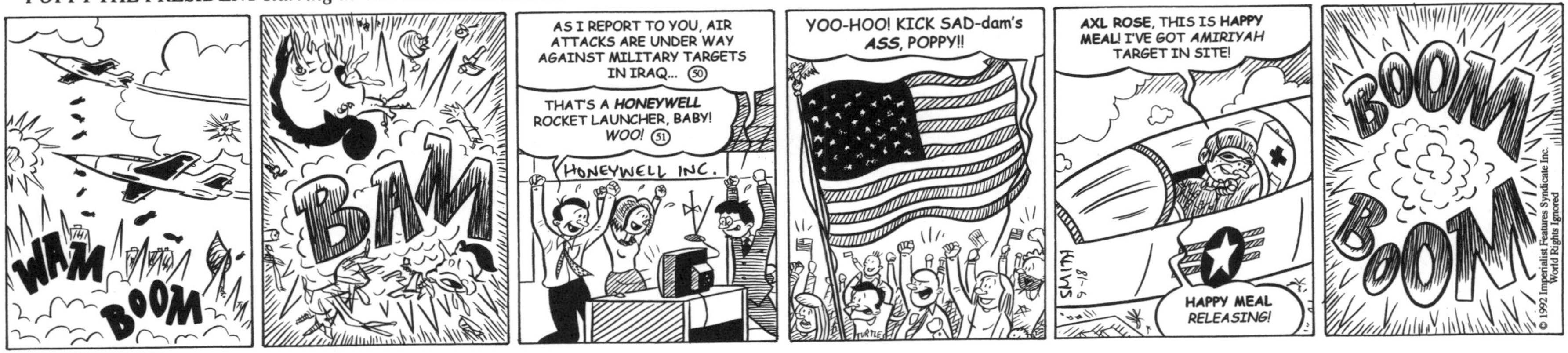
WAM
BOOM
BAM
AS I REPORT TO YOU, AIR ATTACKS ARE UNDER WAY AGAINST MILITARY TARGETS IN IRAQ... (50)
THAT'S A HONEYWELL ROCKET LAUNCHER, BABY! WOO! (51)
HONEYWELL INC.
YOO-HOO! KICK SAD-dam's ASS, POPPY!!
AXL ROSE, THIS IS HAPPY MEAL! I'VE GOT AMIRIYAH TARGET IN SITE!
HAPPY MEAL RELEASING!
SMITH 9-18
BOOM
BOOM
© 1992 Imperialist Features Syndicate Inc. World Rights Ignored

POPPY THE PRESIDENT starring in **A BEDTIME STORY** *by* HACK SMITH

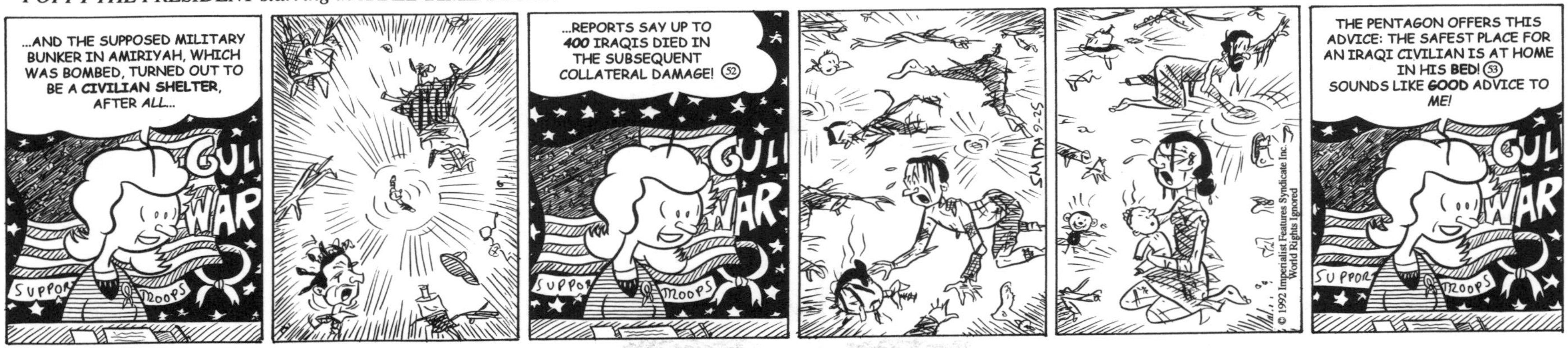
...AND THE SUPPOSED MILITARY BUNKER IN AMIRIYAH, WHICH WAS BOMBED, TURNED OUT TO BE A CIVILIAN SHELTER, AFTER ALL...
GULF WAR
SUPPORT TROOPS
...REPORTS SAY UP TO 400 IRAQIS DIED IN THE SUBSEQUENT COLLATERAL DAMAGE! (52)
SMITH 9-25
© 1992 Imperialist Features Syndicate Inc. World Rights Ignored
THE PENTAGON OFFERS THIS ADVICE: THE SAFEST PLACE FOR AN IRAQI CIVILIAN IS AT HOME IN HIS BED! (53)
SOUNDS LIKE GOOD ADVICE TO ME!

POPPY THE PRESIDENT *starring in* ALL THE TELLING VISIONS

by HACK SMITH

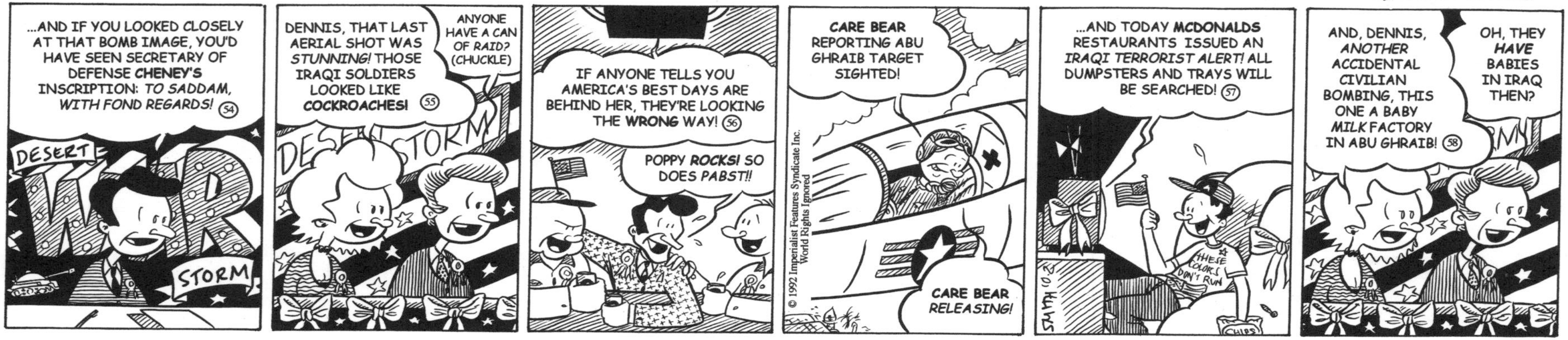
...AND IF YOU LOOKED CLOSELY AT THAT BOMB IMAGE, YOU'D HAVE SEEN SECRETARY OF DEFENSE CHENEY'S INSCRIPTION: TO SADDAM, WITH FOND REGARDS! (54)
DESERT
WAR
STORM
DENNIS, THAT LAST AERIAL SHOT WAS STUNNING! THOSE IRAQI SOLDIERS LOOKED LIKE COCKROACHES! (55)
ANYONE HAVE A CAN OF RAID? (CHUCKLE)
IF ANYONE TELLS YOU AMERICA'S BEST DAYS ARE BEHIND HER, THEY'RE LOOKING THE WRONG WAY! (56)
POPPY ROCKS! SO DOES PABST!!
© 1992 Imperialist Features Syndicate Inc. World Rights Ignored
CARE BEAR REPORTING ABU GHRAIB TARGET SIGHTED!
CARE BEAR RELEASING!
...AND TODAY MCDONALDS RESTAURANTS ISSUED AN IRAQI TERRORIST ALERT! ALL DUMPSTERS AND TRAYS WILL BE SEARCHED! (57)
THESE COLORS DON'T RUN
CHIPS
SMITH 10-2
AND, DENNIS, ANOTHER ACCIDENTAL CIVILIAN BOMBING, THIS ONE A BABY MILK FACTORY IN ABU GHRAIB! (58)
OH, THEY HAVE BABIES IN IRAQ THEN?

POPPY THE PRESIDENT *starring in* DESERT HUMOR

by HACK SMITH

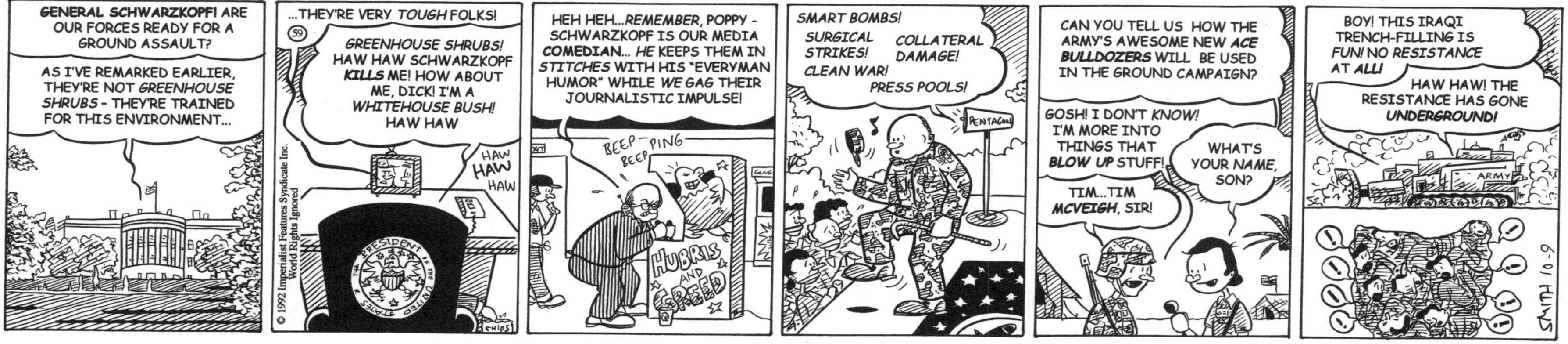
GENERAL SCHWARZKOPF! ARE OUR FORCES READY FOR A GROUND ASSAULT?
AS I'VE REMARKED EARLIER, THEY'RE NOT GREENHOUSE SHRUBS - THEY'RE TRAINED FOR THIS ENVIRONMENT...
...THEY'RE VERY TOUGH FOLKS! (59)
GREENHOUSE SHRUBS! HAW HAW SCHWARZKOPF KILLS ME! HOW ABOUT ME, DICK! I'M A WHITEHOUSE BUSH! HAW HAW
HAW HAW HAW
© 1992 Imperialist Features Syndicate Inc. World Rights Ignored
THE PRESIDENT OF THE UNITED STATES
CHIPS
HEH HEH...REMEMBER, POPPY - SCHWARZKOPF IS OUR MEDIA COMEDIAN... HE KEEPS THEM IN STITCHES WITH HIS "EVERYMAN HUMOR" WHILE WE GAG THEIR JOURNALISTIC IMPULSE!
BEEP BEEP PING
HUBRIS AND GREED
SMART BOMBS!
SURGICAL STRIKES!
COLLATERAL DAMAGE!
CLEAN WAR!
PRESS POOLS!
PENTAGON
CAN YOU TELL US HOW THE ARMY'S AWESOME NEW ACE BULLDOZERS WILL BE USED IN THE GROUND CAMPAIGN?
GOSH! I DON'T KNOW! I'M MORE INTO THINGS THAT BLOW UP STUFF!
WHAT'S YOUR NAME, SON?
TIM...TIM MCVEIGH, SIR!
BOY! THIS IRAQI TRENCH-FILLING IS FUN! NO RESISTANCE AT ALL!
HAW HAW! THE RESISTANCE HAS GONE UNDERGROUND!
ARMY
SMITH 10-9

POPPY THE PRESIDENT *starring in* NICE AND FRIENDLY FIRE

by HACK SMITH

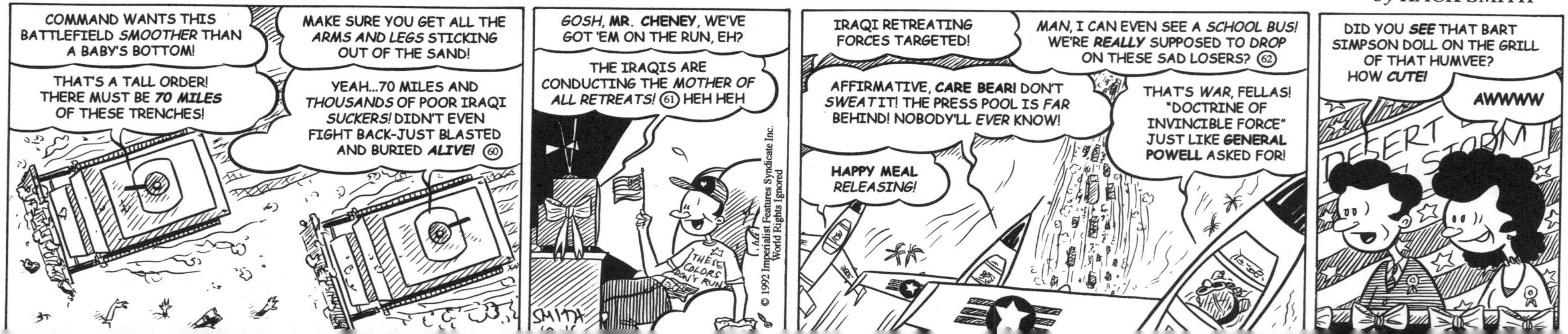
COMMAND WANTS THIS BATTLEFIELD SMOOTHER THAN A BABY'S BOTTOM!
THAT'S A TALL ORDER! THERE MUST BE 70 MILES OF THESE TRENCHES!
MAKE SURE YOU GET ALL THE ARMS AND LEGS STICKING OUT OF THE SAND!
YEAH...70 MILES AND THOUSANDS OF POOR IRAQI SUCKERS! DIDN'T EVEN FIGHT BACK-JUST BLASTED AND BURIED ALIVE! (60)
GOSH, MR. CHENEY, WE'VE GOT 'EM ON THE RUN, EH?
THE IRAQIS ARE CONDUCTING THE MOTHER OF ALL RETREATS! (61) HEH HEH
THESE COLORS DON'T RUN
© 1992 Imperialist Features Syndicate Inc. World Rights Ignored
IRAQI RETREATING FORCES TARGETED!
AFFIRMATIVE, CARE BEAR! DON'T SWEAT IT! THE PRESS POOL IS FAR BEHIND! NOBODY'LL EVER KNOW!
HAPPY MEAL RELEASING!
MAN, I CAN EVEN SEE A SCHOOL BUS! WE'RE REALLY SUPPOSED TO DROP ON THESE SAD LOSERS? (62)
THAT'S WAR, FELLAS! "DOCTRINE OF INVINCIBLE FORCE" JUST LIKE GENERAL POWELL ASKED FOR!
DID YOU SEE THAT BART SIMPSON DOLL ON THE GRILL OF THAT HUMVEE? HOW CUTE!
AWWWW
DESERT STORM

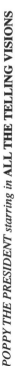

POPPY THE PRESIDENT starring in **PRESS HERE FOR VICTORY**

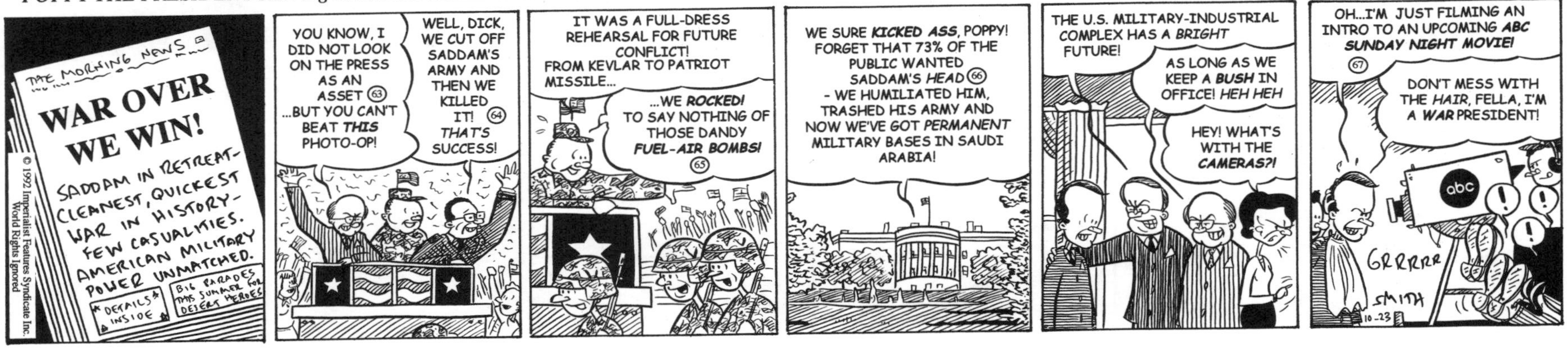
THE MORNING NEWS
WAR OVER
WE WIN!
SADDAM IN RETREAT-
CLEANEST, QUICKEST
WAR IN HISTORY-
FEW CASUALTIES.
AMERICAN MILITARY
POWER UNMATCHED.
DETAILS INSIDE
BIG PARADES THIS SUMMER FOR DESERT HEROES
© 1992 Imperialist Features Syndicate Inc. World Rights Ignored
YOU KNOW, I DID NOT LOOK ON THE PRESS AS AN ASSET (63) ...BUT YOU CAN'T BEAT *THIS* PHOTO-OP!
WELL, DICK, WE CUT OFF SADDAM'S ARMY AND THEN WE KILLED IT! (64) *THAT'S* SUCCESS!
IT WAS A FULL-DRESS REHEARSAL FOR FUTURE CONFLICT! FROM KEVLAR TO PATRIOT MISSILE...
...WE *ROCKED!* TO SAY NOTHING OF THOSE DANDY ***FUEL-AIR BOMBS!*** (65)
WE SURE ***KICKED ASS***, POPPY! FORGET THAT 73% OF THE PUBLIC WANTED SADDAM'S *HEAD* (66) - WE HUMILIATED HIM, TRASHED HIS ARMY AND NOW WE'VE GOT *PERMANENT* MILITARY BASES IN SAUDI ARABIA!
THE U.S. MILITARY-INDUSTRIAL COMPLEX HAS A *BRIGHT* FUTURE!
AS LONG AS WE KEEP A ***BUSH*** IN OFFICE! *HEH HEH*
HEY! WHAT'S WITH THE ***CAMERAS?!***
OH...I'M JUST FILMING AN INTRO TO AN UPCOMING ***ABC SUNDAY NIGHT MOVIE!*** (67)
DON'T MESS WITH THE *HAIR*, FELLA, I'M A ***WAR*** PRESIDENT!
abc
GRRRRR
SMITH 10-23

by HACK SMITH

POPPY THE PRESIDENT starring in **A FINISH YOU CAN SEE YOURSELF IN**

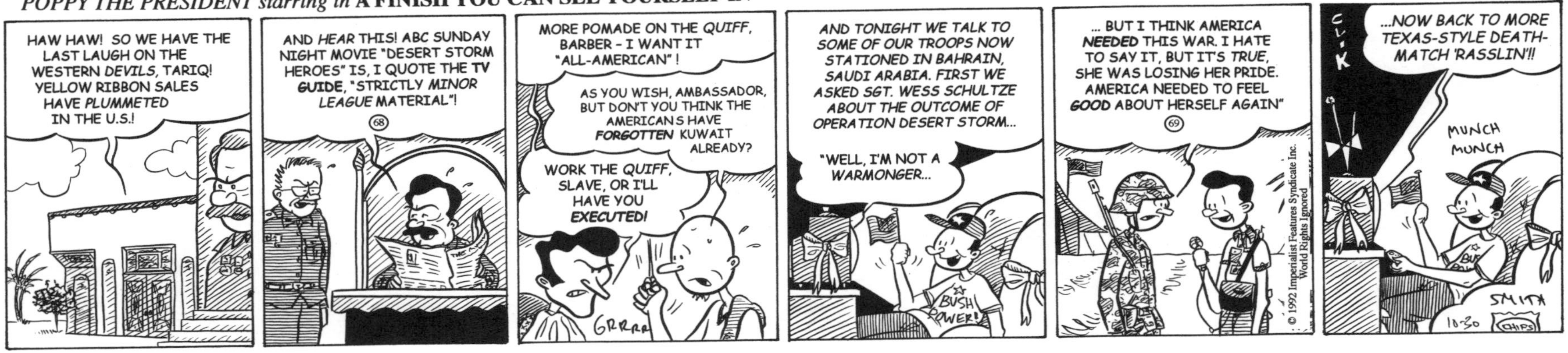
HAW HAW! SO WE HAVE THE LAST LAUGH ON THE WESTERN *DEVILS*, TARIQ! YELLOW RIBBON SALES HAVE *PLUMMETED* IN THE U.S.!
AND *HEAR* THIS! ABC SUNDAY NIGHT MOVIE "DESERT STORM HEROES" IS, I QUOTE THE **TV GUIDE**, "STRICTLY *MINOR LEAGUE* MATERIAL"! (68)
MORE POMADE ON THE *QUIFF*, BARBER - I WANT IT "ALL-AMERICAN"!
AS YOU WISH, AMBASSADOR, BUT DON'T YOU THINK THE AMERICANS HAVE ***FORGOTTEN*** KUWAIT ALREADY?
WORK THE *QUIFF*, SLAVE, OR I'LL HAVE YOU ***EXECUTED!***
GRRRR
AND TONIGHT WE TALK TO SOME OF OUR TROOPS NOW STATIONED IN BAHRAIN, SAUDI ARABIA. FIRST WE ASKED SGT. WESS SCHULTZE ABOUT THE OUTCOME OF OPERATION DESERT STORM...
"WELL, I'M NOT A WARMONGER...
BUSH POWER!
... BUT I THINK AMERICA ***NEEDED*** THIS WAR. I HATE TO SAY IT, BUT IT'S *TRUE*, SHE WAS LOSING HER PRIDE. AMERICA NEEDED TO FEEL ***GOOD*** ABOUT HERSELF AGAIN" (69)
© 1992 Imperialist Features Syndicate Inc. World Rights Ignored
CLIK
...NOW BACK TO MORE TEXAS-STYLE DEATH-MATCH 'RASSLIN'!!
MUNCH MUNCH
CHIPS
SMITH 10-30

by HACK SMITH

POPPY THE PRESIDENT starring in **LET THE SON DO THE FINKING**

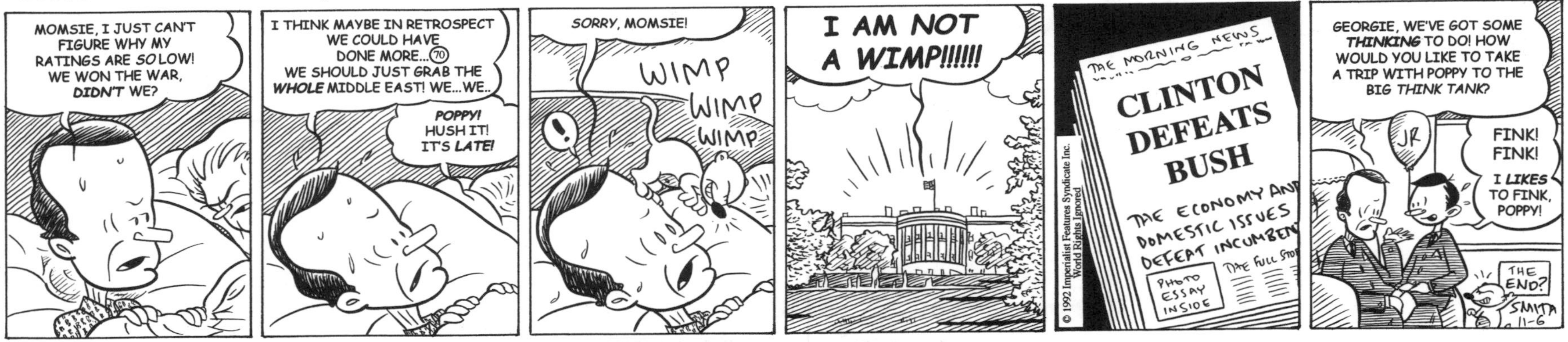
MOMSIE, I JUST CAN'T FIGURE WHY MY RATINGS ARE *SO* LOW! WE WON THE WAR, ***DIDN'T*** WE?
I THINK MAYBE IN RETROSPECT WE COULD HAVE DONE MORE... (70) WE SHOULD JUST GRAB THE ***WHOLE*** MIDDLE EAST! WE...WE..
POPPY! HUSH IT! IT'S ***LATE!***
SORRY, MOMSIE!
WIMP WIMP WIMP
I AM NOT A ***WIMP!!!!!!***
THE MORNING NEWS
CLINTON DEFEATS BUSH
THE ECONOMY AND DOMESTIC ISSUES DEFEAT INCUMBENT
PHOTO ESSAY INSIDE
THE FULL STORY
© 1992 Imperialist Features Syndicate Inc. World Rights Ignored
GEORGIE, WE'VE GOT SOME ***THINKING*** TO DO! HOW WOULD YOU LIKE TO TAKE A TRIP WITH POPPY TO THE BIG *THINK TANK?*
JR
FINK! FINK!
I ***LIKES*** TO FINK, POPPY!
THE END?
SMITH 11-6

BUSH
FAMILY VALUES

IN THE RENAISSANCE the Medicis managed to place three of their murderous clan, Leo X, Clement VII, and Leo XI, in the office of Pope, from which they arranged hits on their family's enemies. The even more nefarious Borgias, in the 1400s and 1500s, got two of their kin into the Papacy, Calixtus III and Alexander VI. The evilest among the Borgias, Cesare, became Machiavelli's model for his amoralist manual of political treachery and deceit, *The Prince*.

The evidence of history is that very little cannot be bought and put to sinister uses. And, as a rule, just as Machiavelli argued, boldness of concept in the honorable criminal culture of politics tends to be rewarded rather than punished, at least in the historical short term.

Roger Ailes, the media strategist who turned around the fortunes of the GOP with the election of Richard Nixon, required all of his political clients—including George H.W. Bush—to study closely Machiavelli's masterwork in amoralist politics, *The Prince*. To make sure they understood every implication and didn't lie about reading it, Ailes gave them tests on it. This text in mendacity and covert criminalism became the Bible of the contemporary Republican politician: the central Neo-Conservatives evidently also got to know this book very well at the feet of Leo Strauss, a major analyst of Machiavelli.

NEIL BUSH & THE S&L PILLAGE

NEIL BUSH SEEMED INCAPABLE throughout the S&L scandals of grasping the biased standards of self-accountability with which he rationalized his behavior. He was remarkably blind even to the existence of the conflicts of interest that, to him, were nothing more than splendid opportunities. His very moral obtuseness "made Neil the poster boy of the savings and loan crisis. He became a window into the board rooms of savings and loans across the country. Through him, the country saw that ethics and business deals went out the window in the 1980s, replaced by the notion that money and importance are the birthright of a small, privileged set. To them, no crime was committed." (p. 198) They had the connections for all the get-out-of-jail-free cards they could possibly want.

One source explained in lengthy detail "how Neil had organized the entire savings and loan crisis from a NORAD-like bunker in New Hampshire." Neil alone could not have masterminded even the failure of his own bank, Silverado. But the 500-billion dollar S&L fiasco as a whole would never have been possible without the luster of his famous name and his connections on-high. "The savings and loan crisis required hundreds of people who believed as Neil Bush did—directors, accountants and regulators. It required a vast abrogation of ethics that for many years have held together the machinery of capitalism, which otherwise would fly apart from the very force that drives it: greed." (pp. 204-5)

It was not ordinary greed for money alone that drove Neil Bush and all the cronies he symbolized. "...It was more destructive and... it lay at the heart not only of the savings and loan crisis, but the entire decade of the eighties. 'I've been prosecuting white collar crime for more than 20 years,' a government attorney told me. 'Financial crimes are always driven by greed for money. But it was different this time. This was vanity. A bunch of nobodies made it big for themselves. That's what this whole thing was about.'" (p. 205) Students of Marx will recall his chapter from The Economic-Philosophic Manuscripts of 1844, "The Power of Money in Bourgeois Society," on the overwhelming authority that great wealth has got to compensate for personal, natural, psychological, moral, and intellectual deficiencies: the archetypal formula for mass-revolution, "I am nothing and I should be everything," describes well this late-twentieth-century shocking mass-looting by conniving mediocrities.

Quotations above from *Silverado: Neil Bush and the Savings & Loan Scandal,* by Steven Wilmsen [National Press Books, 1991]

GEORGE BUSH & THE ORGANIZED CRIMES OF S&L PILLAGE

Pete Brewton's research into the tangled culture of Houston good-old-boy corruption defies ordinary credibility: it is as complex as a street-map of Houston, more incestuous by magnitudes than any Third World dictator's nepotistic scheme. His book portrays graphically a whole subculture of amoralists, of proliferating schemes that are clockwork mechanisms within mechanisms, forms of unscrupulous ingenuity and sophistication far exceeding the plodding methods of journalists, investors' attorneys, federal task forces, or the court system. Formal and respectable business-culture proved utterly porous to the Mafia and to crypto-rightwing forces within the CIA. The money siphoned out of just Texas savings-and-loans funded underground gun- and drug-smuggling operations ("guns down, drugs up"), vanished into offshore bank accounts on the Isle of Jersey and elsewhere, gratified Arab princes on the make for quick money, and fed many, many other predators. — Half a trillion dollars was looted and American taxpayers obtusely footed the bill and continued to regard the official malefactors as worthy of respect and reelection.

Brewton writes that he began to link "the world of [H.K.] Beebe, the Louisiana mob associate connected to the failure of at least a dozen Texas and Louisiana savings and loans, and the world of Mario Renda, the New York mob associate involved in the failure of financial institutions across the country. Not only did the two show up at Mainland Savings, but they also appeared together in other places and at other failed S&Ls, indicating the Mafia involvement in financial institutions had spread like a virus throughout the nation." (pp. 64-5) The most powerful financier in Houston and perhaps in Texas at large, Walter Mischer—a major figure in George Bush's career and in the S&L collapses—has a "reputed relationship to one of the most powerful Mafia families in the country, the [Carlos] Marcello family in New Orleans." (p. 15) The earliest eruption of this network of good-old-boy politics was the Sharpstown scandal in Houston in 1971 (p. 14), powerful enough in its repercussions to wreck the political career of golden-boy onetime-Lt.-Gov. Ben Barnes—but now utterly eclipsed by the scale of 1980s hubris.

What is harder to document definitively than Mafia implication in the lootings is the involvement of the CIA, just because this hypersecretive and long-ago ideologized federal agency has the power to quash the subpoenas needed to track the ultimate terminus of the S&L lucre. ". . .More likely than not . . . someone in the CIA hierarchy knew about and approved, if not instigated, S&L actions of its operatives." (p. xiv)

Quotations above from *The Mafia, C.I.A. and George Bush.*

BREWTON'S HISTORICAL SUMMARY is incisive: ". . . Defrauding a savings and loan before 1980 was like stealing a car that doesn't have an engine: a lot of trouble and hardly worth the effort. But beginning in 1980, Congress and then the Reagan Administration made it a great deal easier by opening the vaults of savings and loans to anyone with the temerity to walk in and take out the money."

Freeing up access to the S&L's vaults was called "deregulation," a feel-good piece of rhetoric that is not truly descriptive of what was actually done. But the term served very well to allay suspicions from ordinarily fiscally fastidious conservatives, and of course it made the whole affair look initially like business-as-usual. "Deregulation loosened the restrictions on the kinds of loans and investments S&Ls could make, while it lifted the ceiling on the interest rates S&Ls could pay on their deposits—which were used for the loans and investments. This meant that S&Ls could pay just about anything they needed to get money and then do just about anything they wanted with it." Combined with federal deposit insurance, requiring the federal government (and taxpayers, in the end) to assume liability for losses to depositors on loans and investments, all this was "an open invitation to the criminal element."

"If deregulation was the engine that made the car easy and worthwhile to steal, then the gasoline was brokered deposits. These are deposits placed in a savings and loan or bank by a middleman (broker) who gathers them together from various individuals and institutions such as pension funds and credit unions. Large amounts of brokered deposits at an S&L were a dead giveaway that the institution was on a fast track to hell. In their most virulent form, brokered deposits were made contingent on loans going to the broker's chosen borrowers. Those in the industry referred to this as 'linked financing.' Bribery, extortion and conspiracy would be more accurate." (pp. 44-5) This was how the cronies steered the loans toward one another, and toward the true principals who were hidden well behind the paper-shells of corporations and agents. The genius of these schemes consisted in all the insidious things that could be done with "other people's money," as one book on the criminal systems was titled.

Quotations above from *The Mafia, C.I.A. and George Bush.*

MANY THINGS OF STRUCTURAL SIGNIFICANCE about the rigged game of American banking and business were exposed by the mass-scale fraud of the S&L looting. "Henry Ford once remarked that if the American public really understood the banking system there would be rioting in the streets. Perhaps he was referring to these facts: (1) it is nearly impossible to succeed in any business without bank credit; (2) banks take in federally insured deposits from everyone and then lend out the money to their selected friends and associates; and (3) bank charters are awarded to the favored few by the government." (p. 269) Like TV stations and other news media and of course the notorious industrial-military complex that the Bush clan would later grow quite fat off of, banks as federally chartered institutions were examples of an exquisitely corruptible selective dispensation of federal largesse: as with the media and the military suppliers, so with banks—fealty flows back from the fiscally bound vassals to their superiors, the lieges or lords.

Taking it as a general characterization of the S&L mass-looting, Brewton cites what Benjamin Stein said of Imperial Savings in *Barron's* (9 October 1989) as a rare case of journalistic candor and indictment: "Imperial's story is about mismanagement, inadequate regulation, organized crime and questionable accounting." (p. 243) One has to remind oneself at every step of the S&L scandals that the power and connections of these upper-class pirates warp even the journalistic descriptions of what they did, and ultimately draw a veil of obscurity over the great hemorrhaging of wealth from public into private hands.

"The destruction of the savings-and-loan industry in Texas, and in some other parts of the country, worked basically like an organized-crime bustout or burnout. This is a mob scam in which a failing company is taken over, built up on credit, then drained of all its assets and purposely put into bankruptcy, leaving the creditors holding the bag." (p. xii) The commonplace system of good-old-boy trust or collegiality meant, of course, that banking and auditing professionals—if not themselves directly in bed with the conmen—were here being played like doddering retirees by those conmen.

The profile and symptoms of crony-capitalism and its propensity for crypto-criminal self-indulgences were evident in the long-standing personal associations among the malefactors. "Asked about all the numerous and curious connections of Kappa Sigmas [a minor but notoriously debauched UT-Austin fraternity] to the S&L debacle, Walt Mischer, Jr., just laughed and said there was nothing to it—ha, ha, ha." (p. 153)

Quotations above from *The Mafia, C.I.A. and George Bush*.

THE MODERN MULTITUDES are, to their exploiters, thoroughly predictable in their mass-psychology: most people want and need to believe specific consoling myths, fictions of meaningfulness that reassure them that the world is, in spite of everything, just continuing in the same-old-same-old order as of yore. All-too-familiar stereotypes of the sort Hollywood and TV long ago ensconced in the public imagination can be profitably deployed for the soporific purposes of mass-deception. "Many journalists. . .focused on the sizzle of this story, rather than on the meat. Their story line goes something like this: Those who looted the S&Ls were just a bunch of good-old-boy, Texas wheeler-dealer developers who blew all that money on wine, women, song, gambling, fast horses, faster cars, yachts, airplanes, Colorado chalets, California beach houses, etc. . . .Now, it may be true that these people spent most of the money they got out of the S&Ls on such things, but as mere front men and middle men they only received 1 or 2 percent of what was looted, and rarely more." (p. 384)

In the world of politics, things that seem stupid or unaccountable are typically forms of acute ingenuity operating under the guise of obtuseness, ways of planning ahead to alleviate future problems of which the public hasn't got a clue. Nothing is done accidentally or inadvertently. ". . .Organized crime strike forces. . .conducted successful S&L prosecutions in Florida, Kansas City and New York City. These strike forces had the background, knowledge and experience to delve into the kinds of large-scale conspiracies, with Mafia involvement, that were occurring in S&Ls across the country. And what did the Reagan and Bush Administrations do with these strike force units? They abolished them right in the middle of the S&L crisis." (p. 385) That is, in itself, graphic evidence of complicity from on high.

"Not one Congressman that I am aware of ever asked these simple questions: What happened to all that money, and why don't we try to get it back?" (p. 386) The most corrupt interests in this way have got an evident stake in making corruption as epidemic as possible: it guarantees that virtually all who may be involved in the official operations of government can be bought off or blackmailed. The already-amnesiac public is encouraged to believe that action is futile and they should just roll over and go back to sleep. Meanwhile the United States is subjected to an outsized kleptocracy whose scale puts in the shade all the most outrageous organized lootings in history.

"Not only did Congress not want to investigate any part of the S&L crisis—for obvious reasons—but they weren't about to take on the CIA either. They had seen . . . what had happened to congressional critics of the CIA in the mid-1970s, for example, Senator Frank Church: They had later been defeated for reelection by powerful, well-financed right-wing organizations and opposition." (p. 369) The popular notion of a "free marketplace of ideas" utterly ignores the reality that great concentrations of power and wealth naturally exude rightwing and authoritarian perspectives as a rationalizing ideology, and such perspectives are invaluable to plutocracy in helping it consolidate its power.

"The final insult is that the Congress and the Justice Department are not tracking down the money stolen from us. Not only do we need to know what it was used for—we need to get it back. The fact that the people who run this country have no desire to do either speaks louder than all the excuses and pious platitudes coming out of Washington, D.C., today." (p. 392)

Quotations above from *The Mafia, C.I.A. and George Bush.*

GEORGE BUSH INDISPUTABLY HAD A SERIES of high positions and a whole resume contrived for him by the interests he served as broker. Like his sons, he is about as charisma-challenged as any public official in living memory; it is nearly unthinkable that he might have accomplished anything in national politics on his own merits and competence. Brewton summarizes his career and demeanor as "former spook chief, transplanted Texas gladhander, standard-bearer for the hands-off, blind-eye government policies that made the S&L crisis possible." It was no accident that all these fiscal horrors came to a head on Bush's watch. "Reagan-Bush deregulation opened a Pandora's box, and George couldn't close it, and didn't want to, considering all his friends, offspring and political backers who were happily getting richer. As America sank in a sea of S&L debt, the President exhorted us to 'stay the course.'

The Bush course of complicity, non-reaction and denial has left the taxpayer over $500 billion poorer." To a far more eminent degree than his dirty-handed son Neal, "Bush is the perfect representative of the real problem in the savings-and-loan crisis: the wealthy businessmen with symbiotic relationships to the Mafia and the CIA. They all used each other to get what they wanted, and most of all they used the government—via semi-monopolistic government charters, government regulation and government deposit insurance—to cheat the taxpayers." (p. 393) Indeed, when Neil Bush's corrupt Silverado S&L had been challenged for its uncollateralized loans, the same supervisory agent for the board who waived these questions—Kermit Mowbray—also "later that year held off seizing deeply insolvent Silverado until the day after George Bush was elected President." (p. 238)

"While Congress, the Justice Department, and the press concentrated on the flamboyant borrowers and managers of the S&Ls, the big recipients of the money—the wealthy, powerful landowners and property owners—crept off quietly with their profits." (p. xi)

In reports of the S&L frauds, we Americans in the end all completely overlooked ". . .the massive transfer of wealth from the American taxpayers to a select group of extremely rich, powerful people. Had the American public taken to heart the real dynamics and power-structures behind the S&L pillage, it might well have known to expect that even more grandiose forms of mass-looting would ensue from the "election" of another Bush to our highest office.

Quotations above from *The Mafia, C.I.A., and George Bush: The Untold Story of America's Greatest Financial Debacle*, by Pete Brewton [S.P.I. Books, 1992])

GEORGE H.W. BUSH
&
SADDAM HUSSEIN

THE FIRST RULE OF SURVIVAL in our hyper-Machiavellian social world is to "watch what people do, not what they say." GHW Bush's rhetoric plays however the prevailing public winds may require it to, but his actions inevitably belie these posturings. "The only way to bring foreign violators of proliferation controls [such as Saddam Hussein] to book is by imposing strict trade sanctions. And yet sanctions legislation passed by Congress has been vetoed again and again by President [GHW] Bush."

"Saddam Hussein's death machine was built almost exclusively by Western companies. The vast majority of the machine tools, computers, and test equipment he needed to build ballistic missiles, bombs, bullets, and guns was provided totally legally by companies who applied for export licenses. A compilation of public sources alone shows that 445 companies cashed in on this macabre bonanza, one third of them in West Germany alone."

"Until concrete steps are taken to curb this type of trade, the 'new world order' President [GHW] Bush is so keen on heralding will turn out to be more death as usual." (p. 397) There is only a brief transitional period during which it is possible to describe the workings of big-money corruptivism as "criminal." Once it acquires the full scope of governmental powers it desires, it will define these criminal acts out of existence as crimes, and make it impossible for the public ever to find out about them. For the forces that drive megamoney interests to consolidate and aggrandize their powers are ultimately aimed at abolishing even the appearance of an opposition. If the public understood what Bush's rhetoric about a "new world order" actually forebodes, they would certainly have risen up in terror and outrage against the abolition of their democratic rights and the expropriation of their hard-won savings, home equity, and retirement accounts. Under the unprecedented dispensation of the "new world order," this once-prosperous nation will get ground down to the status of a Third-World populace of debt-slaves.

Quotations above from *The Death Lobby: How the West Armed Iraq*, by Kenneth R. Timmerman [Houghton Mifflin, 1991]

"WORSE THAN HITLER"

ONE FORMER WHITE HOUSE OFFICIAL acknowledged that "black ops" or "off-the-shelf operations" in the Middle East were standard operating procedures during the first Bush administration even though they were illegal. ". . .People think the Irangate affair was something strange. It wasn't. It was just the one that went public. It was not at all abnormal.'" (p. 24)

That official said, "The government found third parties and private channels for our shipments. I call this our 'dirty policy.' This was all consistent with covert operations at the time. False fronts were used a lot."

Who within the White House aided these covert shipments? asked Friedman. "Two of the most active people. . . were Judge Clark and [CIA director] William Casey. . . . Casey would travel to Saudi Arabia a lot. He went every two or three months to coordinate. . . . Casey had an office in the Old Executive Office Building, right next to the White House. . . . He was frequently at the White House, and he would meet with Reagan all the time," and with VP George Bush, who "knew about the covert operations, and Casey felt he could trust him, with his intelligence orientation and all that." Bush made it quite clear "he wanted to help Iraq. His door was always open to the Iraqis. If they wanted a meeting with Bush, they would get it." (p. 25)

All through the Reagan administration exports were knowingly sent to nuclear installations in Iraq for numerous reasons, a former White House official explained. Some people doubted that Saddam would actually get the programs running. Others argued Saddam would not ever in fact use a nuclear weapon. "There were some very ugly debates about Saddam's intentions in the interagency groups." About the White House position, there was no possible doubt. "Bush as vice president made it clear he wanted to help Iraq." (pp. 156-7.)

Quotations above from *Spider's Web*

Aware of the dramatic growth of Saddam's nuclear program and also of its support by the export policies of the Bush administration, one intelligence agent summed it up tersely: "It was policy. The White House knew what was happening and didn't really care." (p. 157) A secret policy review "articulated a prime US business interest that influenced both Bush and [secretary of state James] Baker in their thinking: Iraq's 'vast oil reserves promising a lucrative market for US goods.' The review noted that US oil imports from Iraq had skyrocketed after Iraq began offering American oil companies 'large price incentives.'" (p.134)

NSD (National Security Directive) 26 expressed the Bush administration's firm determination "to aid and abet Saddam Hussein," said Congressman Sam Gejdenson, a Connecticut Democrat and one of Bush's sharpest critics. "The cop was put in the intersection, and he was waving the sellers on." (p. 134) After the fact, both Bush and his less-than-presidential-timber son would criticize Saddam for his heinous methods and acts of war against his own people; but ". . . [GHW] Bush had been among those in the Reagan administration who resisted congressional efforts to levy sanctions on Iraq . . . to punish Saddam for gassing the Kurds in August 1988." (p. 134)

"For almost ten years Washington had delivered to Saddam enormous amounts of agricultural credits and Eximbank guarantees, weapons and technology, sometimes covertly and sometimes quite openly. Now the Iraqi leader was making speeches like this," threatening to cremate Israel with his weapons. Surely Bush must have been aghast now, hoping against hope that Saddam could not really mean it. (p. 159)

Quotations above from *Spider's Web*

WHEN BUSH'S CATASTROPHICALLY SHORT-SIGHTED FOREIGN POLICY began to crumble as Saddam made his brutal aims all too evident, Bush required someone to interpose himself between the President and Congressional investigators. Nicholas Rostow "triggered congressional complaints of 'stonewalling' when he drafted a White House order instructing the CIA, State Department, and Pentagon not to provide documents or information to an investigation that was examining knowledge that George Bush was alleged to have had of Manuel Noriega's drug-dealings when Bush was CIA director." (p. 212) To squelch Noriega's efforts at blackmailing him, Bush had our military invade the sovereign nation of Panama and, instead of turning Noriega over to the World Court, seized him and brought him to the US, under dubious or fraudulent jurisdiction, for a tightly muzzled trial. The American public never got to hear what the Panamanian dictator wanted to reveal about the dirty deals of our President.

Congressman Henry Gonzalez, investigating the executive branch's role in Middle Eastern illegalities, was infuriated by "the Rostow gang"'s organized meetings and plans to frustrate the process of congressional discovery. Formerly, he said, ". . .cover-ups were sort of ad hoc events, a mad scramble to provide damage control for the moment. The Rostow gang advances the notion that cover-up mechanisms have become an integral cog in the machinery of this administration.'" (p. 216)

"'George Bush is presiding over a cover-up significantly larger than Watergate," charged the Democrats' Vice Presidential candidate, Al Gore. (p. 245) One supposes that, after so many decades of routinely relying on illegal and extralegal measures, the Republicans finally realized they needed to play hardball and suppress information far more rigorously than Nixon had ever tried to do. In the last of the televised presidential debates, Ross Perot made the Iraqgate matter directly public: "If you create Saddam Hussein over a ten-year period using billions of US taxpayer money, step up to the plate and say it was a mistake." (pp. 245-6) Perot was evidently envisioning a hypothetical world in which Bushes actually have courage, candor and scruples.

Quotations above from *Spider's Web*

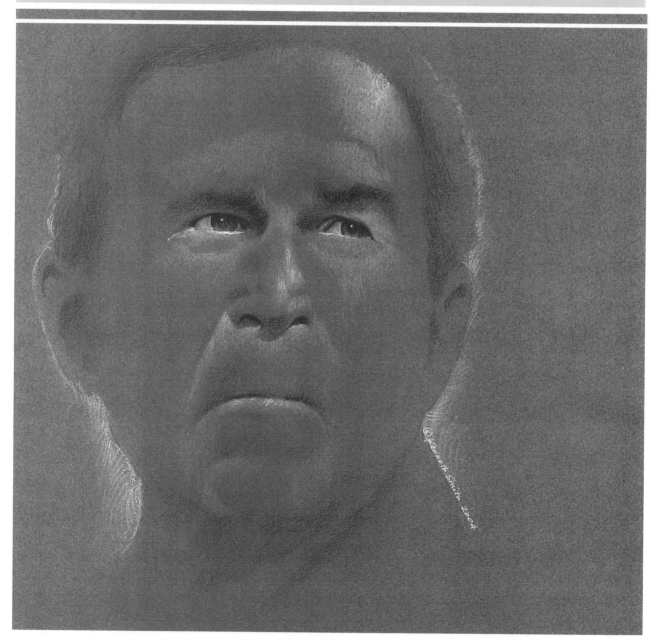

NEARLY A WEEK AFTER KUWAIT WAS INVADED by Iraq ". . .the president [GHW Bush] signed an unusual document that had been drawn up by White House counsel Boyden Gray. It was a financial conflict-of-interest waiver that authorized Baker and ten other cabinet officers and officials—including Brent Scowcroft, Robert Mosbacher, and Robert Gates—to participate in 'current United States policy-making, discussions, decisions, and actions in response to the Iraqi invasion of Kuwait.'"

"Gray had asked the president to sign waivers for all those officials who had substantial oil, defense, or other business holdings that might be affected by the Persian Gulf crisis. A waiver was also issued for Gray himself." (pp. 169-70) We see in this concern for legal formalities a degree of fastidiousness not to be met with again in the subsequent regime of organized corruptions under Bush's son. The more the Bush regimes go on, the more incomprehensible they seem to find the very concept of a "conflict of interest," just like Neal Bush.

The financial holdings of Baker and his immediate family, filed by him in 1989, explain what is so sensitive about his case in particular. "He and his family held interests in the major oil companies Amoco, Exxon, and Texaco, three other oil-related companies, and ten limited partnerships in oil wells or leases." (pp. 170-1)

"In the 1980s,. . .because of the obsessive drive to guarantee access to Persian Gulf oil, the Reagan and Bush administrations, with people like George Bush and James Baker in positions of primary responsibility, did virtually anything they wanted. The government's lack of accountability, either to Congress or to the public, was so egregious as to pose a silent threat to the principles of American democracy." (pp. 285-6) The principles of American democracy have come to be directly and mortally threatened by a tidal wave of rightwing authoritarians and evangelical know-nothings, organized by means of Fox News and Limbaugh and other radio shills for the forces of political darkness.

--quotes above from *Spider's Web: The Secret History Of How the White House Illegally Armed Iraq*, by Alan Friedman (Bantam, 1993)

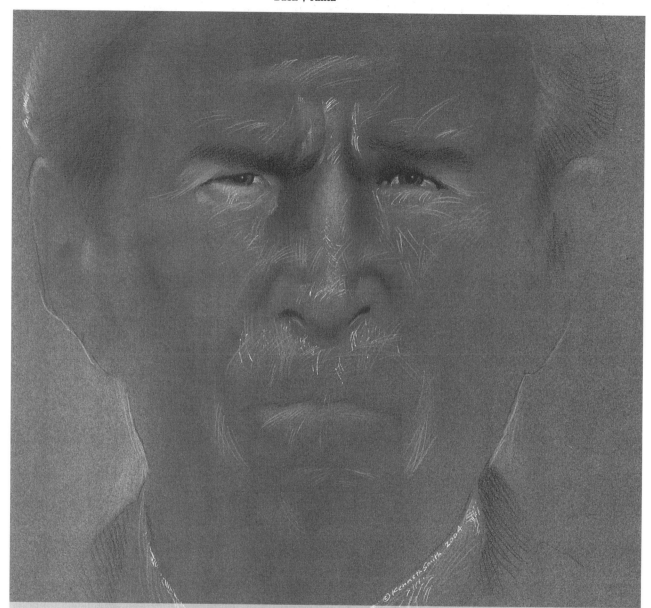

JEB BUSH & THE MURDEROUS DRUGLORD SALINAS-GORTIARI

THE CURRENT PRESIDENT'S BROTHER "JEB" (John Ellis Bush), before he became governor of Florida, was a close friend of Raul Salinas de Gortiari, brother of the former President of Mexico Carlos Salinas, now himself sought of course for massive theft of government funds and bribery. "Raul was a leading member of the Mexican Drug Cartel and is now serving a 27-year jail term for having murdered a political opponent." (Michel Chossudovsky, "Bush Family Links to the Mexican Drug Cartel," <u>Global Outlook</u> issue #5, summer/fall 2003.)

In Mexico there has been much speculation about the full extent and nature of Raul Salinas' intimate friendship with ex-President George Bush's son, Jeb. "It is well known here that for many years the two families spent vacations together—the Salinases at Jeb Bush's home in Miami, the Bushes at Raul's ranch, Las Mendocinas, under the volcano in Puebla. There are many in Mexico who believe that the relation became a back channel for delicate and crucial negotiations between the two governments, leading up to President Bush's sponsorship of NAFTA." (<u>Houston Chronicle</u>, 9 March 1995) But the accusations of Noriega, that

GHW Bush had his hands in the hemisphere's drug traffic, take on greater gravity in the light of these connections; and the implications of Brewton's discoveries about Houston's big-money operatives in Latin American drugs ("Guns down, drugs up"). Bush's son George may have been the first convicted felon to assume the office of president, but he was apparently preceded in his felonies by his unindicted father.

Chossudovsky notes: "The personal relationship between the Bush and Salinas families is a matter of public record. George H.W. Bush (Senior)--when he worked in the oil business in Texas in the 1970s—had developed close personal ties with Carlos Salinas and his father, Raul Salinas Lozano." According to Carl Openheimer, "Witnesses say former Mexican president Carlos Salinas de Gortiari, his imprisoned brother Raul, and other members of the country's ruling elite met with drug lord Juan Garcia Abrego at a Salinas family ranch; Jeb Bush admits he met with Raul Salinas several times but [claims he] has never done any business with him." (<u>The Miami Herald</u>, 17 February 1997)

GODFATHER BUSH & GODFATHER LOZANO

RAUL SALINAS LOZANO, THE FAMILY PATRIARCH and father of Carlos and Raul Jr., was the principal behind the crime syndicate: the former private secretary to Lozano testified to US authorities that "Mr. Salinas Lozano was a leading figure in narcotics dealing that also involved his son, Raul Salinas de Gortiari, his son-in-law, Jose Francisco Ruis Massieu, the No. 2 official in governing Institutional Revolutionary Party, or PRI, and other leading politicians, according to the documents. Mr. Ruiz Massieu was assassinated in 1994 [by Raul Salinas]." (Dallas Morning News, 26 Feb. 1997.)

A former agent of the US Drug Enforcement Administration, Michael Levine, said that the Mexican Drug Cartel was definitely a "family affair." Carlos as well as Raul were major figures in the Cartel, and this was known to Reagan's Attorney-General Edwin Meese already in 1987, a year before Carlos Salinas was inaugurated as president. The Dallas Morning News reported the Bush administration knew quite well about President Salinas' links to organized crime. But the American and Canadian publics were kept in the dark in order to facilitate the signing of NAFTA, which it is now hard to imagine was nothing more than a clean and above-board business-partnership between the US and Mexico. Many of its provisions, permitting for instance Mexican trucks to enter the US without inspections, seem directly to facilitate drug traffic.

Former officials in the US government say they were coerced "to keep mum because Washington was obsessed with approving NAFTA . . . . 'The intelligence on corruption, especially by drug traffickers, has always been there,' said Phil Jordan, who headed DEA's Dallas office from 1984 to 1994. But 'we were under instructions not to say anything negative about Mexico. It was a no-no since NAFTA was a hot political football.'" (Dallas Morning News, 26 February 1997.) Among international drug cartels—including the very lucrative crops of opium in Afghanistan, major supplier to the world at large, in which the US is now the occupying power—the mixed metaphor of a "hot political football" might be more apt than Mr. Jordan knew.

THE LATE 20TH CENTURY SAW WIDESPREAD KLEPTOCRACY, rule by systematic plunderers or massive looters such as the Marcoses in the Philippines, Manuel Noriega in Panama, Idi Amin in Uganda, the Ceaucescus in Romania, Saddam Hussein in Iraq, Fujimori in Peru, Salinas in Mexico, and many, many more.

The United States of America has proved not to be impervious to but rather ideal as a culture-medium for this kind of treacherous and even murderous regime. Although plane crashes involving politicians are quite rare in Europe, they seem to afflict the opponents and critics of the Bush regime all too frequently: before he became GWB's attorney-general, John Ashcroft lost an election to Congress even after his opponent Mel Carnahan died in a plane crash; the skids were greased for GWB's campaign for war on Iraq after his most vocal antagonist in the Senate, Paul Wellstone, perished with his family, aides and pilot in a plane crash; after making an enthusiastically received speech before the Democratic National Convention and later informing close friends that he was considering going into national politics, John F. Kennedy Jr. died in a plane crash with his wife and sister-in-law; and Democratic fund-raiser Ron Brown's plane had gone down in Europe during Clinton's administration. And the ex-con Jim Hatfield who authored an exposé—*Fortunate Son*—of GWB's earlier dissolute, fraudulent and criminal career, died a purported suicide not long after GWB's unelected accession to office as so-called president.

Truth, over against the great forces that shape mass-publicity, is always a fragile and easily extinguished realization. The conduits of public truth can be monopolized and controlled just as readily as water resources and electricity and gasoline—and wealth and power. Any group sufficiently powerful can not just snuff public understanding but also misdirect public curiosity. Every particular scheme and every expose of those schemes can be "managed" and kept obscure, doomed to evaporate in the modern wasteland of superficial and fickle mass-mentalities. What is not so easy to manage is the whole course and profile of a vast criminal conspiracy which is always liable to spring leaks and provoke outrage in repetitive patterns. The shape of something horrible, even though most people will never find out exactly what, can be made out beneath the blankets.

KLEPTOCRACY GROWN INTO AN EMPIRE

AN OPERATIVE FORMERLY IN THE SERVICE of Nelson Rockefeller and the national GOP observed to me in the early 1990s, "The big boys never get their hands dirty, they don't have to. Someone else, a disposable 'cat's paw,' executes everything for them. They buy whatever services they need, from Democrats or from Republicans. They have no party and no ideology. They just use these things." A striking tale from Brewton's *The Mafia, CIA, and George Bush* may illustrate how the billionaire-puppeteers keep their anonymity: Brewton's paper, <u>The Houston Post</u>, was having his articles on the S&L scandals legally vetted by the major Houston law firm of Fulbright and Jaworski, and its attorney was arguing that one of the Houston principals was not a "public figure" and therefore posed a very high risk for rejoining the articles with a libel suit.

Brewton writes: "What [attorney] Wallingford said about [Walter] Mischer's not being a public figure was patently absurd, and everyone on the city desk hooted when they heard it. Mischer is probably the most powerful man in Houston and Texas; he has been appointed to various state government agencies by many governors; he was chairman and largest stockholder of the third largest bank in Houston; he was named to all of Texas Monthly's 'most powerful Texans' lists; he has been named 'The Kingmaker' for his political influence in a book, *Texas Big Rich*, by Sandy Sheehy; he was written about critically in Harvey Katz' book *Shadow on the Alamo*; he had been mentioned in many recent news stories, including one in which he was lobbying members of the City Council not to change a Yellow Cab contract at Houston International Airport (Mischer had an ownership interest in Yellow Cab); and his picture graced the front of the Houston Post's Sunday magazine in November 1987, along with the words 'Texas Power Broker.' In addition, Mischer and his bank were involved in two of the dirtiest S&Ls in the country, Mainland and Continental, whose failures cost taxpayers more than $1 billion. Also, Mischer had many other connections, direct and indirect, to the savings-and-loan scandal, as detailed in this book." (pp. 370-71, *The Mafia, C.I.A, and George Bush*)

But in 21st- as in 20th-century America, one of the utmost privileges of great wealth is invisibility-on-demand: in some countries plutocrats and their militarist minions make their enemies into "disappeareds." In the US, by the magic of money and its regime of "special effects," the megawealthy themselves disappear from accusatory contexts and reappear when it is time for them to take credit for the economic sunshine.

BREWTON FURTHER NOTES that, for his work in obstructing and delaying the publication of the <u>Houston Post</u> exposés—keeping them from appearing when the stories were still hot, in a mass-market format—the Fulbright and Jaworski attorney was evidently rewarded with promotion to partner. Mischer effectively owned the very law firm the Post had turned to for legal advice and defense against him, "a firm that keeps popping up in connection with many of the big S&L players" (Brewton, p. 370). And another crony of George Bush, Hugh Liedtke, the chairman of Pennzoil, may have been instrumental in stymieing major publisher Simon and Schuster's plan to get Brewton's own book out in time to inform voters before the 1990 presidential election. "Liedtke is also a member of the board of directors of Paramount Communications, the parent company of Simon & Schuster." (p. 378)

Brewton's book was stalled and eventually had to be published by a vastly smaller house, S.P.I. Not just what happens but also what doesn't happen is testimony to the insidious and covert powers of megalomoney. Virtually the whole public domain belongs to them or else can be controlled strategically by them. In a political system governed by manipulable numbers games, statistically insignificant critically informed readers can be guaranteed to be kept to a minimum by our whorish media.

In the Renaissance the Medicis managed to place three of their murderous clan, Leo X, Clement VII, and Leo XI, in the office of Pope, from which they arranged hits on their family's enemies. The even more nefarious Borgias, in the 1400s and 1500s, got two of their kin into the Papacy, Calixtus III and Alexander VI. The evilest among the Borgias, Cesare, became Machiavelli's model for his amoralist manual of political treachery and deceit, *The Prince*.

The evidence of history is that very little cannot be bought and put to sinister uses. And, as a rule, just as Machiavelli argued, boldness of concept in the honorable criminal culture of politics tends to be rewarded rather than punished, at least in the historical short term.

Roger Ailes, the media strategist who turned around the fortunes of the GOP with the election of Richard Nixon, required all of his political clients—including George H.W. Bush—to study closely Machiavelli's masterwork in amoralist politics, *The Prince*. To make sure they understood every implication and didn't lie about reading it, Ailes gave them tests on it. This text in mendacity and covert criminalism became the Bible of the contemporary Republican politician: the central Neo-Conservatives evidently also got to know this book very well at the feet of Leo Strauss, a major analyst of Machiavelli.

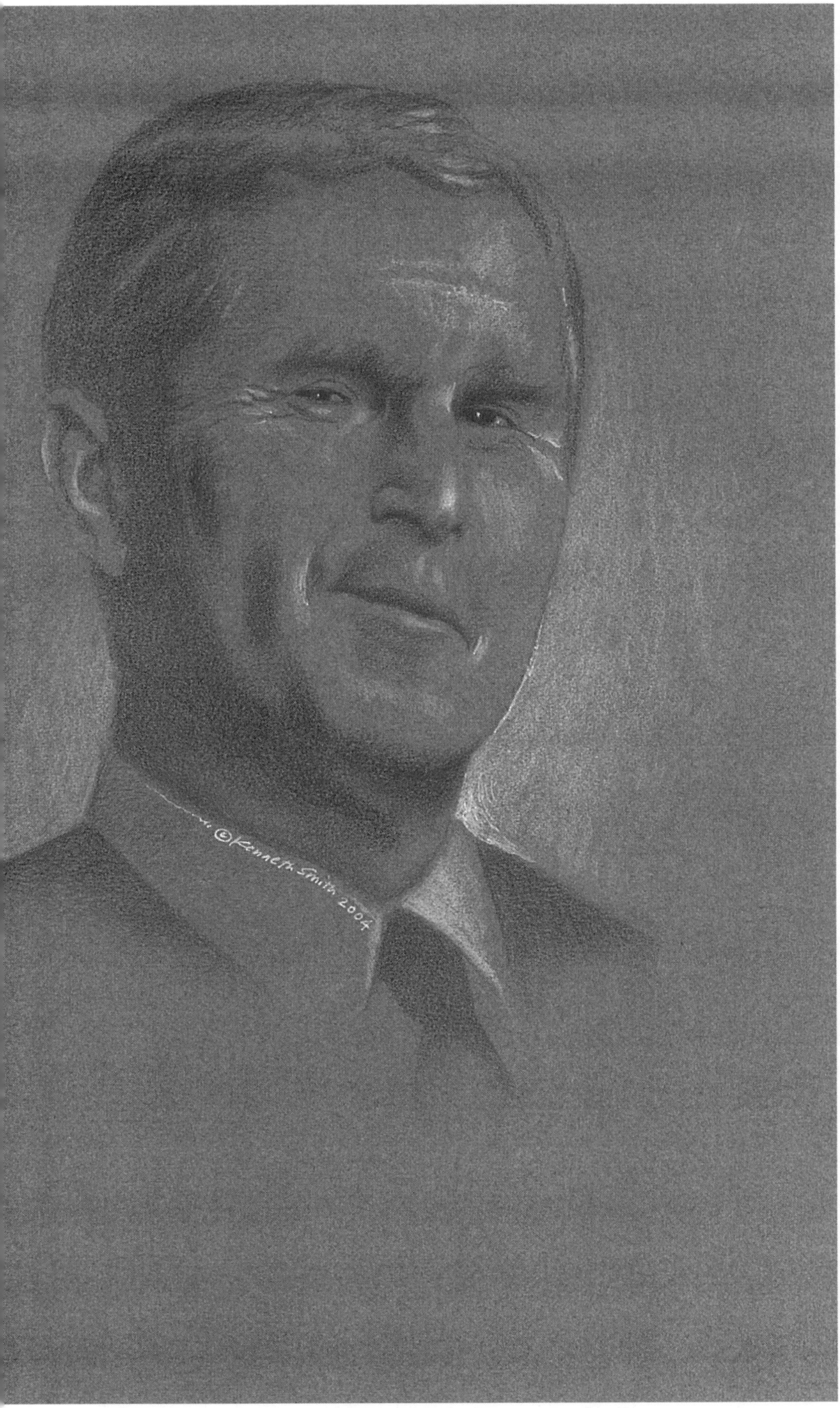
©Kenneth Smith 2004

2
The Son

EARLY MORNING, 1972
ELLINGTON FIELD,
HOUSTON, TEXAS, USA

LT. GEORGE W. BUSH OF THE TEXAS AIR NATIONAL GUARD MOUNTS HIS F-102 FIGHTER JET AND
READIES HIMESELF FOR ANOTHER LONG PATROL, HIS SOLEMN AERIAL VIGIL TO DEFEND...

THE SKIES OF TEXAS

by Scott A. Gilbert

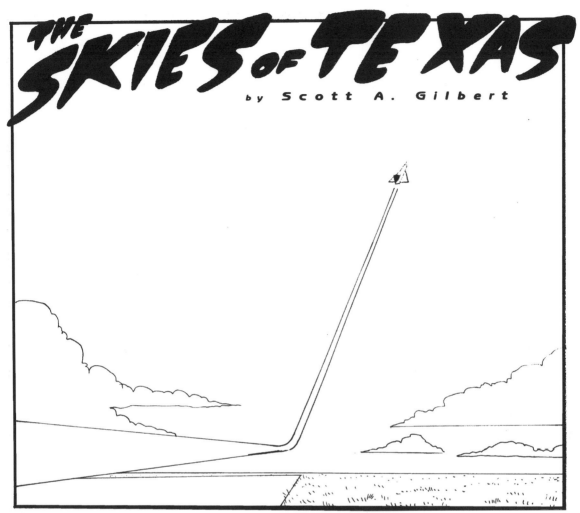

VIGILANCE MUST BE CONSTANT: THE SINISTER VIETCONG MUST NEVER BE ALLOWED TO DIM THE THE LIGHT OF THE LONE STAR.

BUSH'S MISSION IS CLEAR AND HIS RESOLVE STEELY (THE REMNANTS OF HIS PREVIOUS EVENING'S CELEBRATORY ACTIVITIES NOTWITHSTANDING).

BUSH'S WAR MACHINE SHOOTS OUT OVER THE SHIMMERING EXPANSE OF THE GULF OF MEXICO.

FAR BELOW AN OIL DRILLING PLATFORM BREAKS THE GOLDEN MONOTONY OF THE GULF'S WAVES.

ONE SHORT YEAR FROM NOW, SHAWN'S PATROLS WILL END. ALL THAT'S LEFT OF HIM WILL RETURN HOME TO TEXAS.

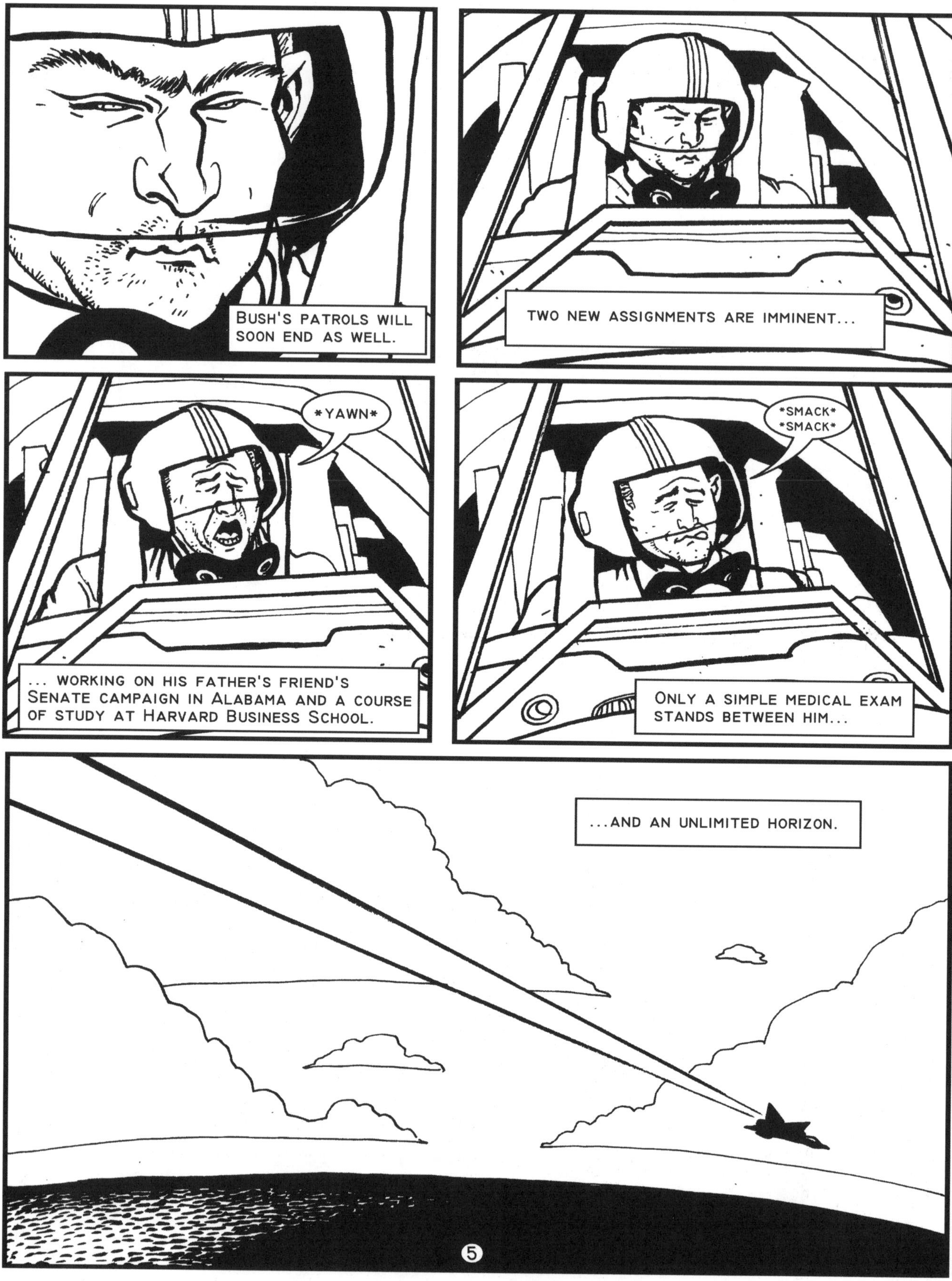
BUSH'S PATROLS WILL SOON END AS WELL.
TWO NEW ASSIGNMENTS ARE IMMINENT...
YAWN
... WORKING ON HIS FATHER'S FRIEND'S SENATE CAMPAIGN IN ALABAMA AND A COURSE OF STUDY AT HARVARD BUSINESS SCHOOL.
SMACK *SMACK*
ONLY A SIMPLE MEDICAL EXAM STANDS BETWEEN HIM...
...AND AN UNLIMITED HORIZON.
5

The COMPASSIONATE CONSERVATIVE ☠

Art by Penny Van Horn • Text by Mack White

George W. Bush is known as a "Compassionate Conservative." He first demonstrated his unique brand of compassion while governor of the state of Texas.

★ ★ ★ ★ ★

When Bush became Governor, the Texas criminal justice system was already widely recognized as the worst in the nation. Amnesty International stated that "at every step in the death penalty process in Texas, a litany of grossly inadequate legal procedures failed to meet recognized minimum international standards for the protection of human rights."

Governor Bush responded to this situation with his characteristic compassion. For instance, he opposed reforms to the death penalty process, and also vetoed legislation which would have provided for basic indigent defense, calling it "a threat to public safety."

Another example of Bush's compassion occurred when convicted murderer Karla Faye Tucker appealed to him to spare her life. In a *Talk* magazine interview, he compassionately mimicked the woman he had put to death, pursing his lips in mock desperation and whimpering:

"Please don't kill me!"

During his governorship, Bush compassionately presided over 152 executions. Many of these prisoners were mentally ill or severely retarded. Others were indigents whose court-appointed attorneys fell asleep during their trials.

Governor Bush's compassion also extended to the environment.

His compassionate protection of the top polluters resulted in Texas being:

Number One ★ in overall toxic releases.
Number One ★ in carcinogens in the air.
Number One ★ in developmental toxin in the air
(affecting the brain and nervous
system development of children).
Also ★ 1/3 of Texas rivers and 44% of Texas bays are so polluted
that they do not meet the minimum standards for recreational
and other uses.

These are just a few examples of Bush's compassion as governor. God help the rest
of the nation now that his compassion extends beyond the borders of Texas.

Florida 11/7/00

* HAITIAN AND HISPANIC VOTERS, UNLIKE WHITES, WERE OFTEN ASKED FOR TWO FORMS OF I.D BEFORE BEING ALLOWED TO VOTE.

— FINANCIAL TIMES. 11/16/00

* MANY BLACK VOTERS' NAMES WERE DROPPED FROM THE ROLLS AS BEING CONVICTED FELONS, THOUGH THESE PEOPLE HAD NEVER BEEN ARRESTED.
—DAILY NEWS 11/11/00

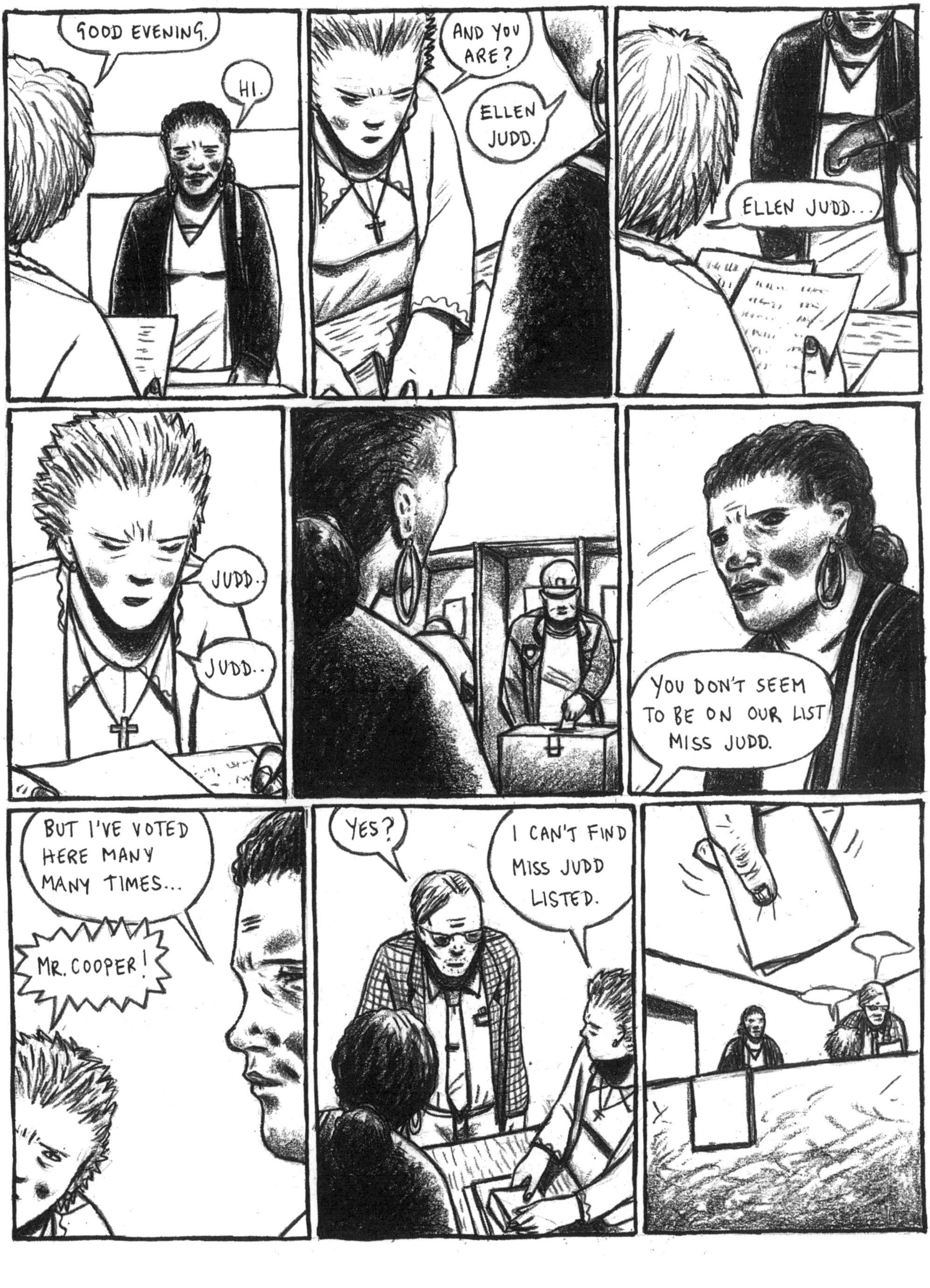
GOOD EVENING.
HI.
AND YOU ARE?
ELLEN JUDD.
ELLEN JUDD...
JUDD..
JUDD..
YOU DON'T SEEM TO BE ON OUR LIST MISS JUDD.
BUT I'VE VOTED HERE MANY MANY TIMES...
MR. COOPER!
YES?
I CAN'T FIND MISS JUDD LISTED.

※ MANY VOTERS WERE RE-DIRECTED FROM THEIR USUAL PRECINCTS WITHOUT EXPLANATION.
— ST. PETERSBURG TIMES. 12/7/00

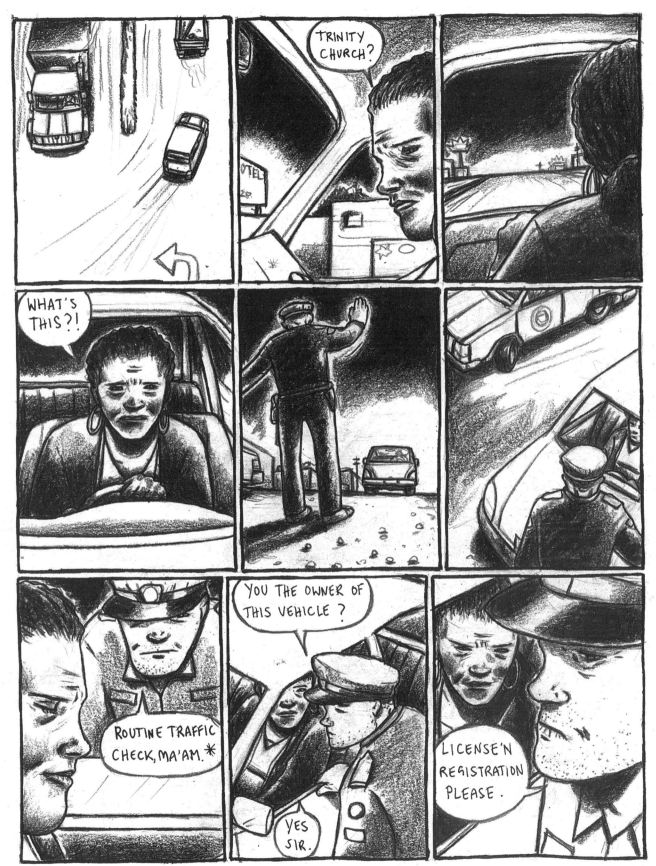

✱ TRAFFIC CHECKS HINDERED VOTERS TRYING TO REACH THEIR PRECINCTS.

INTER PRESS 11/14/00

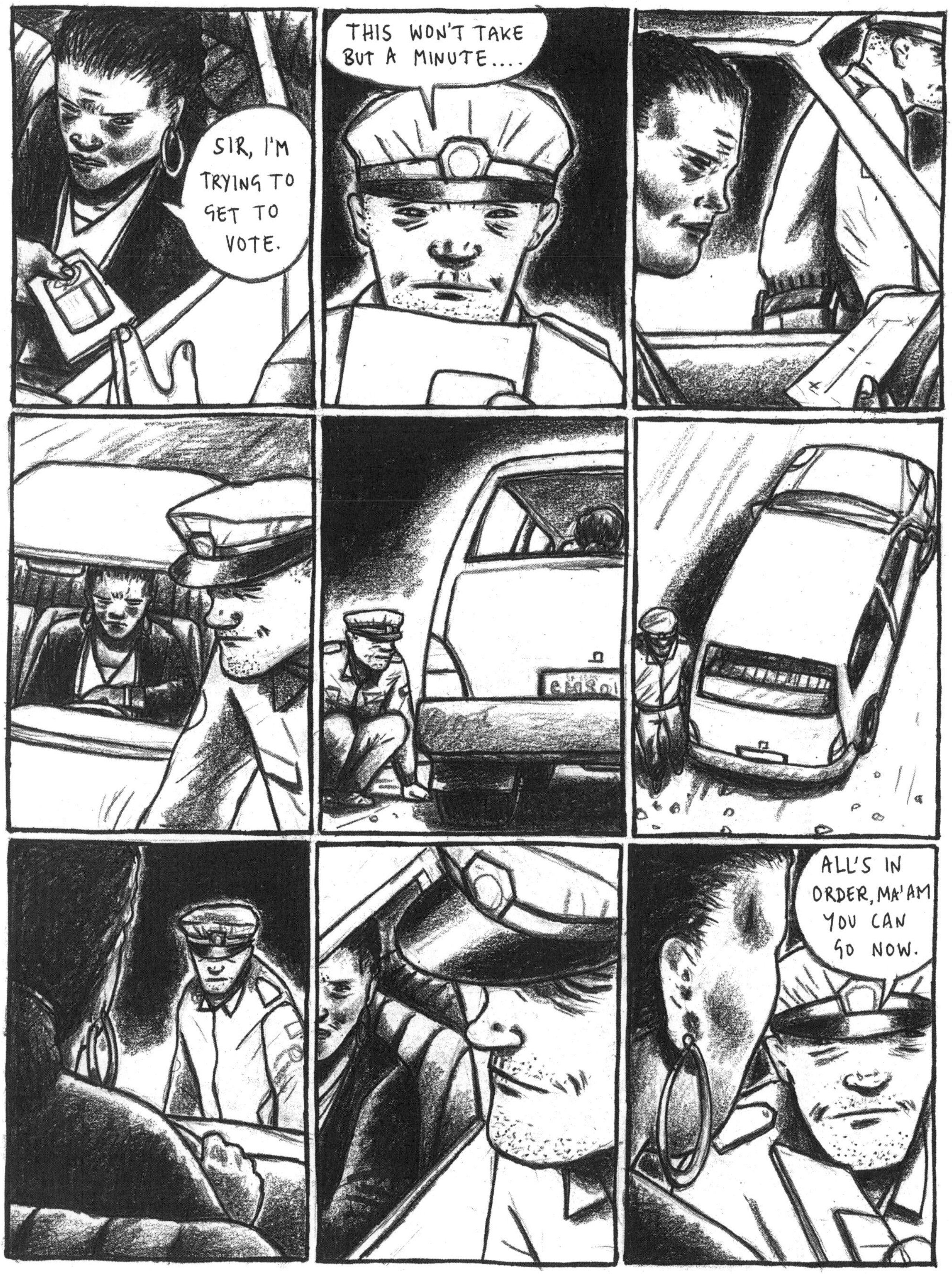
SIR, I'M TRYING TO GET TO VOTE.
THIS WON'T TAKE BUT A MINUTE....
ALL'S IN ORDER, MA'AM YOU CAN GO NOW.

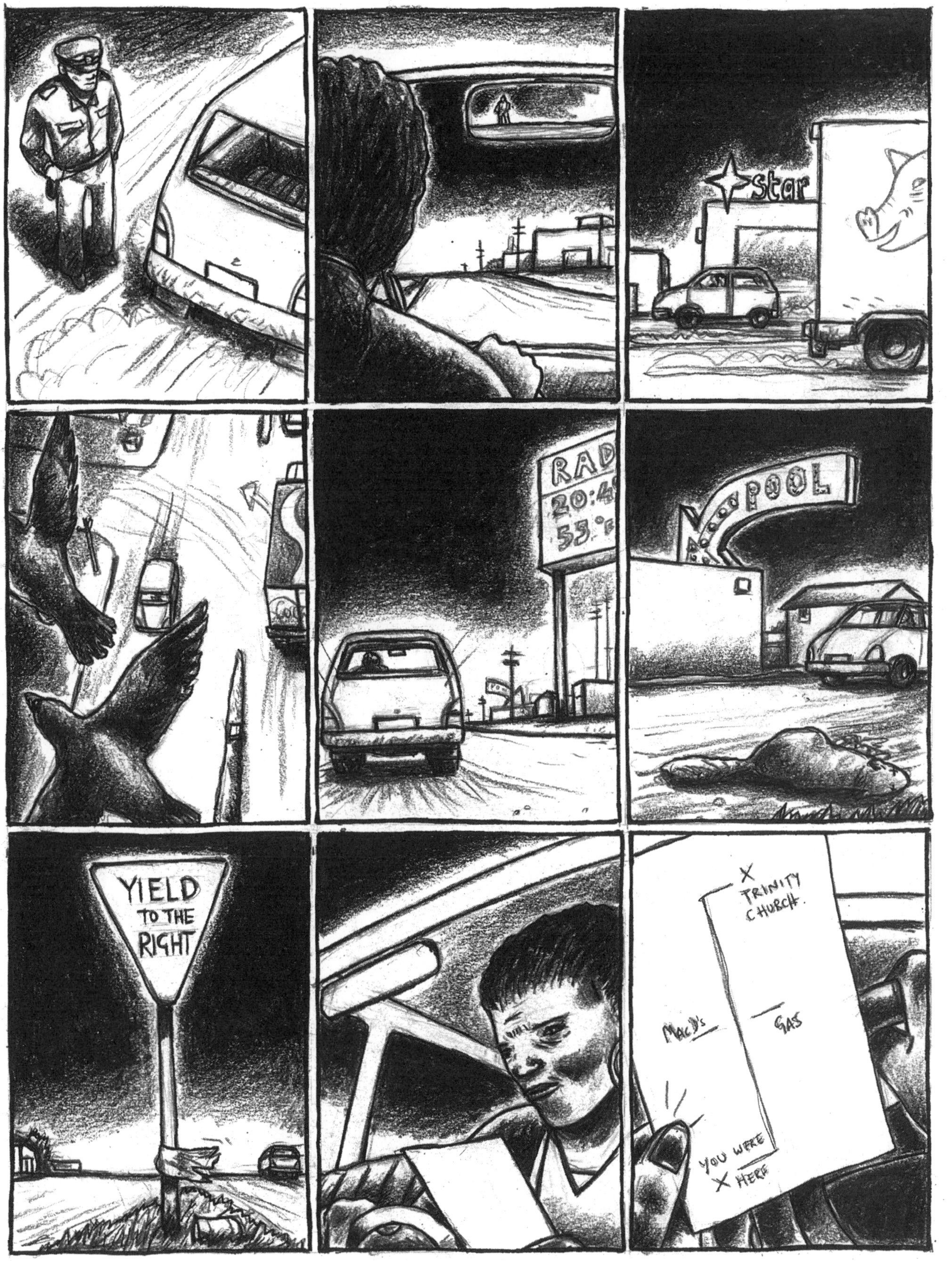
Star
RAD
20:4
53°F
POOL
YIELD
TO THE
RIGHT
X
TRINITY
CHURCH.
MacD's
GAS
YOU WERE
X HERE

✱ GEORGE W. BUSH LED FLORIDA'S STATE OFFICIAL COUNT BY ONLY 537 VOTES.

ABC NEWS 1/12/01

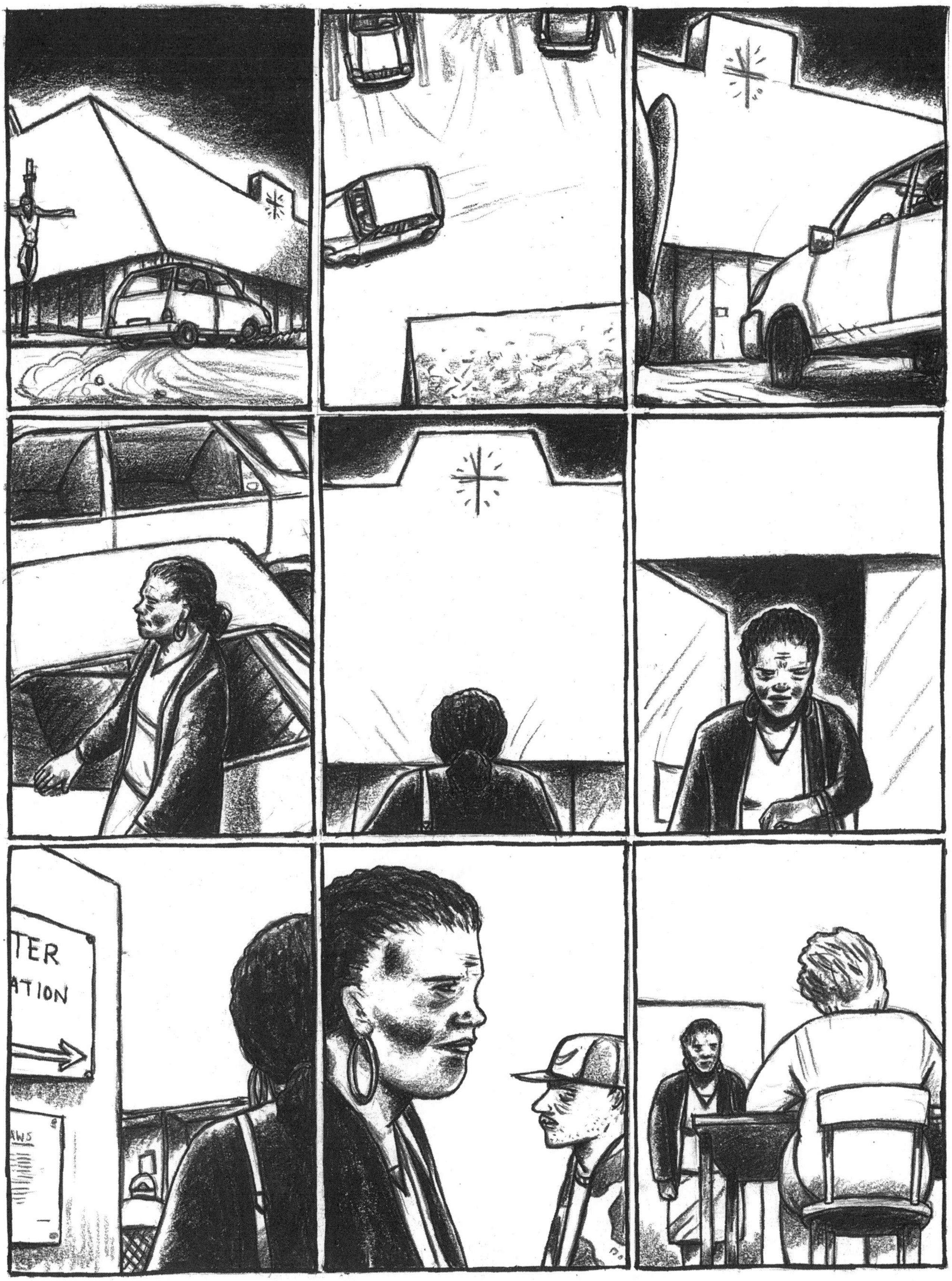
TER
ATION

✱[1] VOTERS WERE TOLD POLLS WERE CLOSED EVEN THOUGH IT WAS FIVE MINUTES INSIDE TIME.
ST. PETERSBURG TIMES. 12/7/00

✱[2] AS TOLD TO CONCHITA MITCHEL IN JACKSONVILLE FLORIDA ON 11/7/00
ABC NEWS 1/12/01

CAROL 88 SWAIN

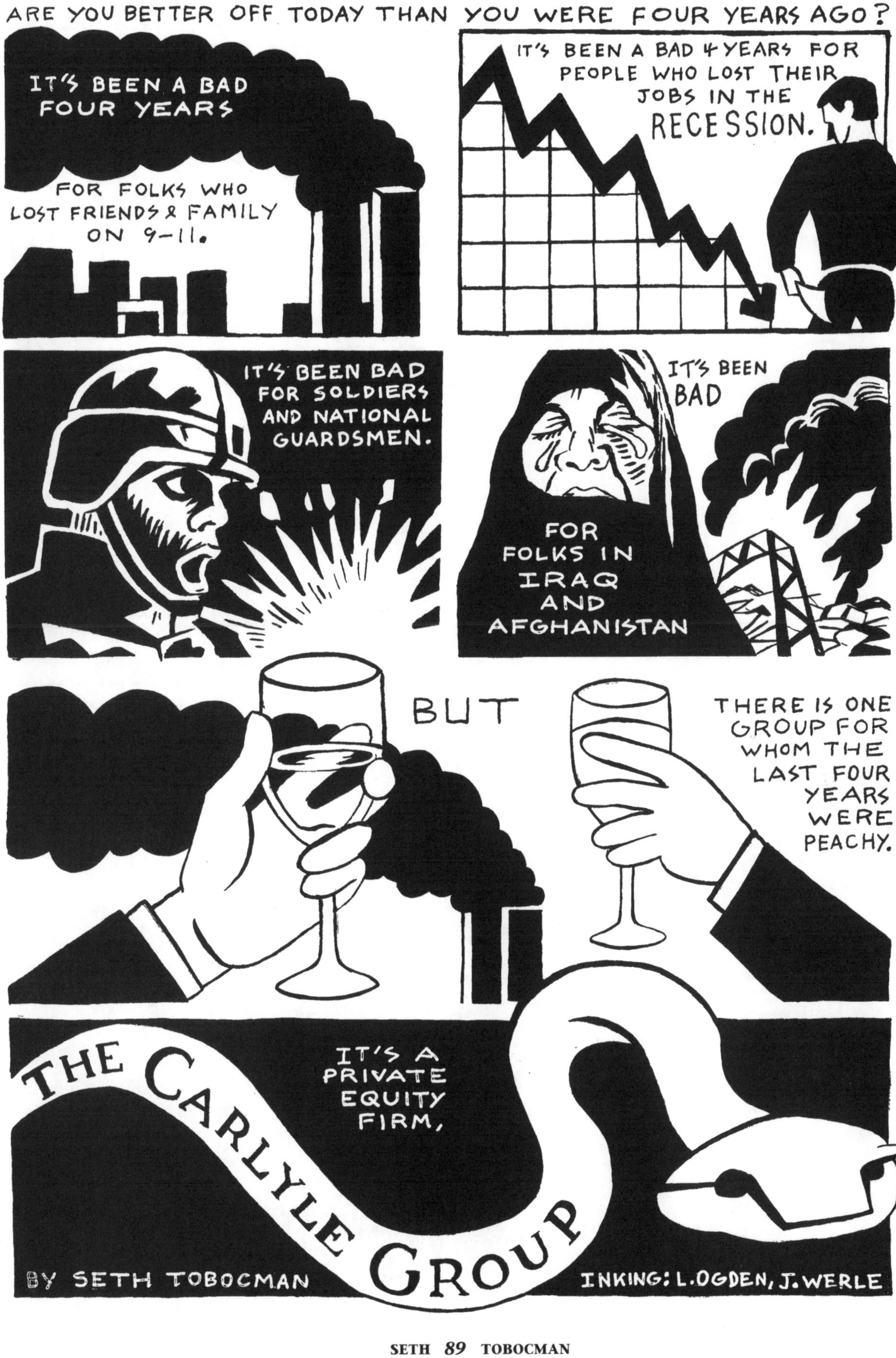
ARE YOU BETTER OFF TODAY THAN YOU WERE FOUR YEARS AGO?
IT'S BEEN A BAD FOUR YEARS
FOR FOLKS WHO LOST FRIENDS & FAMILY ON 9-11.
IT'S BEEN A BAD 4 YEARS FOR PEOPLE WHO LOST THEIR JOBS IN THE RECESSION.
IT'S BEEN BAD FOR SOLDIERS AND NATIONAL GUARDSMEN.
IT'S BEEN BAD
FOR FOLKS IN IRAQ AND AFGHANISTAN
BUT
THERE IS ONE GROUP FOR WHOM THE LAST FOUR YEARS WERE PEACHY.
THE CARLYLE GROUP
IT'S A PRIVATE EQUITY FIRM,
BY SETH TOBOCMAN
INKING: L. OGDEN, J. WERLE

A PRIVATE EQUITY FIRM IS A COMPANY THAT BUYS OTHER COMPANIES, USUALLY FAILING COMPANIES.

IDEALLY, THEY MAKE THESE COMPANIES SUCCEED,

THEN SELL THEM AT A PROFIT.

CARLYLE PREFERS TO BUY COMPANIES THAT DO BUSINESS WITH THE GOVERNMENT.

1991, THE BERLIN WALL FELL THE COLD WAR WAS OVER. THE MILITARY BUDGET WAS CUT.

HARD TIMES FOR WAR RELATED INDUSTRIES.

CARLYLE BOUGHT UP MILITARY COMPANIES DIRT CHEAP.

THEY BOUGHT VAUGHT AIR CRAFT.

THEY BOUGHT U.S.I.S. WHO DO BACKGROUND CHECKS ON AIR-LINE EM-PLOYEES.

THEY BOUGHT B.D.M., A COMPANY WORKING WITH THE GOVERNMENT OF SAUDI ARABIA. B.D.M. IN TURN OWNED VINNELL, A MERCENARY CORPORATION WHO GUARD SAUDI OIL FIELDS.

CARLYLE BOUGHT UNITED DEFENSE INDUSTRIES, WOULD-BE MAKERS OF A GIANT CANNON CALLED THE CRUSADER. IT WAS TOO BIG, TOO HEAVY, FOR MODERN WARFARE. THE ARMY DIDN'T WANT THE CRUSADER.

TO GET CONGRESS TO BUY THE CRUSADER, CARLYLE WOULD NEED POLITICAL CONNECTIONS

SUCH CONNECTIONS ARE CARLYLE'S SPECIALTY.

CARLYLE HIRES POLITICIANS WHEN THEY LEAVE OFFICE.

FRANK CARLUCCI HAD A LONG CAREER OF COVERT OVERSEAS WORK FOR UNCLE SAM.

HE EVENTUALLY BECAME DEPUTY C.I.A. DIRECTOR AND SECRETARY OF STATE.

CARLUCCI BECAME CHAIRMAN OF THE CARLYLE GROUP

JAMES BAKER THE 2ND

WORKED IN TWO REPUBLICAN ADMINISTRATIONS BEFORE HE CAME TO CARLYLE

IN 1990, CARLYLE MADE G.W. BUSH DIRECTOR OF CATERAIR

THIS COMPANY SERVED MEALS IN FLIGHT.

UNDER W'S LEADERSHIP CATERAIR WENT OUT OF BUSINESS

CARLYLE HAD LOST A COMPANY BUT GAINED

THE BUSH FAMILY.

AFTER LEAVING OFFICE, GEORGE SENIOR BECAME A CARLYLE BOARD MEMBER.

CARLYLE ALSO HAS DEALINGS WITH MANY WEALTHY SAUDIS INCLUDING THE FAMILY OF OSAMA BIN LADEN.

CARLYLE GROUP

AND SO, ON THE MORNING OF SEPTEMBER 11th 2001, GEORGE BUSH SENIOR AND THE BROTHER OF OSAMA BIN LADEN WERE BOTH ATTENDING A MEETING OF THE CARLYLE GROUP AT A FANCY WASHINGTON HOTEL.

DID THESE MEN KNOW WHAT WAS ABOUT TO HAPPEN?

WE MAY NEVER KNOW THE ANSWER.

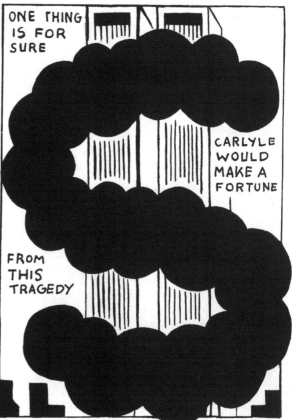

ONE THING IS FOR SURE

CARLYLE WOULD MAKE A FORTUNE

FROM THIS TRAGEDY

VAUGHT WOULD MAKE THE STEALTH BOMBERS

USED IN IRAQ AND AFGHANISTAN

USIS WOULD HAVE LOTS OF WORK DOING BACKGROUND CHECKS ON AIRLINE EMPLOYEES AFTER 9-11

CONGRESS FINALLY APPROVED THE CRUSADER.

CARLYLE WOULD GO PUBLIC WITH STOCK IN UNITED DEFENSE AND MAKE A KILLING ON THE STOCK MARKET.

ONCE CARLYLE HAD SOLD LOTS OF U.D.I. STOCK, CONGRESS CHANGED ITS MIND. THEY CANCELED THE CRUSADER.

CONGRESS GAVE UNITED DEFENSE A CONTRACT FOR A SMALLER CANNON INSTEAD.

BUT UNITED DEFENSE WOULD STILL MAKE A FORTUNE PRODUCING THE BRADLEY FIGHTING VEHICLES USED IN IRAQ AND AFGHANISTAN.

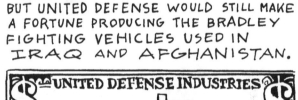

UNITED DEFENSE INDUSTRIES

VINNELL IS ONE OF MANY "CIVILIAN CONTRACTORS" IN IRAQ.

PEOPLE HAVE BEGUN TO ASK QUESTIONS ABOUT THE CARLYLE GROUP.

WHAT DID THEY KNOW

WHEN DID THEY KNOW IT?

CONGRESSWOMAN MCKINNEY

PEOPLE HELD A PROTEST AT THE OFFICES OF THE CARLYLE GROUP.

MOST PROTESTERS WERE ARRESTED.

BUT

IN COURT ALL CHARGES WERE DROPPED.

IT IS STILL LEGAL TO PROTEST AT THE CARLYLE GROUP.

PEACE

CARLYLE HAS TRIED TO CHANGE ITS IMAGE. BUSH & BIN LADEN HAVE LEFT THE COMPANY.

AND THEY HAVE SOLD OFF MANY OF THEIR MILITARY HOLDINGS.

BUY LOW, SELL HIGH, MISSION ACCOMPLISHED.

AS THE WORLD MOVES TOWARD A WIDER WAR IN THE MIDDLE EAST,

THERE IS AN ECONOMIC AND POLITICAL RULING CLASS WHO MAKE MONEY OFF OF EVERY DROP OF BLOOD SPILLED. THE BUSH AND BIN LADEN FAMILIES ARE PART OF THIS RULING ELITE.

NONE OF US SHOULD DIE IN THEIR WARS.

CHECKLIST FOR THE NEOFASCISTS

"AFTER REREADING *MEIN KAMPF*, I REALIZED THAT HITLER HAD TOLD THE WORLD EXACTLY WHAT HE WAS GOING TO DO WITH REGARDS TO THE JEWS AND THAT NO ONE PAID ATTENTION."
— RAOUL WALLENBERG.

THE **PROJECT FOR THE NEW AMERICAN CENTURY** IS "A NON-PROFIT EDUCATIONAL ORGANIZATION DEDICATED TO A FEW FUNDAMENTAL PROPOSITIONS: THAT AMERICAN LEADERSHIP IS GOOD BOTH FOR AMERICA AND THE WORLD; THAT SUCH LEADERSHIP REQUIRES MILITARY STRENGTH, DIPLOMATIC ENERGY AND COMMITMENT TO MORAL PRINCIPLE; AND THAT TOO FEW POLITICAL LEADERS TODAY ARE MAKING THE CASE FOR GLOBAL LEADERSHIP." FOUNDED IN 1997 BY NEOCONSERVATIVES DISMAYED BY 5 LONG YEARS IN POLITICAL EXILE, THE PNAC THINK TANK HAS BECOME THE BUSH ADMINISTRATION'S *MEIN KAMPF*: A BLUEPRINT FOR ITS FOREIGN POLICY OBJECTIVES WRITTEN BY POLITICAL IDEOLOGUES WHO NOW HOLD UNPARALLED CONTROL OF ALL 3 BRANCHES OF OUR GOVERNMENT. THE PNAC ISN'T A CONSPIRACY. IT'S WHAT'S GOING ON.

ON JUNE 3, 1997, 25 MEN AND WOMEN SIGNED THE PNAC'S "STATEMENT OF PRINCIPLES." DECRYING BILL CLINTON'S "ADRIFT"— I.E., PEACEFUL — FOREIGN POLICY, THEY CALLED FOR:

A RETURN TO REAGAN-LEVEL DEFENSE SPENDING

REGIME CHANGE FOR HOSTILE REGIMES

CREATING AN "INTER-NATIONAL ORDER" FRIENDLY TO THE U.S.

THE PNAC'S CHARTER MEMBERS READS LIKE A WHO'S WHO OF FUTURE BUSHISTS:

PAUL WOLFOWITZ DEPUTY SECRETARY OF DEFENSE

JEB BUSH DUBYA'S BROTHER, FLORIDA GOVERNOR AND FIXER

I'M A HUMANE BOMBER.

DONALD RUMSFELD SECRETARY OF DEFENSE

WEST BANK

GAZA

ELIOT ABRAMS SPECIAL ASSISTANT TO THE PRESIDENT FOR NEAR EAST & NORTH AFRICAN AFFAIRS

AFTER A CAREFUL SEARCH FOR V.P. I'VE DECIDED ON ME!

DICK CHENEY VICE PRESIDENT

"THE PET AFGHAN"

UNOCAL

ZALMAY KHALILZAD SPECIAL ENVOY TO AFGHANISTAN AND IRAQ

PETER RODMAN ASSISTANT SECRETARY OF DEFENSE

STOP RIGHT THERE.

OVA OFFI

I. LEWIS LIBBY ASSISTANT TO THE PRESIDENT AND V.P.'S CHIEF OF STAFF

COMMUNISM LOST. CAPITALISM WON. C'EST TOUT.

FRANCIS FUKUYAMA HISTORIAN, AUTHOR OF "THE END OF HISTORY"

HENRY KOWEN MEMBER OF BUSH'S WMD COMMISSION

A FLAT TAX IS SIMPLER

A SIMPLER WAY TO STEAL!

STEVE FORBES PERENNIAL REPUBLICAN PRESIDENTIAL CANDIDATE

YOU GOT RID OF THE LADIES' ROOM?!

PAULA DOBRIANSKY UNDERSECRETARY FOR GLOBAL AFFAIRS

IT WOULD BE ABSURD TO SUGGEST, AS SOME HAVE, THAT THE PNAC IS A CONSPIRATORIAL CABAL OF NEOCONS USING GEORGE W. BUSH AS A TOOL IN THEIR QUEST FOR GLOBAL DOMINATION.

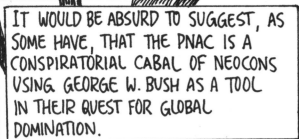

DON'T YOU UNDERSTAND?! THEY'RE ALL <u>INSANE</u>!!

↑

KIND OF TRUE, ACTUALLY.

IT IS TRUE, HOWEVER, THAT BUSH DIDN'T HAVE MUCH OF A FOREIGN POLICY IN MIND BEFORE COMING TO POWER.

"I'M WORRIED ABOUT... [USING] NATION-BUILDING AND THE MILITARY IN THE SAME SENTENCE."

— GEORGE W. BUSH NOV. 6, 2000

HIS FOREIGN POLICY TEAM WAS COMPOSED ALMOST EXCLUSIVELY OF PNAC MEMBERS AND PNAC SYMPATHIZERS LIKE CONDI RICE.

FUCK AFGHANISTAN! IRAQ HAS BETTER TARGETS!

WAIT UNTIL NEXT YEAR, SWEETIE.

MEOW

SEPT. 11 2001

COLIN POWELL, THE SOLE EXCEPTION, BECAME A SECRETARY OF STATE WITHOUT PORTFOLIO: ROUTINELY EXCLUDED AND IGNORED WHEN MAJOR DECISIONS OF WAR AND PEACE WERE MADE.

ON THE PLUS SIDE, I GET TO CATCH UP ON QUALITY TIME.

BUSH'S AGGRESSIVE ACTIONS, THE RESULT OF PNAC-ORIENTED ADVISORS, CAREFULLY ADHERED TO THE VISION OF AN EXPANSIONIST AMERICAN EMPIRE DETERMINED TO BEND THE WORLD TO ITS WILL VIA MILITARY MIGHT.

GENEVA? WHAT'S THAT?!

NOW THAT WE'VE SEEN THE PNAC AGENDA AT WORK, THE QUESTION IS...

OCCUPIED IRAQ

OCCUPIED AFGHANISTAN

WHAT'S NEXT?

THE PNAC'S ADHERENTS BELIEVE IN MACHIAVELLI'S ADVICE ABOUT WAR: IT ISN'T ENOUGH TO BUILD AN ARMY. TO BUILD STRENGTH AND INFLUENCE, MILITARY FORCE MUST BE USED FREQUENTLY.

IT'S YOUR CHOICE — RIDE A CARPET OF GOLD OR LIVE UNDER A CARPET OF BOMBS.

NEGOTIATIONS BTWN. BUSH ADMINISTRATION AND TALIBAN OFFICIALS RE: PIPELINE, 2001

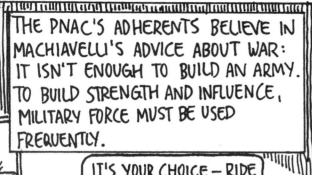

THE PHILOSOPHY OF CONTINUOUS, ESCALATING — EACH ATTACK'S "SHOCK AND AWE" MUST OUTDO ITS PREDECESSORS — WAR ECHOS FASCISM'S DYNAMIC IMPULSE. PEACE WILL REIGN UNTIL ELECTION DAY 2004, BUT SHOULD BUSH WIN, THE NEOCONS WILL PUSH FOR WAR.

FIRST AFGHANISTAN. THEN IRAQ. THE NEXT ONE HAS TO BE IRAN. ALWAYS BIGGER AND BETTER. SYRIA'S TOO TINY.

9 DAYS AFTER 9/11, BUSH RELEASED A NEW "NATIONAL SECURITY STRATEGY OF THE UNITED STATES," A VIRTUAL COPY OF THE PNAC'S "REBUILDING AMERICA'S DEFENSES" REPORT (2000). ONE OF THE HIGHLIGHTS: FORCING OIL-RICH NATIONS TO ACCEPT PERMANENT U.S. MILITARY BASES.

CAMP FREEDOM
U.S.M.C.

STOP

ALL VEH MUST S

AFTER 9/11, THE U.S. LEANED ON ITS CENTRAL ASIAN CLIENT DICTATOR-SHIPS — UZBEKISTAN, KYRGYZSTAN, KAZAKHSTAN, TAJIKISTAN — TO DEMAND BASES ON FORMER SOVIET TERRITORY. ALL SUCCUMBED.

SO I GIVE YOU BASE, I CAN TORTURE MUSLIM DISSIDENTS, DA?

DA! IT'S THE "WAR ON TERROR"!

EVEN THE WORLD'S WEALTHIEST NATION, HOWEVER, CANNOT SUSTAIN THE BREADTH OF EMPIRE THE BUSHIST PNAC DISCIPLES ENVISION. AS TAXES RISE TO PAY FOR A GROWING MILITARY, PERMANENT WAR AND FOREIGN CANTONMENTS, THE ECONOMY WILL SUFFER.

MOREOVER, WE WILL MAKE NEW ENEMIES. WE WILL BE THE SOURCE OF MOST OF THE WORLD'S ILLS; WE WILL SUFFER THEIR WRATH.

TED RALL 2001

"THE PUBLIC SUPPORTED AMERICA'S ENGAGEMENT IN WORLD WAR II LARGELY BECAUSE OF THE SHOCK EFFECT OF THE JAPANESE ATTACK ON *PEARL HARBOR* ..."

Zbigniew Brzezinski, founder of the Trilateral Commission and advisor to Democrat and Republican presidents, advocating what it will take to put the American public in a "supportive mood" for a U.S. takeover of Middle Eastern oil and gas reserves. *The Grand Chessboard: American Primacy and Its Geostrategic Imperatives*, 1997.

"THE PROCESS OF TRANSFORMATION IS LIKELY TO BE A LONG ONE, ABSENT SOME CATASTROPHIC AND CATALYZING EVENT— LIKE *A NEW PEARL HARBOR* ..."

Richard Perle, former Deputy Secretary of Defense under President Ronald Reagan, describing "the need for a substantial American force presence" in the Middle East and a "transformation" of the U.S. military that would let it "fight and decisively win multiple, simultaneous major theater wars." Papers of the Project for a New American Century, September 2000.

SEPTEMBER 11
by MACK WHITE

1985. President Ronald Reagan signs National Security Directive 166, authorizing increased covert aid to the *mujahideen* to defeat Soviet troops in Afghanistan. Pakistan's ISI, a publicly known front for the CIA, is funneling the money and weaponry through the Maktab al-Khidamar, an organization run by **Osama bin Laden**, heir to the Saudi Binladen Group construction fortune.

MSNBC, 8/24/98; Michel Chossudovsky, "Who is Osama bin Laden?"

1988. Osama bin Laden forms a new guerilla group, Al Qaeda.

1998-2000. Working for the Carlyle Group, a defense contractor, former **President Bush** twice meets with the bin Laden family, major investors in the firm. *The Wall Street Journal, 9/27/01; Guardian, 10/31/01*

July 3, 2000. **Mohammed Atta** and **Marwan Alshehri**, later identified as September 11 hijackers, begin flight training in Venice, Florida, at Huffman Aviation, owned by **Wallace Hilliard**, a friend of Florida **Governor Jeb Bush**. Atta and the other alleged hijackers have also received training at secure U.S. military installations.

Washington Post, 9/16/2001 / *Knight Ridder/Tribune*, 9/16/2001 / *Newsweek*, 9/15/01 / Daniel Hopsicker, "Did Terrorist Pilots Train at U.S. Military Schools?", "Terror Flight School Owner's Plane Seized for Heroin Trafficking."

August. Wiretaps by Italian police reveal that suspected Al Qaeda operatives are planning major attacks on airports and airplanes in the U.S.

Los Angeles Times, 5/29/2002. The *Times* suggests that the information might not have been passed along to U.S. authorities, but notes that "Italian and U.S. anti-terrorism experts cooperate closely."

October 24-26. The Pentagon stages an emergency drill based on the crashing of a hijacked airliner into the Pentagon.

The Mirror, 5/24/02.

Summer. The German BSD warns the CIA that terrorists are planning to hijack aircraft and use them as weapons. According to FBI agent **Coleen Rowley**, the FBI receives and ignores similar warnings from French intelligence, as well as warnings from FBI agents investigating **Zacaris Moussaoui** who is receiving flight training in Phoenix. One agent states that bin Laden may be planning to crash planes into the World Trade Center. The FBI, Rowley says, "deliberately sabotaged" her efforts to secure a warrant to search Moussaoui's computer. Also, agent **Robert Wright** finds his attempts to shut off funding to Al Qaeda "obstructed" by the FBI.

The New York Times, May 14, 2002
Frankfurter Allgemeine Zeitung, Sept. 14, 2001
Associated Press, May 21, 2002
Robert G. Wright, Jr., Press Conference, CSPAN, 5/31/02

January 2001. The Bush administration orders the FBI to "back off" investigations into the bin Laden family's connection to terrorist organizations.

Greg Palast, *BBC Newsnight*, 11/6/01

Deputy Director **John O'Neill** quits the FBI, charging that his investigation of bin Laden has been stymied ...

"THE MAIN OBSTACLES TO INVESTIGATE ISLAMIC TERRORISM WERE U.S. OIL CORPORATE INTERESTS AND THE ROLE PLAYED BY SAUDI ARABIA IN IT ..."

John O'Neill, quoted in Charles Brisard and Guillaume Dasquie, *Forbidden Truth*

JOHN P. O'NEILL
(1952 - 2001)

July. While at a Dubai hospital to receive treatment for a kidney infection, Osama bin Laden meets with a top CIA official ...

Le Figaro, 11/2/01

August-September. Lt. Gen. **Mahmud Ahmad**, head of Pakistan's ISI, wires $100,000 to **Mohammed Atta**. Later, Mahmud and President **Musharraf** meet with US congressmen **Bob Graham**, **Porter Goss**, and **John Kyl** to discuss terrorism; they will meet again on the morning of September 11 in Washington. A Mahmud subordinate tells a US undercover agent that the World Trade Center is going to be destroyed.

The Times of India, 10/11/01
Washington Post, 5/18/02
Agence France Press, 8/28/01
Palm Beach Post, 10/17/02
Vero Beach Press Journal, 9/12/01

In the weeks before September 11, a "threat assessment" causes Attorney General **John Ashcroft** to begin flying by chartered jets instead of commercial airlines. Also, the FAA bans author **Salman Rushdie** from internal flights in the US, airport security warns San Francisco Mayor **Willie Brown** not to fly on September 11, and top Pentagon officials suddenly cancel travel plans for the same day.

CBS.com, 7/26/01
Ananova,.com 9/27/01
San Francisco Chronicle, 9/12/01
Newsweek, 9/13/03.

September 11, 5:45 a.m. In Portland, Maine, **Mohammed Atta** and **Abdulaziz Alomari** board a flight for Boston, where they will later board American Airlines Flight 11 ...

9-11-01 24H
5:45:13

Meanwhile, other suspected Al Qaeda members are boarding other flights ...

8:20 a.m. Flight controllers decide Flight 11 has been hijacked, but wait 20 minutes to inform NORAD.

8:43 a.m. NORAD is notified that United Airlines Flight 175 has been hijacked.

8:46 a.m. NORAD orders F-15 fighters to find Flight 11.

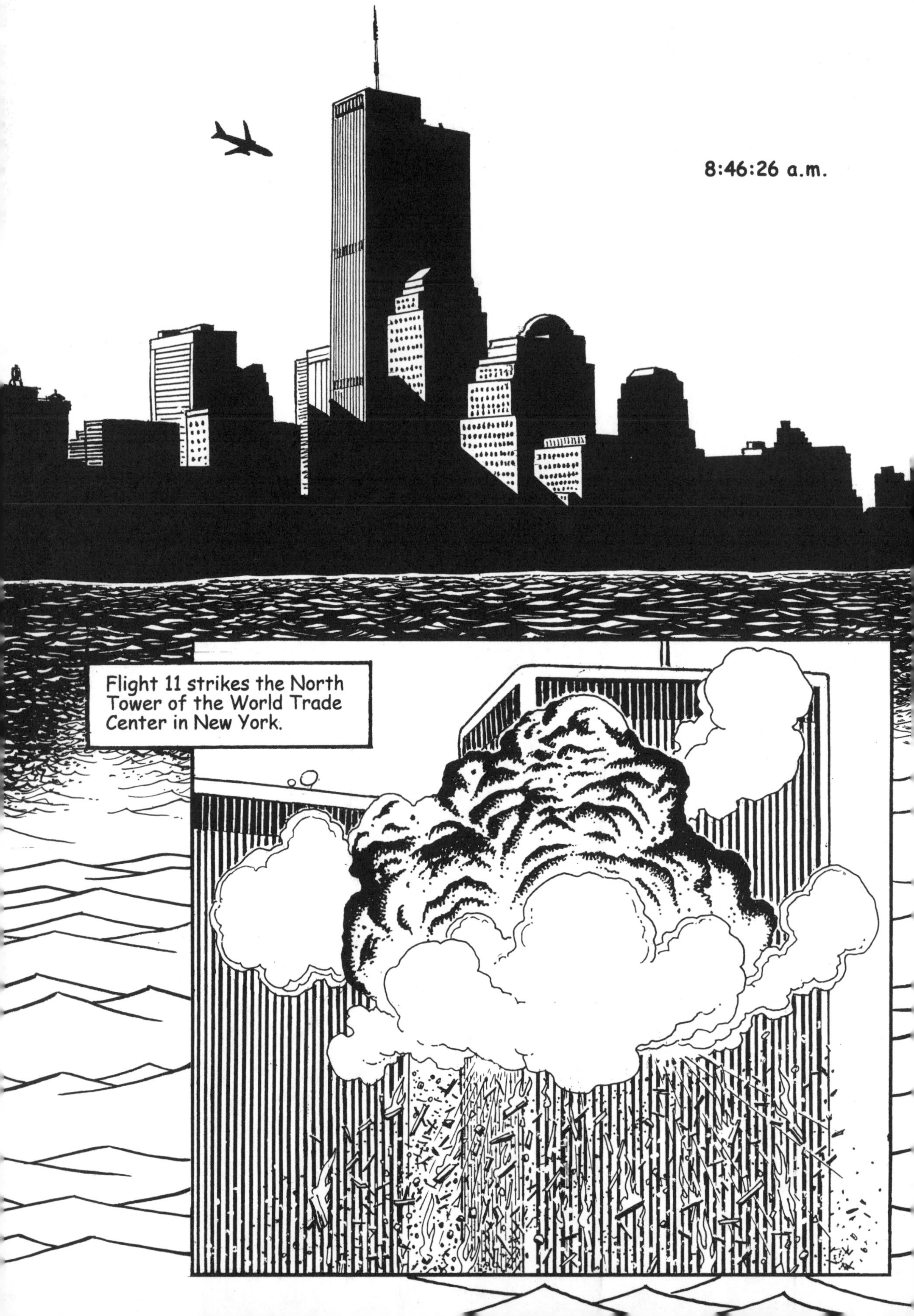
8:46:26 a.m.
Flight 11 strikes the North Tower of the World Trade Center in New York.

8:52 a.m. By now, it is known that Flight 175 is heading towards New York. Two F-15s take off from Otis Air National Guard Base in Massachusetts, bound for New York.

9:02 a.m. Flight 175 hits the south tower of the World Trade Center.

Killed in the south tower is John O'Neill, who two weeks earlier became security chief of the World Trade Center.

9:11 a.m. The F-15s arrive in New York, apparently having traveled less than 600 mph. Had they been traveling at maximum speed (over 1857 mph) they would have reached New York ahead of Flight 175.

Complete 9/11 Timeline,
www.cooperativeresearch.org

WORLD TRADE CENTER
DEATH TOLL: **2,752**

9:07 a.m. At Booker Elementary, **Bush** is about to participate in a reading drill with second grade students when White House Chief of Staff **Andrew Card** interrupts ...

A SECOND PLANE HAS HIT THE SECOND TOWER. AMERICA IS UNDER ATTACK ...

READING MAKES A COUNTRY GREAT!

Knowing that the country is under attack, **Bush** does not excuse himself to begin making decisions as Commander in Chief. Instead, he begins reading to the schoolchildren ...

9:16 a.m. NORAD is notified that United Airlines Flight 93 "may" have been hijacked ...

9:24 a.m. NORAD is notified that American Airlines Flight 77 "may" have been hijacked. Though the plane appears to be heading towards Washington, DC, no order is given to evacuate federal buildings ...

9:20 a.m. Secret Service agents escort Vice President **Richard Cheney** and other White House staffers into an underground bunker where they monitor the progress of Flight 77 ...

IT'S *TEN MILES OUT.* DO THE ORDERS STILL STAND?

OF COURSE THE ORDERS STILL STAND. HAVE YOU HEARD ANYTHING TO THE CONTRARY? ...

Congressional Testimony, Norman Mineta, Secretary of Transportation, May 21, 2003 Mineta did not describe Cheney's orders, but stated on the record that Cheney gave no orders to shoot down Flight 77.

9:27 a.m. NORAD orders F-16s scrambled from Langley Air Force Base (129 miles away) to intercept Flight 77.

9:38 a.m. The Pentagon is hit.

9:49 a.m. The F-16s scrambled from Langley arrive, having flown at less than half their maximum speed of 1500 mph.

PENTAGON DEATH TOLL: 189

By now, it is known that Flight 93 is heading towards Washington. Also, the FBI is monitoring cell phone calls from passengers to friends and family describing a possible passenger takeover of the plane. (Two passengers—Don Greene and Andrew Garcia—are capable of safely landing the plane.) Presumably, the FBI is passing this information along to the White House.

MSNBC, 7/30/02; Telegraph, 8/6/02; Newsweek, 11/25/01; Observer, 12/2/01; Complete 9/11 Timeline, www.cooperativeresearch.org

9:56 a.m. Cheney authorizes F-16s to shoot down Flight 93.

Washington Post, 1/27/02; ABC News, 9/11/02

Later, a New Hampshire flight controller will state that an F-16 closely pursued Flight 93, making 360-degree turns to remain close.

AP, 9/13/01; Nashua Telegraph,, 9/13/01

"I KNOW OF TWO PEOPLE ... THAT HEARD A MISSILE. THEY BOTH LIVE VERY CLOSE, WITHIN A COUPLE OF HUNDRED YARDS ... THIS ONE FELLOW'S SERVED IN VIETNAM AND HE SAYS HE'S HEARD THEM, AND HEARD ONE THAT DAY ..."

Ernie Stuhl, Mayor of Shanksville, quoted in *Philadelphia Daily News*, 11/15/01

10:06 a.m. Flight 93 crashes in a field near Shanksville, Pennsylvania. Eyewitnesses describe explosions prior to the crash and the plane breaking apart in the air. Debris and human remains will later be discovered many miles from the point of impact, indicating that the jet was indeed falling apart before it hit the ground. All of this is consistent with a shoot-down and refutes the government's claim that a struggle in the cockpit caused the plane to simply crash.

US Army Authorized Seismic Study; Philadelphia Daily News, 9/16/02, 11/15/01; Pittsburgh Post-Gazette, 9/13/01; Complete 9/11 Timeline, www.cooperativeresearch.org

FLIGHT 93 DEATH TOLL: 44

During the terror attacks, **former President George H. W. Bush** is attending a meeting of Carlyle Group investors at the Ritz-Carlton in Washington. The guest of honor is **Shafig bin Laden**, brother of Osama bin Laden.

The Observer, 6/16/02; The Fifth Estate, CBC, 10/29/03

In the aftermath of September 11, all US flights are grounded. However, members of the bin Laden family and other Saudi elites travel under FBI supervision to a secret assembly point in Texas where they are flown out of the country.

CBS, 9/30/01; New York Times, 10/29/03, 6/1/04

Later, unknown officials leak a censored section of the 9/11 Congressional Inquiry's report describing links "between the hijacking plot and the very top levels of the Saudi royal family."

New Republic,, 8/1/03

September 17. President Bush signs a document outlining an invasion of Afghanistan, where energy giants Enron and Unocal have long wanted to build a gas pipeline. The document also directs the Pentagon to begin planning an invasion of Iraq to oust **Saddam Hussein**—one of the goals of the Project for the New American Century.

Washington Post, 1/12/02; Seymour Hersh, "The Price of Oil," The New Yorker; Asia Times, 1/26/02; BBC, 12/4/97

October 26. President Bush signs the PATRIOT Act. The law empowers the federal government to "fight terrorism" and severely damages the Bill of Rights.

© Mack White

ENVIRONMENTAL PLU
TAKING   IN

QUESTION: WHY ARE MORE AND MORE CHILDREN SUFFERING FROM ASTHMA?

COAL BURNING POWER PLANTS WHICH HAVE BEEN EXEMPTED BY BUSH FROM THE CLEAN AIR ACT ARE A BIG CONTRIBUTOR

THEY HAVE ALSO STERILIZED ONE HALF THE LAKES IN THE ADIRONDACKS

ON INAUGURATION DAY, BUSH HALTED ALL RECENT ECO-REGULATIONS

THE EPA HAS STOPPED WORK ON 62 STANDARDS
OSHA HAS STOPPED 57 STANDARDS

BUSH ENVIRONMENTAL POLICIES ARE CLEVERLY HIDDEN BY ORWELLIAN LANGUAGE-TWISTER FRANK LUNTZ. "HEALTHY FORESTS", "CLEAR SKIES", "REFORM", ETC. ARE POLL-TESTED RUSES TO GET ECO-BASHING UNDER THE RADAR.

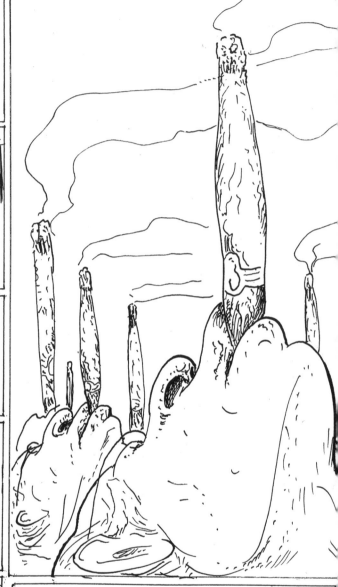

THE EPA'S INSPECTOR GENERAL REVEALED BUSH CONCEALED RISKS OF POISONED AIR FOLLOWING THE 9-11 ATTACKS

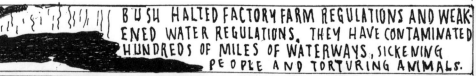

BUSH HALTED FACTORY FARM REGULATIONS AND WEAKENED WATER REGULATIONS. THEY HAVE CONTAMINATED HUNDREDS OF MILES OF WATERWAYS, SICKENING PEOPLE AND TORTURING ANIMALS.

NDER ADMINISTRATION
THE BUSH RECORD

INTERIOR SECRETARY GAIL NORTON HAS REWRITTEN STUDIES; HIDING THE EFFECTS OF

MOUNTAINTOP MINING...

...AND ENDANGERING SPECIES LIKE POLAR BEARS AND TRUMPETER SWANS.

DICK CHENEY'S ENERGY TASK FORCE WAS COMPRISED OF FELLOW ENERGY INDUSTRY SHILLS

INCLUDING ENRON'S KEN LAY

WHO ENGINEERED THE CALIFORNIA ENERGY CRISIS

WHICH BUILT SUPPORT FOR OIL DRILLING IN ALASKA

CO_2 IS NOW CLASSIFIED AS A "NON POLLUTANT". IT WILL KILL AS MANY AS 30,000 PEOPLE THIS YEAR.

DENYING **GLOBAL WARMING** HAS BEEN A BUSH OBSESSION. HE HAS SUPPRESSED OVER A DOZEN STUDIES ON THE ISSUE.

AS OVERWHELMING AS THIS ATTACK ON THE NATURAL WORLD HAS BEEN, ITS HAS GONE UNREPORTED BY MAINSTREAM MEDIA— ADDING DEMOCRACY TO THE ENDANGERED SPECIES LIST.

NEWS! KOBE, LACI, JACKO

STEVE BRODNER '04

INTRODUCTION

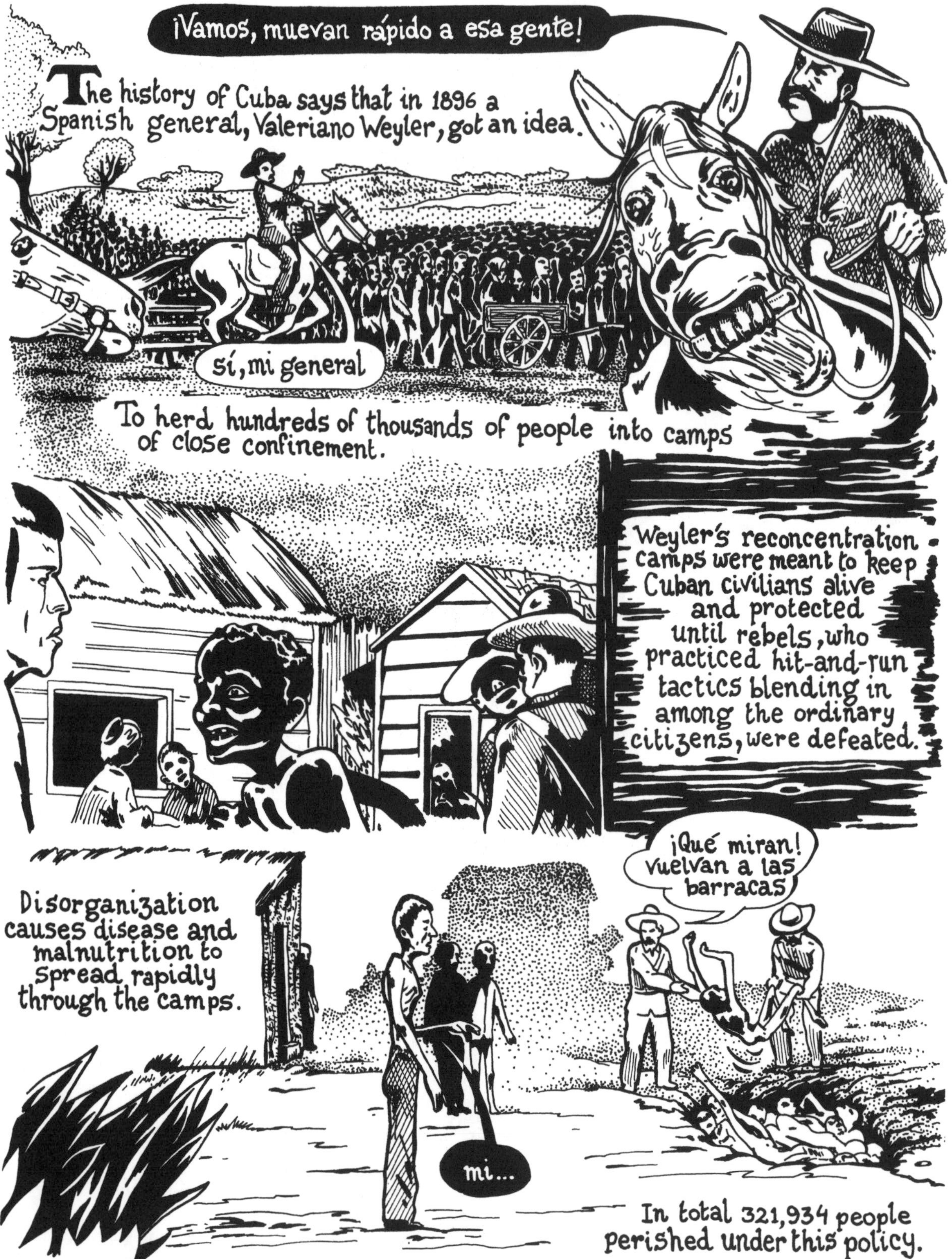
¡Vamos, muevan rápido a esa gente!
The history of Cuba says that in 1896 a Spanish general, Valeriano Weyler, got an idea.
sí, mi general
To herd hundreds of thousands of people into camps of close confinement.
Weyler's reconcentration camps were meant to keep Cuban civilians alive and protected until rebels, who practiced hit-and-run tactics blending in among the ordinary citizens, were defeated.
Disorganization causes disease and malnutrition to spread rapidly through the camps.
¡Qué miran! Vuelvan a las barracas
mi...
In total 321,934 people perished under this policy.

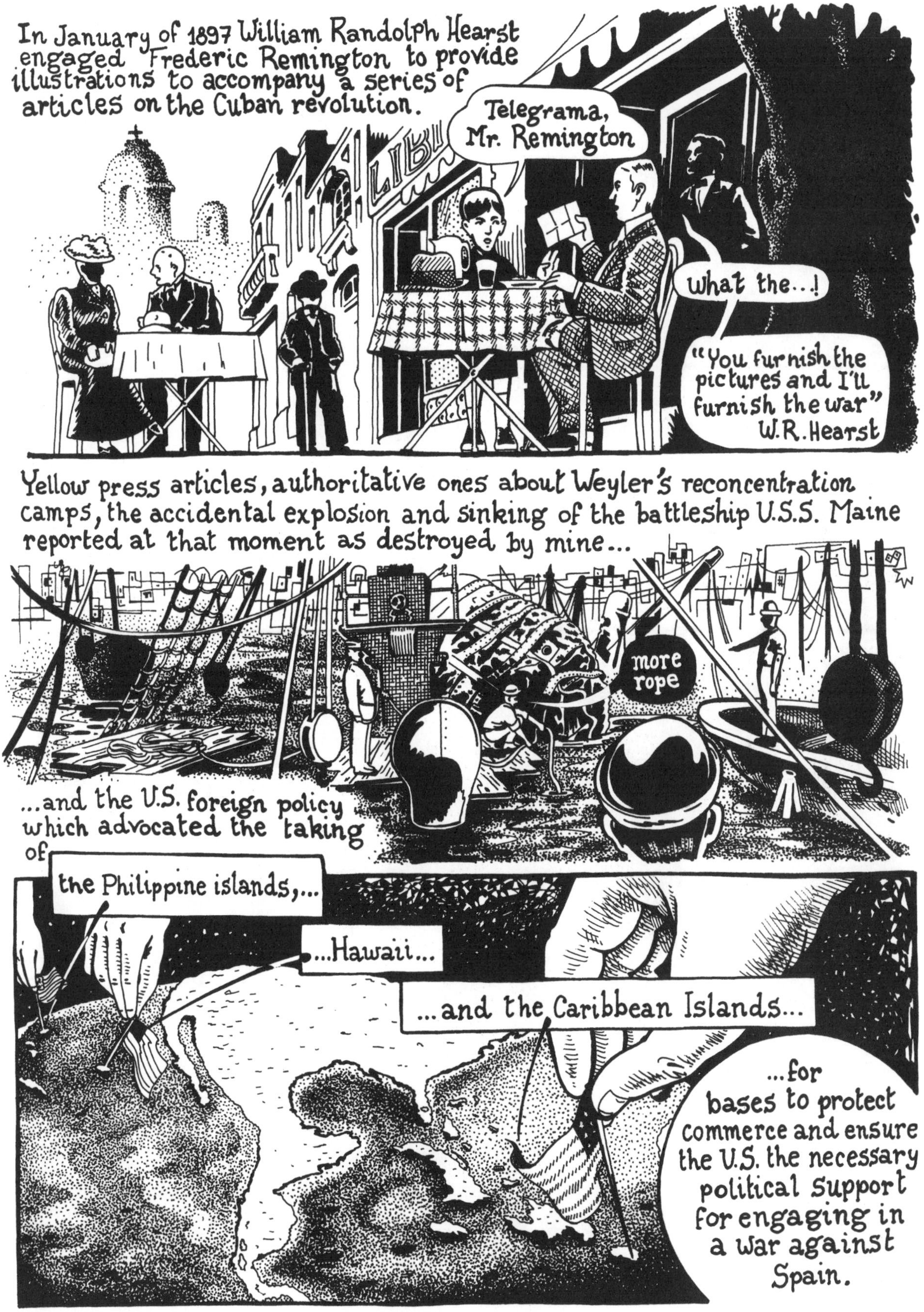
In January of 1897 William Randolph Hearst engaged Frederic Remington to provide illustrations to accompany a series of articles on the Cuban revolution.
Telegrama, Mr. Remington
What the...!
"You furnish the pictures and I'll furnish the war" W.R. Hearst
Yellow press articles, authoritative ones about Weyler's reconcentration camps, the accidental explosion and sinking of the battleship U.S.S. Maine reported at that moment as destroyed by mine...
more rope
...and the U.S. foreign policy which advocated the taking of
the Philippine islands,...
...Hawaii...
...and the Caribbean Islands...
...for bases to protect commerce and ensure the U.S. the necessary political support for engaging in a war against Spain.

In June of 1898 600 Marines landed in Guantanamo Bay for the first time.

"Stars and stripes flew in the harbor and had come to stay."

On July 8 the U.S. acquired Hawaii. With the signing of a treaty of peace in December 10, Spain acknowledged Cuban independence, ceded Puerto Rico, the island of Guam and sold the Philippines for $20,000,000. to the U.S.

In 1903 the U.S. and Cuba signed a treaty which leases the Guantanamo Bay site to the U.S. for $4,085 per year. The treaty requires the consent of both governments to revoke or change it. The U.S. will not agree to a revocation. Cuba, in protest, has refused to accept the rent payment.

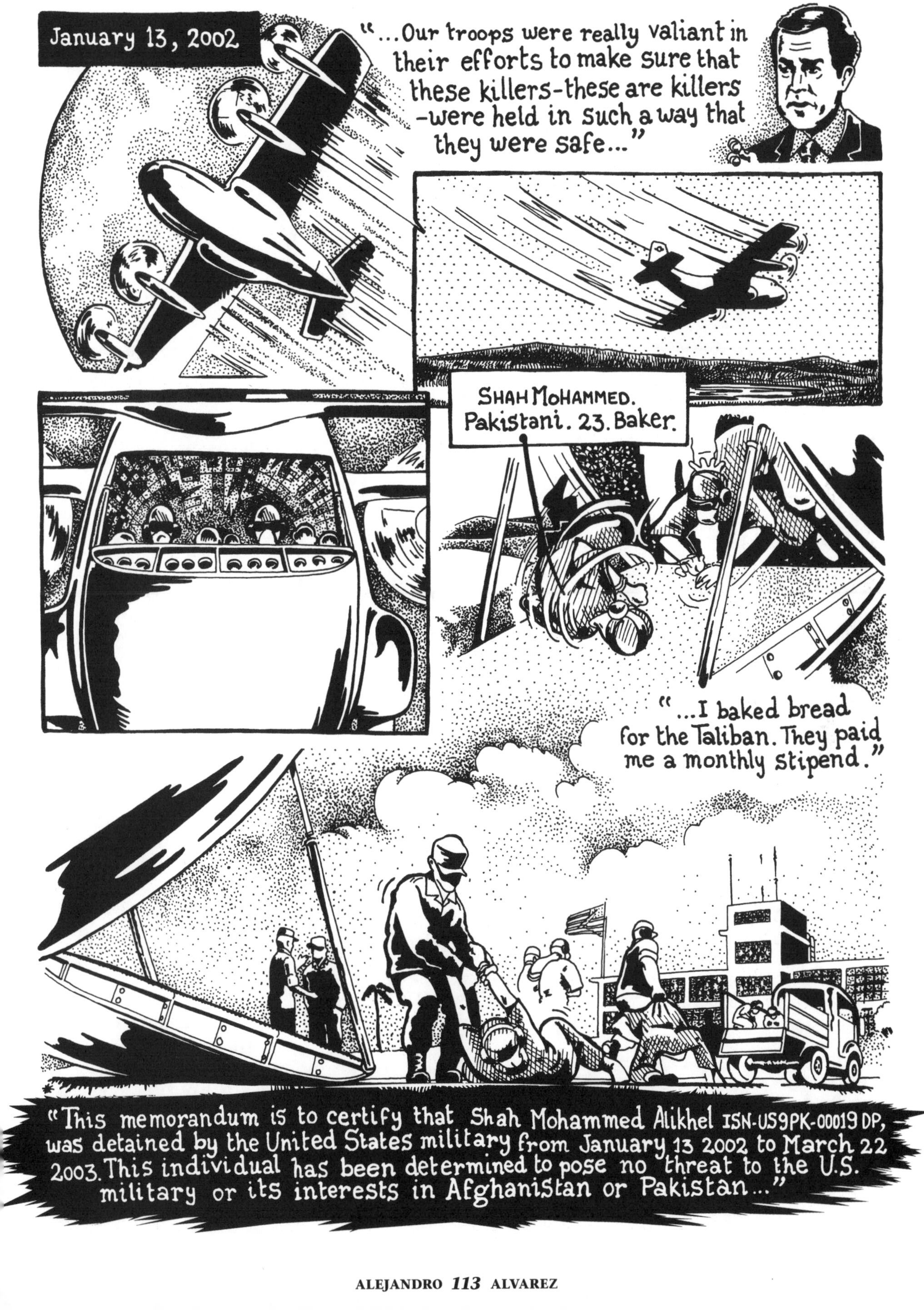
January 13, 2002
"...Our troops were really valiant in their efforts to make sure that these killers-these are killers -were held in such a way that they were safe..."
SHAH MOHAMMED. Pakistani. 23. Baker.
"...I baked bread for the Taliban. They paid me a monthly stipend."
"This memorandum is to certify that Shah Mohammed Alikhel ISN-US9PK-00019 DP, was detained by the United States military from January 13 2002 to March 22 2003. This individual has been determined to pose no threat to the U.S. military or its interests in Afghanistan or Pakistan..."

"...There are no charges pending from the U.S. against this individual. The U.S. goverment intends that this person be fully rejoined with his family."

This letter was given to Shah Mohammed when released. He was one of the first prisoners to be taken to:

CAMP X-RAY
GUANTANAMO

a. alvarez 2004

Sited on the northern side of the U.S. naval base it was named after one of the symbols in the phonetic alphabet used for official military radio communication (ie: Alpha, Bravo, Golf, x-Ray)

keep your head down!!

Originally constructed to hold Haitian refugees in the 1990s, it was now to serve as a holding facility for Al Qaeda, Taliban and other detainees under U.S. control during the war on terror.

The U.S. Southern Command activated Joint Task Force 160 to take care of the captured enemies in Guantanamo.

Told you to keep your head down!!

Asif Iqbal, Briton, 22

We travelled to Pakistan ahead of the marriage my parents arranged for me. He was going to be best man

I hoped to do a computer course after the wedding.

Asif Iqbal, Ruhal Ahmed and Shafiq Rasul after being released, in the sitting room of a suburban House in Tipton, England. Sunday March 14, 2004.

"We were travelling through Afghanistan in a taxi trying to escape to a safer place..."

"...but when we reached Kunduz the city was surrounded by the Northern Alliance Forces."

"One thing made us dangerously visible, we had no beards."

"We were captured and taken through the open desert with thousands of prisoners outside Shebargan prison."

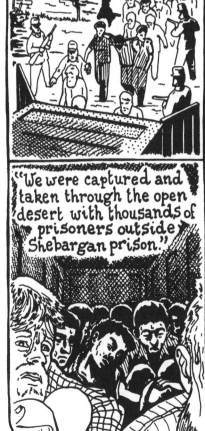

"There they herded us into containers, maybe 300 of us into each one."

"We were suffocating. It got really hot and everyone started screaming and banging."

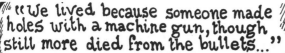

"We lived because someone made holes with a machine gun, though still more died from the bullets..."

"..I had not drunk for more than two days. We stank, we were covered in blood, urine and the smell of death."

"Freed from the containers we were taken into Shebargan prison. People died daily there..."

"I'll never forget one Arab who was missing half his jaw. For 10 days until his death he was screaming continuously begging to be killed."

"One day we were put in chains, hooded and handed over to the U.S. Special Forces. They took us to Kandahar."

ABDUL RAZAQ
Pakistani. 31.
English teacher.

Many of the people taken to Kandahar and then to Guantanamo Bay were simple bystanders. In an interview, after being released, Abdul Razaq declared: "I'm convinced that the only reason I was sent to Kandahar was because I spoke English. When a soldier came and asked who among the prisoners spoke English I stepped forward..."

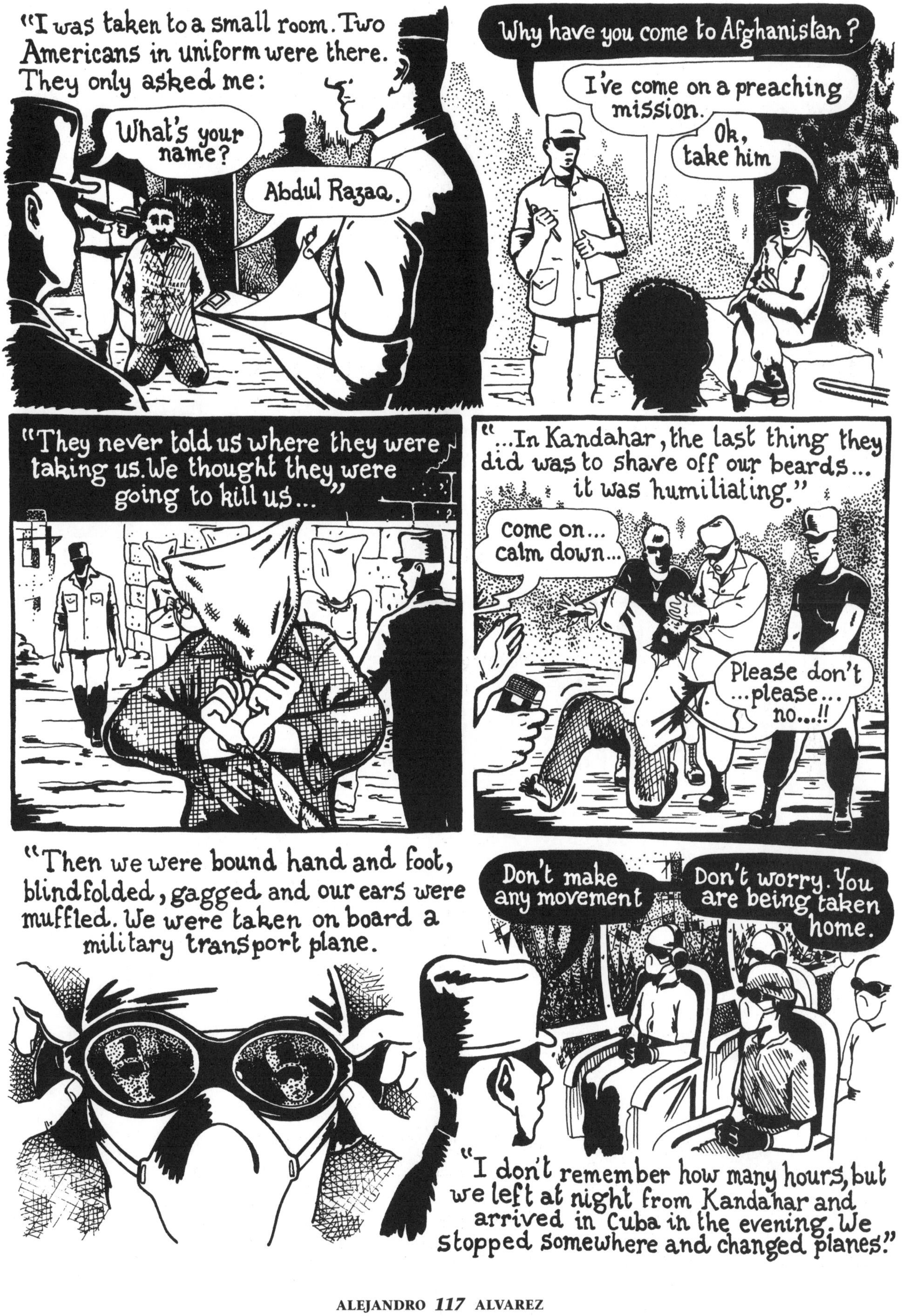
"I was taken to a small room. Two Americans in uniform were there. They only asked me:
What's your name?
Abdul Razaq.
Why have you come to Afghanistan?
I've come on a preaching mission.
Ok, take him
"They never told us where they were taking us. We thought they were going to kill us..."
"...In Kandahar, the last thing they did was to shave off our beards... it was humiliating."
come on... calm down...
Please don't ...please... no...!!
"Then we were bound hand and foot, blindfolded, gagged and our ears were muffled. We were taken on board a military transport plane.
Don't make any movement
Don't worry. You are being taken home.
"I don't remember how many hours, but we left at night from Kandahar and arrived in Cuba in the evening. We stopped somewhere and changed planes."

"I don't have the slightest concern about their treatment after what they have done." Defense Secretary Donald Rumsfeld.

"...In the first one-and-a-half months in Guantanamo they wouldn't let us speak to anyone, there was almost nothing to do. You just stare and the hours go clicking by. You'd look at people and see they'd lost it. There was nothing in their eyes anymore. They didn't talk..."

Mohamed Saghir, Pakistani. 53. Sawmill owner

"...They wouldn't let us call for prayers or pray in the room..."

✳Allahu akbar
Allahu akbar
Allahu akbar
Allahu akbar

✳ God is most great.

Who is it ?!!

✳Ashhadu anna Muhammada-rasulu-llah
Ashhadu anna Muhammada-rasulu-llah
Hayya 'ala-salah Hayya 'ala-salah.

✳ Ashhadu an la ilaha illa-llah
Ashhadu an la ilaha illa-llah

✳ I witness that there is no god except God

✳I witness that Muhammad is the messenger of God. Come to prayer.

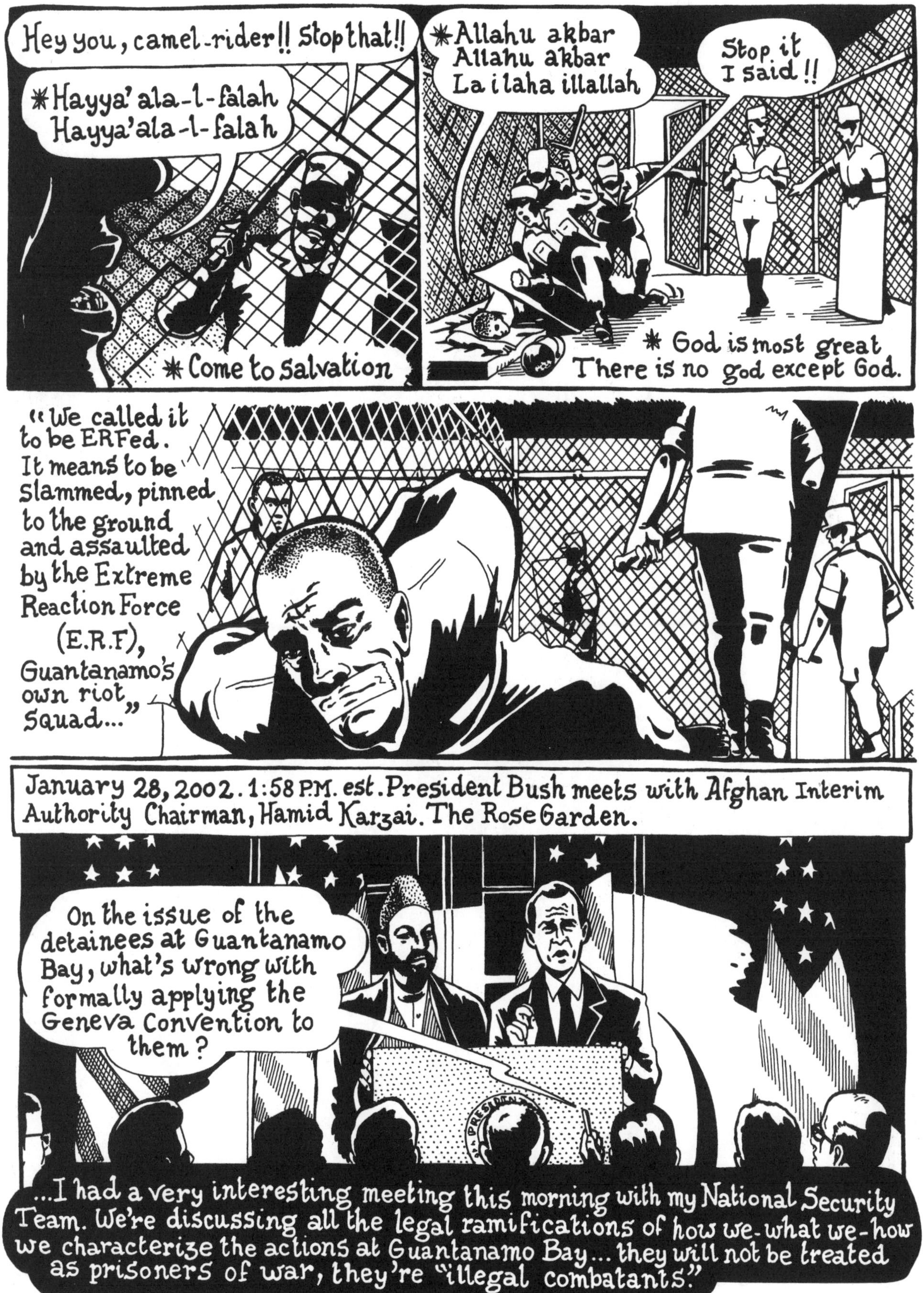
Hey you, camel-rider!! Stop that!!
✱Hayya'ala-l-falah
Hayya'ala-l-falah
✱Come to Salvation
✱Allahu akbar
Allahu akbar
La ilaha illallah
Stop it
I said!!
✱ God is most great
There is no god except God.
"We called it to be ERFed. It means to be slammed, pinned to the ground and assaulted by the Extreme Reaction Force (E.R.F), Guantanamo's own riot Squad..."
January 28, 2002. 1:58 P.M. est. President Bush meets with Afghan Interim Authority Chairman, Hamid Karzai. The Rose Garden.
On the issue of the detainees at Guantanamo Bay, what's wrong with formally applying the Geneva Convention to them?
...I had a very interesting meeting this morning with my National Security Team. We're discussing all the legal ramifications of how we-what we-how we characterize the actions at Guantanamo Bay... they will not be treated as prisoners of war, they're "illegal combatants."

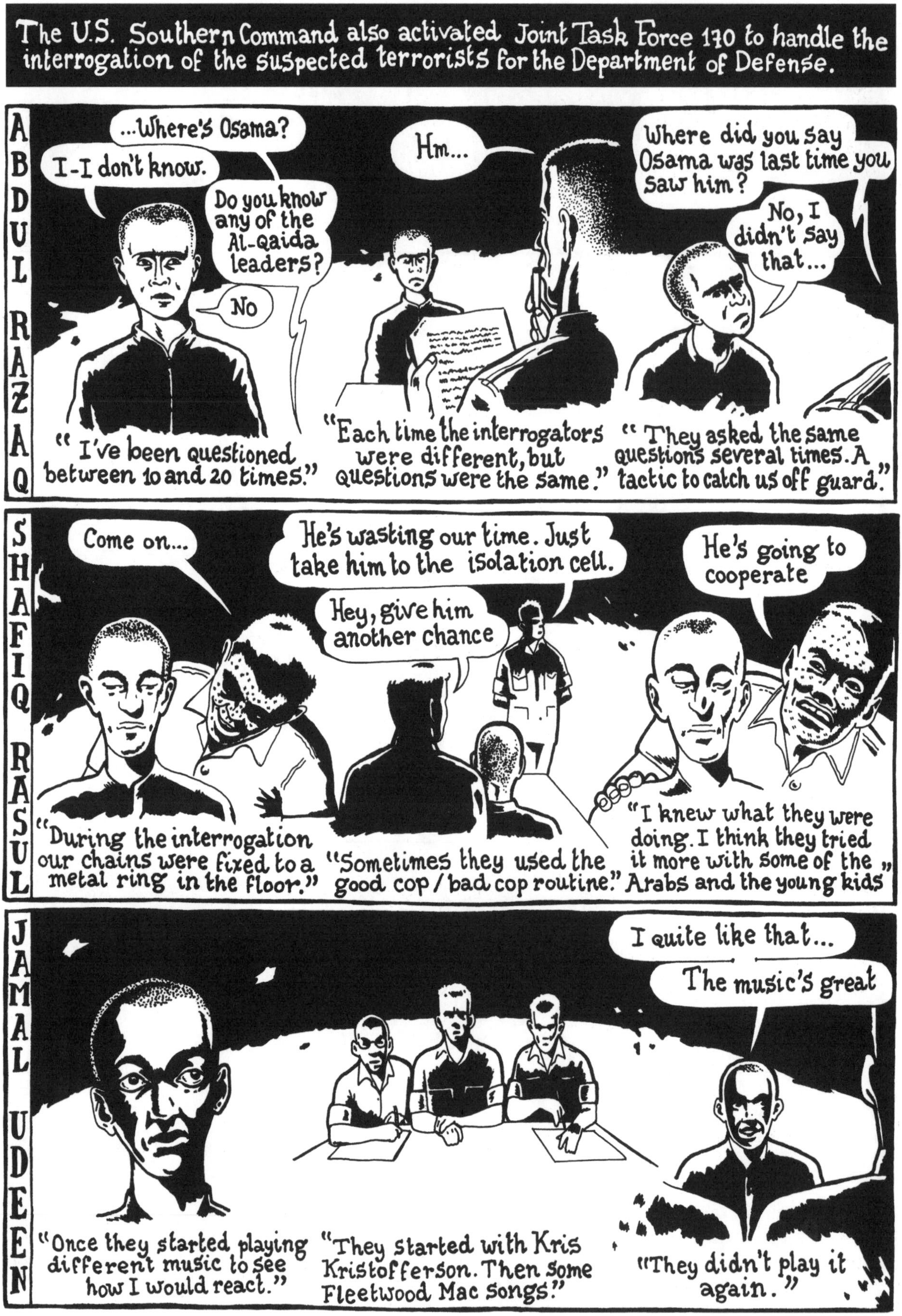
The U.S. Southern Command also activated Joint Task Force 170 to handle the interrogation of the suspected terrorists for the Department of Defense.
ABDUL RAZAQ
...Where's Osama?
I-I don't know.
Do you know any of the Al-Qaida leaders?
No
"I've been questioned between 10 and 20 times."
Hm...
"Each time the interrogators were different, but questions were the same."
Where did you say Osama was last time you saw him?
No, I didn't say that...
"They asked the same questions several times. A tactic to catch us off guard."
SHAFIQ RASUL
Come on...
"During the interrogation our chains were fixed to a metal ring in the floor."
He's wasting our time. Just take him to the isolation cell.
Hey, give him another chance
"Sometimes they used the good cop / bad cop routine."
He's going to cooperate
"I knew what they were doing. I think they tried it more with some of the Arabs and the young kids"
JAMAL UDEEN
"Once they started playing different music to see how I would react."
"They started with Kris Kristofferson. Then some Fleetwood Mac songs."
I quite like that...
The music's great
"They didn't play it again."

By the end of 2003 20 percent of the detainess in Guantanamo were on anti-depressants. 32 of them had attempted suicide. Shah Mohammed tried it four times.

"...Why?...I was worried over troubles at home...my mother's health and my own problems..."

Shit!!

GUARDS!

GUARDS!

ARRG

To the hospital

call the doctor

yes

"...Inmates in a normal prison are focused on how much time they are going to serve, on contacting their lawyers, on being able to take constructive efforts to get out...and these guys can't do anything..." (Daryl Matthews: forensic psychiatrist)

Good boy

"They told me my brain wasn't working properly. As treatment for my suicidal state of mind..."

"...they forced me to take these injections and tablets. I couldn't see down, I couldn't see up..."

"...I felt paralysed for one month. Some people were being injected regularly..."

"...After one and a half months we went on a hunger strike..."

It follows several days of growing tension among the detainees, caused by uncertainty about what is going to happen to them in the future.

Press

Marine Major Stephen Cox, Detention Mission Spokesman.

"...in the beginning there was mass hunger strikes but later on there were individual cases of people not eating..."

"At its height, nearly 200 inmates took part. Some were fed intravenously."

I could not tell you how long you will be here or what will happen to you in the future, but you'll be judged fairly.

"...Sometimes we take off our plastic tags carrying the U.S. identification codes and throw them to the guards..."

Hand over your blanket!!

"...two colleagues didn't oblige so they sprayed them, make them unconscious and took them to the isolation cells..."

This is civilization's fight. This is the fight of all who believe in progress and pluralism tolerance and freedom.

In April 2002 prisoners were moved to Camp Delta and Camp X-Ray was closed. At that time more than 600 people were held there, including four children.

May, 2003

Here you are.

Shah Mohammed was transported from Cuba back to Pakistan "in chains."

And like Abdul Razaq, Mohammed Saghir, Shafiq Rasul, Asif Iqbal, Ruhal Ahmed and many others was released to go free.

During more than a year he was held without formal charges or access to legal counsel

And so I'm looking at the legalities involved with the Geneva Convention. We are not going to call them prisoners of war. And the reason why is Al-Qaeda is not a known military.

These are killers. These are terrorists.

"...They promised me some money but at the end they gave me this bag with a pair of jeans, a shirt and a pack of tissues..."

"These guys get shipped to somebody else's country, held there so they don't get the same rights as in the U.S., and then get treated by rules made up by the government to suit their interests..."

"...If we are trying to say to the rest of the world we have due process and best practice in our country... we shouldn't be treating other people in ways that are unfair." James Harrington. New York lawyer.

The Bush administration's decision is that the few detainees facing trial should stand before a military commission, which would take place without juries or appeal to a higher court but with the power to impose a death sentence.

PAUL WOLFOWITZ
Deputy Secretary of Defense and the Commission's Appointing Authority

• The judges for the military commissions are appointed by Wolfowitz.

• Any judge can be substituted up to the moment of the verdict by Wolfowitz.

• The military prosecutors are chosen by Wolfowitz.

• The suspects they charge and the charges they make are determined by Wolfowitz.

• All defendants are entitled to a military defense lawyer from a pool chosen by Wolfowitz.

• If convicted, defendants can appeal to a panel of three people appointed by Wolfowitz, and then the panel sends its recommendation for a final decision to... WolfDwitz

In June 2003 the U.S. military officials were making preparations for the construction of a "death chamber" in Guantanamo.

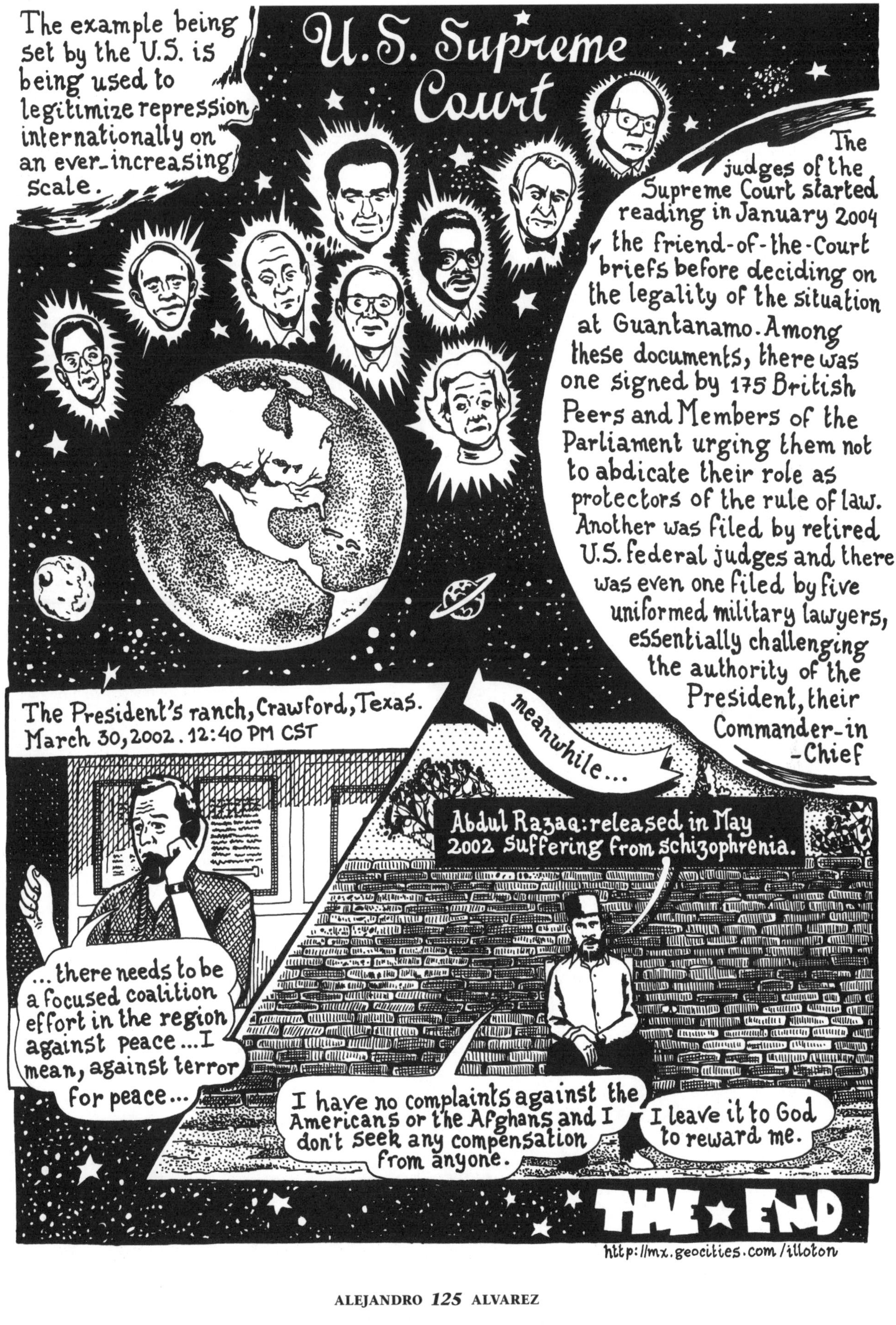

The example being set by the U.S. is being used to legitimize repression internationally on an ever-increasing scale.
U.S. Supreme Court
The judges of the Supreme Court started reading in January 2004 the friend-of-the-Court briefs before deciding on the legality of the situation at Guantanamo. Among these documents, there was one signed by 175 British Peers and Members of the Parliament urging them not to abdicate their role as protectors of the rule of law. Another was filed by retired U.S. federal judges and there was even one filed by five uniformed military lawyers, essentially challenging the authority of the President, their Commander-in-Chief
The President's ranch, Crawford, Texas. March 30, 2002. 12:40 PM CST
meanwhile...
...there needs to be a focused coalition effort in the region against peace...I mean, against terror for peace...
Abdul Razaq: released in May 2002 suffering from schizophrenia.
I have no complaints against the Americans or the Afghans and I don't seek any compensation from anyone.
I leave it to God to reward me.
THE ★ END
http://mx.geocities.com/illoton

THE WAR

ON JANUARY, 28, 2003 GEORGE BUSH GOT UP BEFORE CONGRESS AND IN HIS STATE OF THE UNION ADDRESS SAID...

SADDAM HUSSEIN...PURSUED CHEMICAL, BIOLOGICAL AND NUCLEAR WEAPONS, EVEN WHILE INSPECTORS WERE IN HIS COUNTRY.

IT WAS A LIE.

ON FEBRUARY 5, SECRETARY OF STATE COLIN POWELL ADDRESSED THE UNITED NATIONS.

...TWO OUT OF THREE COMPONENTS FOR A NUCLEAR BOMB.

SCARE TACTICS AND CONCOCTED EVIDENCE FAILED TO CONVINCE CANADA OR MEXICO, CRUDE BULLYING FAILED TO INTIMIDATE EVEN CAMEROON.

ON MARCH 19 GEORGE BUSH, WITHOUT U.N. SANCTION, UNLEASHED A WAR OF AGGRESSION ON ITS FORMER ALLY.

AMERICA'S OVERWHELMING TECHNOLOGICAL RESOURCES WERE BROUGHT TO BEAR FOR A QUICK AND PAINLESS VICTORY.

ON MARCH 31, THE ALHILLAH MARKET WAS CLUSTER BOMBED. THE AMOUNT OF "COLLATERAL DAMAGE" WAS NOT REPORTED.

DESPITE THE CONTINUING CAMPAIGN OF "SHOCK AND AWE," RESISTANCE AGAINST THE INVADERS CONTINUED.

THEY WERE TOLD THEY WOULD BE GREETED WITH FLOWERS...THAT DIDN'T TURN OUT TO BE THE CASE

THE CONFUSION OF BATTLE LEADS TO TRAGIC MISTAKES. THIS DOES NOTHING TO ENDEAR U.S. FORCES TO THE LOCAL POPULATION.

THE TEMPERATURE WAS SOMETIMES 120°, BRINGING THE TEMPERATURE INSIDE BULLET-PROOF VESTS, TO 140° THIS TOOK A FURTHER TOLL ON THE TROOPS MORALE.

BUT, USING SHELLS OF DEPLETED URANIUM THAT COULD PENETRATE ANYTHING, AMERICAN FORCES ROLLED ON.

NUMEROUS STUDIES HAVE SHOWN LINKS BETWEEN THE USE OF DEPLETED URANIUM AND SYMPTOMS OF RADIATION SICKNESS IN RETURNING G.I.S.

DESPITE THESE STUDIES, THE GOVERNMENT DENIED THE ADVERSE EFFECTS OF DEPLETED URANIUM MUCH THE WAY IT DENIED THE EFFECTS OF AGENT ORANGE AFTER THE VIETNAM WAR.

TELEVISION COVERED THE TOPPLING OF THE SADDAM HUSSEIN STATUE IN BAGHDAD'S FIRDOS SQUARE, BY WHAT SEEMED LIKE A HUGE CROWD

A WIDER SHOT OF THE EVENT GAVE A DISTINCTLY DIFFERENT IMPRESSION.

ONE OF THE FIRST ACTS OF THE OCCUPATION GOVERNMENT WAS TO INSTALL CONVICTED EMBEZZLER AHMAD CHALABI IN THE GOVERNING COUNCIL.

ON MAY 1, 2003 A TWO SEAT JET LANDED ON AN AIRCRAFT CARRIER, ANCHORED OFF THE COAST OF SAN DIEGO, WITH A VERY SPECIAL PASSENGER.

MISSION ACCOMPLISHED

AFTER SWAGGERING ACROSS THE DECK IN HIS FLIGHT SUIT "PRESIDENT" BUSH DECLARED VICTORY IN IRAQ

SOON AFTER, THE FIRST G.I.S DIED IN AN AMBUSH SOMEWHERE NEAR BAGHDAD.

*Frustrated and concerned about this country's growing assault on your civil liberties?
Here is one way for you to help educate others, and to work towards changing things.*

Presenting ...

YOUR VERY OWN
INFORMATION CAMPAIGN

Included here are five pages of ready-made flyers, fifteen flyers total, covering the <u>PATRIOT</u> Act and subsequent anti-terrorist legislation — addressing topics as varied as, but not limited to: computer confiscation, surveillance, private abductions and indefinite detainment without the aid of legal counsel.

Each of these flyers is designed to be easily photocopied. Please copy and distribute throughout your local town or city. Additional distribution and printing instructions are on the last page of this piece — Thank you.

Brought to you by

Ethan Persoff .... (words and layout)
and Jasun Huerta ...... (illustrations)

Austin, Texas USA

Fear and Paranoia surrounding recent anti-Terrorism Laws

Does the PATRIOT Act and other recently passed anti-terrorism legislation trouble you? Do you worry that these laws are aimed at harming you and your civil rights, more than protecting you from terrorists? Do you not trust the law-makers thoughtlessly pushing this sort of legislation through Congress?

If so, you are not being paranoid. Your concern is justified. Many Americans do not trust these laws, and for good reason. These laws threaten our entire Constitution, and these laws especially threaten our Bill of Rights.

This legislation has little to do with fighting enemies abroad, and more to do with increasing the powers of law officers to invade our homes without warrants, seize our property, and even spy on us. These laws give new power to police and federal agents to operate (with force) outside the protection of the courts. If these laws don't upset and anger you, why not? What would?

Yes, there is a lot to be worried about. Learn more. Speak out against these laws.

There is an abundant amount of information on this topic on the Internet and in public libraries. Start with Web sites like HTTP://WWW.ACLU.ORG/

The PATRIOT Act and similarly passed anti-terrorism laws are ruining America. These laws harm you and do not protect you. Get informed.

Federal agents and your privacy

Imagine someone spying on you. Looking through your diary. Secretly taking photos of you, or setting up a recording device on your phone. Tracking your email and Internet use. Or searching through your home at any hour of the day or night. What if this person was a federal agent? And what if all this snooping and information gathering was done without your knowledge, and without you ever finding out?

The U.S. Government has always had the authority to track someone in this manner, but the possibility that this would ever happen to you personally used to be highly unlikely, due to the need for securing court-approved warrants, and for providing evidence

that such an invasion of your privacy was justified.

But due to recent anti-terrorism legislation like the PATRIOT Act, such legal formalities are a thing of the past. Your privacy can now be easily intruded upon, and for no reason whatsoever, all in the name of national security. All it takes is for you to match a preexisting profile, based on your race, religion, sexual preference, kind of income, and/or political beliefs.

This has nothing to do with terrorism. Keep the Government out of your closet. Learn more. Speak out against these laws.

There is an abundant amount of information on this topic on the Internet and in public libraries. Start with Web sites like HTTP://WWW.ACLU.ORG/

The PATRIOT Act and similarly passed anti-terrorism laws are ruining America. These laws harm you and do not protect you. Get informed.

Search and Seizure

Recent anti-terrorism legislation allows federal agents and police officers to look through and confiscate anything you own, without cause or reason. And not return it to you. Ever.

That book bag of yours could have nothing threatening in it. Maybe some personal notes to friends, and some gadgets like a cellular phone or an mp3 player. But what if a policeman stopped you for some minor offense like jaywalking and demanded to look through your things? Under recent anti-terrorism laws, he'd be perfectly able to confiscate these items from you. And it's likely you'd never see them again. Why? because that's the way the laws have been written. But what if it's not a book bag? What if it's your car? Or computer. Same rules apply. Policemen now have

the authority to confiscate anything you own, and never return it to you, in the name of protecting this country from terrorists.

What's worse is if you end up possessing something that is potentially a terrorist weapon (including an ever-expanding list of commonly available household items), then you can get in even more serious trouble and even face jail time. And fines.

Learn more. Speak out against these laws.

There is an abundant amount of information on this topic on the Internet and in public libraries. Start with Web sites like HTTP://WWW.ACLU.ORG/

The PATRIOT Act and similarly passed anti-terrorism laws are ruining America. These laws harm you and do not protect you. Get informed.

False Imprisonment

You wake up to the sound of yelling and a harsh spotlight shining on your face. Where are you? What could be going on? Have you been kidnapped? No, suddenly you remember ...

This all began days ago with a knock on your door. A man showed you a badge and asked you to follow him to his car. You were placed in handcuffs and brought into a jail. You were not told of any reason for your arrest, not even charged with a crime, but you were escorted down a hallway and into a jail cell. You've been here now for five days and you have yet to speak with a lawyer, take a shower, or make a phone call.

You would like to speak with your family. You worry they don't know where you are. And alone, in your cell, you sit, waiting ...

This might sound like an unbelievable scenario, but to many innocent, law-abiding immigrants in this country, it is far more real than you can imagine.

Since 9-11, thousands of immigrants have been arrested and detained, without charge, for days, weeks, months. Many are still missing, held in undisclosed locations. Few are guilty of any crime. This is all permissible due to the Patriot Act and other anti-terrorism legislation. These laws also apply to the arrest and detainment of naturally-born American citizens.

Learn more. Speak out against these laws.

> There is an abundant amount of information on this topic on the Internet and in public libraries. Start with Web sites like HTTP://WWW.ACLU.ORG/

The PATRIOT Act and similarly passed anti-terrorism laws are ruining America. These laws harm you and do not protect you. Get informed.

Indefinite Detainment

Your story, if you'll consider it, begins at an American airport. You are visiting the country for business and to see close friends. Suddenly, you are asked questions by Customs. There is something wrong with your work visa, and your luggage also raises an alarm with an inspector. They escort you down a hallway.

You are shuttled off into a holding room in the airport. The next day you are taken to a local jail. You are never allowed a phone call, and you are not allowed to see a judge or allowed counsel with a lawyer.

It has now been months. You've been kept in a jail cell, away from any legal counsel. Your family fears you are dead. You begin to worry you're here for good. How could this happen while visiting, of all places, the United States?

This might sound like an unbelievable scenario, but to many innocent visitors to this country, it is happening, and often.

Since 9-11, thousands of foreign visitors have been arrested in airports and detained without charge, for days, weeks, months. The detained are from all over the globe: The Middle East, Europe, Russia, etc ... Few have criminal records. Due to the PATRIOT Act and similar legislation, this is all legal. These laws also apply to the arrest and detainment of natural-born American citizens.

Do you have any friends or family flying? Learn more. Speak out against these laws.

> There is an abundant amount of information on this topic on the Internet and in public libraries. Start with Web sites like HTTP://WWW.ACLU.ORG/

The PATRIOT Act and similarly passed anti-terrorism laws are ruining America. These laws harm you and do not protect you. Get informed.

The New Drug War
Pot smokers are now considered financial supporters of Terrorists

Next time you're at a party or a concert, look around. Due to the PATRIOT Act, and other supposed anti-terrorism legislation, such gatherings are now, suddenly, very risky.

Not because terrorists might be lurking about, but because if you're caught smoking pot, you might, as absurd as this sounds, be labeled a financial supporter of terrorism — and given an FBI file. This information might even be kept from you. Your name would just be added to a growing list. For prosecution at a later date.

The government has declared war on you with this legislation, and you need to be aware of the risks. It is urgent that you fight to repeal these laws. Let's discuss why:

These new laws target you. They allow agents full access to your credit history and medical records. Your Internet activity and phone can also be monitored without any court approval. And all of this can easily be shared with any law enforcement agency.

A federal file like this will follow you everywhere, affecting future employment, future bank loans, credit cards, insurance premiums, etc ... Other more serious threats include seizure of banking funds, prison, and even possible deportation for natural born American citizens. This is not a joke.

Learn more. Speak out against these laws.

> There is an abundant amount of information on this topic on the Internet and in public libraries. Start with Web sites like HTTP://WWW.ACLU.ORG/

The PATRIOT Act and similarly passed anti-terrorism laws are ruining America. These laws harm you and do not protect you. Get informed.

Your Computer Is Now Considered A Weapon

Use of a computer adds a FIVE-YEAR PENALTY TO ANY CRIME

Due to the PATRIOT Act and similar anti-terrorist legislation, your ownership (or use) of a computer now threatens you with a potential penalty of up to five years added to the jail sentence for any crime.

Portions of anti-terrorism legislation refer to "computers and encryption," punishing any criminal using "encryption" with a five year penalty. Unfortunately, this vague and generalized wording puts any modern computer-user at risk for this charge. You use encryption to enter passwords to log into your computer, to use a credit card, etc. And what crime is this attempting to prevent? It's not just terrorism. The vague wording of these laws are not on your side.

These laws do not separate crimes from misdemeanors, or violent crimes from accidental ones. The Patriot Act has, in fact, labeled any crime a possible act of terrorism. Potentially, you can now go to jail for five years for writing an email joking about the government, or for using a credit card online to purchase household cleaners. This is not a joke. This is an inexcusable assault on your Constitutional freedoms. Your computer is an appliance, not a weapon.

Learn more. Speak out against these laws.

There is an abundant amount of information on this topic on the Internet and in public libraries. Start with Web sites like HTTP://WWW.ACLU.ORG/

The PATRIOT Act and similarly passed anti-terrorism laws are ruining America. These laws harm you and do not protect you. Get informed.

Computer Confiscation

If you are like many Americans, a large amount of your life is spent on and around a computer. You correspond with others through a computer, you pay your bills with a computer. And on the Web you do everything from check the weather to watch a movie. You also use a computer as a word processor, and as a place to keep photos and other personally sensitive documents. Your computer is an indispensable part of your life.

Our computers are also one of our most personal possessions. They are our diary and they keep private details about us, storing emails, bookmarked Web sites, etc.

Imagine a stranger going through your home computer. What would they find?

Due to the PATRIOT Act and other related anti-terrorism legislation, federal agents (and even local police) can now invade your home and confiscate your computer. You don't even need to be home. They can then dissect your machine, and, if possible arrest and detain you based on information found, such as Web sites visited, text files and photos stored, etc. They do not need a court approved warrant to do this, nor are they required to ever return the computer or pay for any damage done to your property.

This is a troubling invasion of your rights. Learn more. Speak out against these laws.

There is an abundant amount of information on this topic on the Internet and in public libraries. Start with Web sites like HTTP://WWW.ACLU.ORG/

The PATRIOT Act and similarly passed anti-terrorism laws are ruining America. These laws harm you and do not protect you. Get informed.

Wiretap/Surveillance

Our legal system has always had a series of checks and balances that keep certain element of law enforcement from abusing your rights. Extreme measures, like entering your home or tapping your phone, have always demanded the approval of the court system. This is because law enforcement can make mistakes. And they can also abuse their authority. But due to the PATRIOT Act and similar anti-terrorism legislation, police no longer need court approval to secure warrants to impose wiretaps on you. And not only can they monitor you without court approval, they can now monitor you in unheard-of ways that violate the entire Constitution, especially your Bill of Rights.

... **Also:** Previous laws used to impose a maximum time limit on information gathering. It can now go on for years.

Electronic surveillance is the most invasive and threatening. Internet use can be tracked, compiling information on people, IP addresses and groups. Computer systems are being designed to flag you, searching out keywords criticizing the government. Your phone, email, etc. can now all be monitored. You do not need to have ever committed a crime. If you fit a profile, you can be tracked. This has little to do with catching terrorists and more to do with setting up a system to monitor normal citizens. What is this leading to? Certainly not a safer country. Something worse is going on. It should trouble you.

Learn more. Speak out against these laws.

There is an abundant amount of information on this topic on the Internet and in public libraries. Start with Web sites like HTTP://WWW.ACLU.ORG/

The PATRIOT Act and similarly passed anti-terrorism laws are ruining America. These laws harm you and do not protect you. Get informed.

Encouraging False Accusations

How smart, would you say, are your neighbors? Not the ones you count as friends, but the other ones. The nosey ones that always seem to be in everyone else's business. Looking out their window when you and others pass by.

How would you feel if these people were suddenly as powerful as a policeman, able to report suspicions of you being a threat to this country — and for this information to not only be valued by local authorities, but for a permanent file to be opened up on you based solely on their phone call?

Recent anti-terrorism legislation like the PATRIOT Act not only allows for this sort of strange witch hunt, it actually encourages it.

These laws empower the most ignorant, racist, over-reactive and paranoid in our society to accuse others of terrorism. Proof is not important, they just want names. All tips are taken seriously. Attempts have also been made to even force postal workers to inform on others. Imagine this happening to you. Would this be justified if you were a terrorist? Possibly ... but are you a terrorist? Doubtful. This might be laughable if the threats of an FBI file weren't so life altering and permanent. What is going on here?

Learn more. Speak out against these laws.

There is an abundant amount of information on this topic on the Internet and in public libraries. Start with Web sites like HTTP://WWW.ACLU.ORG/

The PATRIOT Act and similarly passed anti-terrorism laws are ruining America. These laws harm you and do not protect you. Get informed.

Secret Arrests

TARGETS INCLUDE:
Social protesters at peace rallies

During the Cold War, Americans were told the enemy was Russia. We were warned of a Russian society that not only kept close watch on its citizens, but that the Russians were also freedom haters who, if need be, would abduct and detain free-thinking people who spoke out against the government.

The Cold War is long finished, but the possibility of a government abducting and detaining its citizens is still a very real threat. But it's not Russia. No, quite ironically, the threat comes from within this very country.

Recent anti-terrorism legislation like the PATRIOT Act allows for police and federal agents to not only abduct and detain you, but to do it secretly, and with no one — not even your family — ever being told.

Once in custody, you will very likely not be allowed to appear in front of a judge, or speak with a lawyer. These laws completely ignore your Constitutionally guaranteed civil rights. Under the concept of a "War on Terrorism" law enforcement can now arrest and detain any suspect of their choosing as a prisoner of war ... This includes abducting naturally-born American citizens right off the street.

Ironic for an America so previously bent on defeating fascist regimes and Communism, isn't it? ... BUT this is only happening because we're allowing it to happen.

Learn more. Speak out against these laws.

There is an abundant amount of information on this topic on the Internet and in public libraries. Start with Web sites like HTTP://WWW.ACLU.ORG/

The PATRIOT Act and similarly passed anti-terrorism laws are ruining America. These laws harm you and do not protect you. Get informed.

No one will know where you've gone

Missing Persons   ?????

One of the most threatening aspects of the PATRIOT Act and other recent anti-terrorism legislation is how it authorizes law-enforcement to abduct and detain thousands of Americans, and often without providing any charge, all in the shadowy interest of national security.

But what about the families and friends of these arrested citizens? Are they informed? No. Nothing in these laws assures that family of detained citizens will ever be notified of their loved one's whereabouts.

What this means, in a worst-case scenario, is that people will suddenly begin to just disappear from the streets. It might sound farfetched, since we live in America after all — but to immigrants and other less-empowered members of our society, it has

already begun. Detained persons numbered in the thousands directly following 9-11. If another terrorist attack occurs (which is likely) such measures are sure to increase into mass scale. And from there, what next?

The anxiety over a missing loved one who may or may not be detained by the government can destroy families, especially when the government refuses to help answer yes or no as to whether their loved one has been taken into custody. What is this leading to? Certainly not a safer country. Something worse is going on. It should trouble you.

Learn more. Speak out against these laws.

There is an abundant amount of information on this topic on the Internet and in public libraries. Start with Web sites like HTTP://WWW.ACLU.ORG/

The PATRIOT Act and similarly passed anti-terrorism laws are ruining America. These laws harm you and do not protect you. Get informed.

Revoked Citizenship

Good Bye

ANTI-GOVERNMENT OPINIONS CARRY A CONSEQUENCE WORSE THAN MURDER OR RAPE

The design of America has always had certain absolute guarantees. The 14th Amendment of the Constitution guarantees that if you are born in this country, you are guaranteed citizenship, no matter how terrible you behave. Rapists, thieves, even mass murderers are guaranteed citizenship even though they are imprisoned for committing horrible violent crimes. But due to recent anti-terrorist legislation like the Patriot Act, you can now be stripped of this birthright. And the consequences are severe.

If you show any support or endorsement to any organization (foreign or **domestic**) that is considered a terrorist organization, then the Attorney General can deem you a threat to this country and deport you ... or worse.

But what exactly is a terrorist organization? This is still being debated. After 9-11, it was simple: terrorists were Al Qaeda and other violent military groups. But as the laws get written, the definitions get looser. Soon it can be as simple as a political affiliation, or a subscription to a left-wing political magazine. Many lawmakers consider criticism of this government as an act of treason. Musicians and artists are now as much risk as militias.

What will happen if you are stripped of your U.S. citizenship? Well, you will have no nationality at all, allowing America to detain you indefinitely as an undocumented alien. And you will not be allowed a lawyer.

This is really happening, and is a real threat. Learn more. Speak out against these laws.

There is an abundant amount of information on this topic on the Internet and in public libraries. Start with Web sites like HTTP://WWW.ACLU.ORG/

The PATRIOT Act and similarly passed anti-terrorism laws are ruining America. These laws harm you and do not protect you. Get informed.

Enemy Combatant Status

ENEMY COMBATANT

Since 9-11, we, as Americans, have seen our personal freedoms and civil liberties threatened in historic, unheard of ways ... In the interest of national security, we have given away basic Constitutional freedoms, and we have especially given away our Bill of Rights.

Has our sacrifice been worth it? Not at all. We are no more secure or safe than before. Actually, we are now more vulnerable. The threat from a foreign attack might be less of a possibility, but we have given dangerous authority to a dishonest, unjust and corrupt presidential administration.

The arrogance of this administration is well illustrated by George W. Bush's use of "Enemy Combatant" status to abduct and detain anyone of his choosing as a threat.

Since the president has declared us to be engaged in an ongoing "War on Terrorism" then (by the rule of war) anyone can be arrested and held in a military brig, indefinitely, without legal counsel — jailed until this "war" is finished.

But who are these enemies? There are the obvious ones: actual militant soldiers who plot to harm others. But who else? You'll be surprised to realize that recent laws like the PATRIOT Act allow any of us to be considered a threat. Any crime (violent or not) is now considered a potential act of terrorism. And any terrorist is a potential enemy combatant.

Learn more. Speak out against these laws.

There is an abundant amount of information on this topic on the Internet and in public libraries. Start with Web sites like HTTP://WWW.ACLU.ORG/

The PATRIOT Act and similarly passed anti-terrorism laws are ruining America. These laws harm you and do not protect you. Get informed.

Twenty-three (and counting) New Death Penalties

Now Serving: No. 15

The laws just keep on showing up, don't they? It's here — yet more new legislation from our government, now adding death penalties to their arsenal of threats to keep us from protesting recent legislation like the PATRIOT Act.

Fortunately, however, protests have proven successful. The second PATRIOT Act (also dubbed the Victory Act) will likely never see congressional approval — due largely to **your** public outcry over the extreme and largely un-American ideas involved with these bills. *BUT WE ARE NOW AT RISK* for these laws to be passed quietly, UNDER DIFFERENT NAMES. Case in point: the **Terrorist Penalties Enhancement Act** (T.P.E.A.)

The T.P.E.A. allows for 23 new death penalties for acts of terrorism. But what is an act of terrorism? Unfortunately, since passage of the PATRIOT Act, literally ANY CRIME is a potential act of terrorism. What can we do? It is important to keep informed, and follow legislation as it changes names and as new penalties are added. We can overcome these laws, but it takes a country-wide effort, and a constant criticism of our often corrupt lawmakers.

Learn more! Speak out against these laws!

There is an abundant amount of information on this topic on the Internet and in public libraries. Start with Web sites like HTTP://WWW.ACLU.ORG/

The PATRIOT Act and similarly passed anti-terrorism laws are ruining America. These laws harm you and do not protect you. Get informed.

IT IS IMPORTANT to realize that even if Bush is voted out of office, these laws will remain, and that much of the public are pushing for even more legislation to be written (but this is because they do not know what these laws are about).

Please take a minute to consider participating in photocopying and distributing these flyers, or making your own. These flyers don't pretend to be all the information available on these laws, either. There is a good chance you can do your own research and find something worse to tell people about. However, one benefit to these flyers is that they're already made for you, so distributing them is all that is asked of you. And your participation is very appreciated, too.

Distribution Suggestions

These flyers are designed to be distributed separately. If only one of these flyers seems interesting to you, make three copies of it and arrange these three copies of that flyer on a single sheet of paper. Xerox this single sheet and you will have three copies of each flyer per photocopy. So one hundred photocopies will yield three hundred flyers, etc.... a good paper cutter will be useful, found at any office supply store.

The Campaign

Of course, if all of these flyers appeal to you, you should make copies of all of them. Develop your own strategies for distribution. To get you started, here are a few suggestions.

These are designed to be released, one at a time, over a fifteen-week long period.

one: IDENTIFY PLACES TO DROP OFF FLYERS

Coffee houses and music stores are good places to start. Drop off a stack of flyers, once a week, for fifteen weeks. Only choose one flyer at a time (see directions above for making multiple copies of a single flyer) and always drop flyers off in the exact same place, be it a table or bulletin board — these flyers have been designed with a sequence in mind. Begin with the first ("Fear and Paranoia Surrounding Recent Anti-Terrorism Laws") then, a week later go on to the second ("Federal Agents and Your Privacy") followed the next week by the third, and so on. If you are lucky, people might begin to anticipate these flyers and welcome you. Repeat this fifteen-week cycle of distribution as necessary. Try and find multiple areas in your city to drop off flyers. If you return to a stack of flyers that have not been taken, replace them with the new ones. Don't become discouraged, return to these same places weekly.

TIP: If you want to only do this once, make a random stack of flyers, shuffling them up, and drop them off at various places around town.

two: THE HANDOUT METHOD

Go out on the town for a day or a night and hand out flyers to people. You'll be amazed at what an opportunity this can be to meet and make friends with other like-minded people. A consideration: This method can be complicated, and is up to your own social skills. Keep in mind that many people will not be receptive, and a few might even become confrontational. Most people expect you to be either a religious pamphleteer or salesmen if you have something in your hand. It is better to walk around and hand out flyers than it is to stay in one place. People will think you are selling something if you stay on a street corner with a stack of paper in your hands. Also consider dropping off flyers anonymously in places like the sinks at restaurant and club bathrooms and in phone booths. Social festivals or concerts are the best places to hand out flyers, since people are in good moods and receptive.

If possible, do this for five weekends in a row, using three separate flyers each week, or make a stack of all fifteen flyers and distribute them randomly in one evening or afternoon. (Legal notice: obey local laws regarding littering and handbill distribution.)

three: THE CITY-WIDE ENLARGED POSTER DISTRIBUTION METHOD

In cities that legally allow you places to post on walls and poles, this is a great opportunity for you. Each flyer, when enlarged 245% will fit well on a tabloid-sized sheet of paper (the 11" x 17" size — or enlarged to fit even larger sizes of paper if you can screen-print) Staple, glue or tape these enlarged flyers to walls. Repeat weekly with new flyers or bombard your town with all of these messages at once, at various places — shopping centers, downtown, etc. Make a day out of it. Have fun. People need to know this information.

— Thank you very much for your interest and participation in
Your Very Own Information Campaign. —

Considered A Weap...

Due to the Patriot Act and similar anti-terrorist legislation, your ownership (or use) of a computer now threatens you with a potential penalty of up to five years added to the jail sentence for any crime.

Portions of anti-terrorism legislation refer to "computers and encryption", punishing any criminal using "encryption" with a five year penalty. Unfortunately, this vague and generalized wording puts any modern computer-user at risk for this charge. You use encryption to enter passwords to log into your computer, to use a credit card, etc. And what crime is this attempting to prevent? It's not just terrorism. The vague wording of these laws are not on your side.

These laws do not separ... misdemeanors, or viole... accidental ones. The Patri... labeled any crime a... terrorism. Potentially, yo... jail for five years for writi... about the government, or... card online to purchase h... This is not a joke. This... assault on your Consti... Your computer is an appl...

Learn more. Speak out...

There is an abundant amou... topic on the Internet and i... with Web sites like HTTP:

Him?

The Patriot Act and similarly passe...

...ct and similarly passed anti-terrorism laws are ruining America. These laws harm you and do not prote...

Fo...

If so, ... concern is ... do not trust th... reason. These laws ... Constitution, and these ... threaten our Bill of Rights.

...passed anti-terrorism laws are ruining America. These...

No one will know where you've gone

The Patriot Act and similarly passed anti-terrorism laws are ruining America. These la...

Missing P...

One of the most threatening aspects of the Patriot Act and other recent anti-terrorism legislation is how it authorizes law-enforcement to abduct and detain thousands of Americans, and often without providing any charge, all in the shadowy interest of national security.

But what about the families and friends of these arrested citizens? Are they informed? No. Nothing in these laws assures that family of detained citizens will ever be notified of their loved one's whereabouts.

What this means, in a worst-case scenario, is that people will suddenly begin to just disappear from the streets. It might sound farfetched, since we live in America after all — but to immigrants and other less-empowered members of our society, it has

The...
Pot sm...

Narc.

Bait.

THE EY...

an... migh... would j... prosecutio...

The government... with this legislatio... aware of the risks. It i... to repeal these laws. Let's

...rism laws are ruining America. These la...

...er ...confiscate anyt...

Indefinite Detainment

Your story, if you'll consider it, begins at an American airport. You are visiting the country for business and to see close friends. Suddenly, you are asked questions by Customs. There is something wrong with your work visa, and your luggage also raises an alarm with an inspector. They escort you down a hallway.

You are shuttled off into a holding room in the airport. The next day you are taken to local jail. You are never allow... and you are ...

This might sound like an unbelievable scenario, but to many innocent visitors to this country, it is happening, and often.

Since 9-11, thousands of foreign visitors have been arrested in airports and detained without charge, for days, weeks, months. The detained are from all over the globe... Middle East, Europe... crimina...

There is an abundant amou... topic on the Internet and in... with Web sites like HTTP://

3
Key Players

Snowflake

THE PARANOID-DELUSIONAL WORLD OF DONALD RUMSFELD

But just what sort of person **IS** Donald Rumsfeld — the man behind the Jocular Reaper mask?

The events of 9/11/01 and subsequent USA adventures in Afghanistan and Iraq have made Secretary of Defense Donald Rumsfeld into something of a media star. He is fond of the camera and the microphone, and peppers his speech with affable Boy Scout expletives like "Golly!" or "Goodness gracious!" He has also been one of the main motivating forces behind the Bush Junta's genocidal strategy of "pre-emption"; which, concomitantly, has also been a fantastically profitable boondoggle for members of his inner Cabal, especially Co-UnPresident Dick Cheney (originally, a Rumsfeld protégé) [Jane Mayer, "Contract Sport", *The New Yorker*, 2/16-23/04]. Rumsfeld has had a long career in the public and private sectors as a hired executive henchman, a reaper of souls, a corporate and bureaucratic axe-man.

written and illustrated by Scott Marshall

He was born July 1932 in Chicago; but soon after, the family moved up to haute-bourgeois Winnetka, IL.

He attended the high-achiever High School of New Trier; alma mater of such entertainment figures as Rock Hudson, Charlton Heston, Ann-Margaret, Christie Hefner, and others.

As a teen, he is remembered as always being unusually clean and neatly dressed, with a mother like a wholesome 1940s movie character. Midge Decter, <u>Rumsfeld: a personal portrait</u>, Random House, New York, 2003]

Father bought and sold real estate, enlisting in WW2 after hostilities erupted.

While the family was in North Carolina (where Dad was stationed), young Donald saw an old black man trying to sell watermelons with "an ineffective mumble and unintelligible accent". Rumsfeld decided to help the old man, proposing that for every ten he sold he got to keep one for himself. [ibid.]

The scheme was a success, thus instilling in him a belief at an early age in Enterprise and Outsourcing.

Back in Winnetka at war's end, Rumsfeld made his mark as a wrestler; a sport where, it has been observed, there are only winners and losers, no second place.

Upon graduation, Rumsfeld earned a scholarship to Princeton (the most military of the Ivy League schools), where he studied government and politics. His sophomore year, he was selected in a national competition for a naval ROTC scholarship. He became a Navy flight instructor, and then an instructor of flight instructors. He also won the All-Navy Wrestling Championship. [ibid.]

In 1962 Rumsfeld decided to run for the House of Representatives in the conservative Illinois 13th District. He was elected, then re-elected, to a total of four terms. In the House, he was noted for his aggression and staunch defense of Jewish rights in the face of Soviet persecution. In 1967, he urged Congress to refrain from demanding Israeli withdrawal from land taken in the 6-Day War. [ibid.]

In 1963, he made Washington DC news when he saw a hot-rod youth being pursued by cops. When the kid tried to flee on foot, Rumsfeld jumped out of his own car, tackled the kid, and held him until the cops arrived. [ibid.]

During the 1968 Republican Convention, Rumsfeld was a member of Richard Nixon's "Flying Truth Squad" — free-ranging party hacks mandated to spreading Nixon's gospel to members of the media. [ibid.]

After Nixon's victory, Rumsfeld was awarded with his first Executive assignment: heading the Office of Economic Opportunity. Formerly, it was a progressive liberal-activist bureaucracy known for the Head Start program. Donald quickly changed all that. He delegated Head Start to the Dept. of Health, Education, and Welfare and cut off all funding for radical regional offices. [ibid.] It was at this time that Rumsfeld hired a young grad student from Nebraska named Richard Cheney. Together, "Rumsfeld and Cheney greatly diminished the power of the OEO [by outsourcing many jobs]...

...their tactics were not subtle. On the morning of 9/17/69, Rumsfeld distributed a new agency phone directory; without explanation, 108 employee names had been dropped. The vast majority were senior civil servants who had been appointed by Democrats." [Mayer, op. cit.]

Upon Nixon's resignation, Rumsfeld's old friend from the House of Representatives Gerald Ford asked him to put together a transition team for the new Administration. Rumsfeld made Cheney his deputy.

It was at this point that Rumsfeld became US history's youngest Secretary of Defense, with Cheney becoming White House chief of staff. [Decter, op. cit.]

After Ford's defeat in 1976, Rumsfeld left government and took as his first job an appointment as CEO/axe-man for the floundering Searle Pharmaceutical Co., Skokie, IL. Under his direction, numerous personnel were summarily fired, certain functions were outsourced, extraneous industry holdings were sold off, and Searle successfully sued the FDA over the licensing of Aspartame.

Finally, he negotiated a lucrative sale of Searle to Monsanto Co. Other corporate appointments and executive boards came and went, until...

RONNY RAYGUN DAZE! Under Reagan, the marginalized right-wing lunatic fringe in Washington entered the mainstream with a new mandate...

...and American politics and policy haven't been the same since.

Rumsfeld was appointed Special Envoy for the Middle East (the official conduit for American military intelligence, hardware, and strategic advice) at which point he met with Saddam Hussein. As a conciliatory gesture to Iraq in 1982, the US removed them from the list of state sponsors of terrorism, thus paving the way for munitions (including anthrax, bubonic plague, and components to make sarin and ricin gas) and Rumsfeld's visit.

Saddam was given large amounts of materiel, though Hussein was already known to have used nerve agents against Iran and the Kurds.

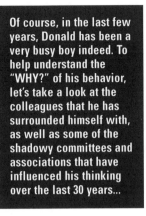

Of course, in the last few years, Donald has been a very busy boy indeed. To help understand the "WHY?" of his behavior, let's take a look at the colleagues that he has surrounded himself with, as well as some of the shadowy committees and associations that have influenced his thinking over the last 30 years...

Beginning with Irving Kristol (neocon godfather), Norman Podhoretz (former editor, Commentary — monthly sphincter of the *American Jewish Committee*), Midge Decter (poseur-writer, wife of Podhoretz and mother of rabid neocon columnist John Podhoretz), and Rumsfeld; all were members of *The Committee on the Present Danger* (1976) which effectively undermined President Jimmy Carter's arms-control policies, and the Raygun-era offshoot, *Coalition for the Free World*. Rumsfeld was the first advocate of the MX missile.
[Jim Lobe, "Family ties connect US right, Zionists", *disinfopedia.org*, 3/9/03]

Rumsfeld, Decter, Podhoretz, Cheney, "Scooter" Libby [present Chief of Staff for Cheney], [mumbling psychopath and present Deputy Secretary of Defense] Paul Wolfowitz, et al., were co-signers of *The Project for the New American Century* manifesto (1997-98), a blueprint for the "wrestle-the-world-to-the-mat" pre-emptive foreign policy that became doctrine, once Cheney and Libby installed it in Dubya's blank head. The invasion of Iraq was a part of this proposal [years before the Junta's assertion].
[Maureen Dowd, "A neoconservative's love ode to Rumsfeld", *The New York Times*, 9/29/03]

There is also a Moonie component to this scummy rogue's gallery: John Podhoretz, "has spent virtually his entire life supping at the table of strange right-wing foreigners seeking to buy their way into respectability by courting the American right wing... [starting with Rev. Moon] who hired John and his college roommate Todd Lindberg to provide a Nice-Jewish-Boy front for his nefarious activities."
[Eric Alterman, writing for *Salon.com*, as quoted on *english.daralhayat.com*, 6/03]

Also heavily in the mix is *The Jewish Institute for National Security Affairs* (JINSA)'s Michael Ledeen (Ollie North's Iran/Contra liaison with the Israelis). JINSA advocates "total war... by any means necessary in Iraq, Iran, Syria, Saudi Arabia, and the Palestinian Authority... a total hegemony achieved with the traditional Cold War recipe of feints, force, clientism, and covert action...

...almost every retired officer who sits on JINSA's board of advisers or has participated in its Israel trips or signed a JINSA letter works or has worked with military contractors who *do business with the Pentagon and with Israel...*

...other JINSA advisers include Cheney, John Bolton (now Under-secretary of State for Arms Control), James Woolsey [former head of CIA], Jeane Kirkpatrick, and Douglas Feith ." [Jason Vest, "The Men from JINSA and CSP", *archives.econ.utah.edu*, 9/2/02 (emphasis added)]

And lest we forget, there is also the *Center for Security Policy* (CSP) — founder, President, CEO: Frank Gaffney. Gaffney was a protégé of Richard Perle (former Zionist member of the Pentagon's *Defense Policy Board*), going back to their days as staffers for late Sen. Henry "Scoop" Jackson (a.k.a. "the Senator from Boeing", and the Senate's most zealous champion of Israel in his day). Gaffney reconstituted the latest incarnation of the *Committee on the Present Danger*, and has articles published regularly in the psychotically far-right Moonie paper <u>The Washington Times</u>. CSP was heavily rep-resented in Rumsfeld's *Commission to Assess the Ballistic Missile Threat to the USA* during the Clinton years. [ibid.]

HALLIBURTON

CSP

JINSA

It was during the 2000 election campaign that the coterie of military/industrial fiends surrounding Bush the Stooge coined a charming nickname for themselves: "The Vulcans" — drawn not from the super-rational beings in *Star Trek* episodes, but, rather, from the Roman god of fire and the forge; meant to convey a sense of god-like Power and supremacy. After the successful outcome of their election coup d'état, the Vulcans seemingly resolved their internecine differences and ordained Condoleezza Rice (protégé of Raygun flunky Brent Scowcroft) to draft a new National Security Strategy that officially laid the framework for the war these monsters had lusted after for so long. [Michiko Kakutani, "How Bush's Advisers Confront the World", review of <u>Rise of the Vulcans: The History of Bush's War Cabinet</u> by James Mann (Viking), *The New York Times*, 3/4/04]

"[Highly influential to neocon thinking are] the writings of political philosopher Leo Strauss. Strauss, who taught at the University of Chicago, was a Holocaust survivor and conservative thinker who is best known for his argument that the works of ancient philosophers contain deliberately concealed esoteric messages whose truths can be comprehended only by a very few, and would be misunderstood by the masses... Strauss believed that good statesmen have powers of judgment and must rely on an inner circle. The person who whispers in the King's ear is more important than the King. If you have that talent, what you do or say in public cannot be held accountable in the same way... The whole story is complicated by Strauss' idea — actually Plato's — that philosophers need to tell noble lies not only to the people at large but also to powerful politicians... [The Vulcans] see themselves as outsiders. There's a high degree of [delusional] paranoia. They've convinced themselves that they're on the side of angels, and everybody else in government is a fool."

[Seymour Hersh, "Selective Intelligence", *The New Yorker*, 5/6/03]

Oy vey! What a mess!
What it all boils down to is this:

In spite of all his fawning subservient attitude to his Führer Bush, Donald Rumsfeld and his Cabal [**HIS term!**] of Vulcans — psychopathic über-hawks in the White House, *Office of Special Plans*, the *Defense Policy Board*, JINSA, CSP, and elsewhere — **have decided to run US foreign policy from the Pentagon,** [W. Patrick Lang, former chief of Middle East intelligence at the DIA, quoted in Hersh, ibid.] while also conveniently turning immense profits for all his defense-contractor-connected buddies through obsessive privatizing of military functions and support. "The Pentagon has banded together to dominate the government's foreign policy, and they've pulled it off... the DIA has been intimidated and beaten to a pulp. And there's no guts at all in the CIA." [ibid.]

"[Like other members of the Bush Junta, Rumsfeld suffers] from a sociopathic inability to see things as the other party sees them... [Rumsfeld's Vulcan Cabal is] disastrously unable to perceive the impact of their own behavior on the other people of the world... If you read Rumsfeld's planning documents... you find that an eventual war with China is still in the cards...

...as the pure products of America's Cold War, Rumsfeld and his cohorts never gave up on the Manichaean fantasy of Armageddon... they're only starting with the Middle East, not ending with it... This is how the Bush regime rules: by terror... [the Junta] requires eternal war."

[Scott Thill, *morphizm.com,* interview with Mark Crispin Miller, author of <u>The Bush Dyslexicon</u>,1/7/03]

OK *So there is the deranged ideological context, the Method behind the Madness. Now, let's take a look at some details of Rumsfeld's personality...*

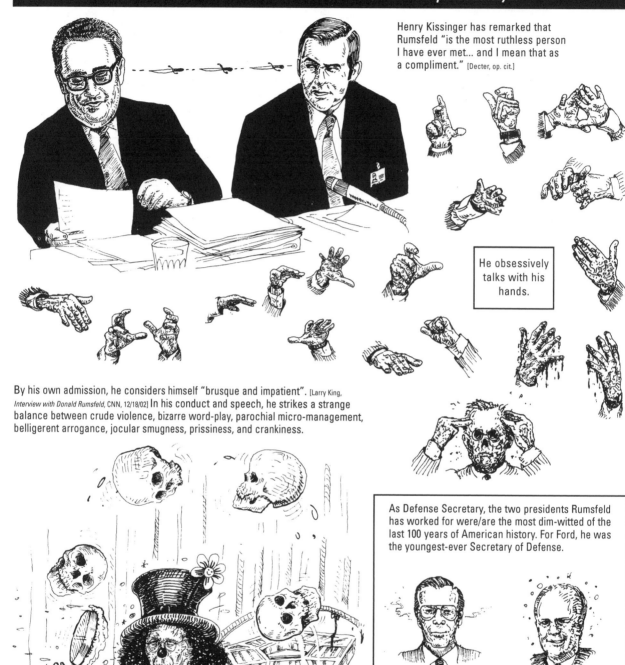

Henry Kissinger has remarked that Rumsfeld "is the most ruthless person I have ever met... and I mean that as a compliment." [Decter, op. cit.]

He obsessively talks with his hands.

By his own admission, he considers himself "brusque and impatient". [Larry King, *Interview with Donald Rumsfeld*, CNN, 12/18/02] In his conduct and speech, he strikes a strange balance between crude violence, bizarre word-play, parochial micro-management, belligerent arrogance, jocular smugness, prissiness, and crankiness.

As Defense Secretary, the two presidents Rumsfeld has worked for were/are the most dim-witted of the last 100 years of American history. For Ford, he was the youngest-ever Secretary of Defense.

And now, for Bush, he is the oldest-ever Secretary of Defense.

Rumsfeld works standing up at a high desk, and is fond of producing a daily barrage of personal, off-the-cuff Memos, or **"snowflakes"**, as they're called in the Pentagon.

"[During his tenure in the Bush Junta] Rumsfeld [has] succeeded in replacing those officers in senior Joint Staff positions who challenged his view. 'All the Joint Staff people now are hand-picked, and churn out products to make the Secretary of Defense happy. They don't make military judgments — they just respond to his snowflakes.'"

[Seymour Hersh, "Offense and Defense", *The New Yorker*, 4/7/03]

His "Soultype" has been defined as "Number 6: Insight: Constructs reality from the soul's love". Other famous No. 6's: Karl Rove, Arnold Schwarzenegger, Regis Philbin, Jack Kerouac, Sigmund Freud, George Bush Sr. [*newequations.com*]

"Rumsfeld used to get even with guys in the White House by leaking stuff to Dan Rather that didn't have any basis in fact."

[Tom Brokaw, *rotten.com*, 8/13/96, from a satellite transmission he didn't know was being broadcast.]

But don't just take my, or anyone else's, word for it. Here's Donald Rumsfeld in his OWN words:

"What I'm about is we've got a wonderful conflict."
[Larry King, *Interview with Donald Rumsfeld*, CNN, 12/5/01]

"Baghdad today is a whale of a lot better than Boise."
[Jim Lehrer, *Interview with Donald Rumsfeld*, PBS, 9/11/03]

"I'm not a physician. But when you've got three bullet holes, it's not like one, two, three — it's three is five." [Dept. of Defense, "DoD Press Briefing" *defenselink.mil*, 4/3/02, in reference to the capture of an alleged al-Qaeda operative who had been wounded.]

Secretary of State Colin Powell has commented that he "detests Rumsfeld's circuitous manner of speaking... which [I call] 'third-person passive once removed.'"
[Bryan Curtis, "The Condensed Bob Woodward", review of Plan of Attack, Bob Woodward, (Simon & Schuster), 4/21/04, slate.msn.com/id/2099277]

And here are a few samples of Rumsfeld's famous "existential poetry", as collected by Hart Seely on Slate.com:

"As we know
there are known knowns.
There are things
we know we know.
We also know
there are known unknowns.
That is to say,
we know there are some things
we do not know.
But there are also
unknown unknowns:
the ones we don't know
we don't know."
[DoD briefing, 2/12/02]

On NATO
"You may think it's something
I ought to know,
But I happen not to.
That's life."
[DoD briefing, 7/9/03]

On Democracy
"People elected
Those people to office.
That's what they think,
and That's life."
[DoD briefing, 2/20/03]

On Criticism
"It makes it complicated.
Sometimes, it makes
It difficult.
That's life."
[DoD briefing, 9/11/03]

On People
"They're going to have
Some impact on
What happens in that country
And that's not wrong.
That's life." [DoD briefing, 11/16/01]

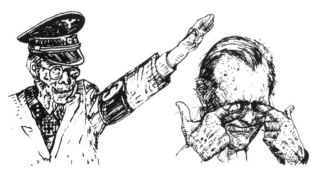

AND THEN THERE IS THE INFAMOUS ABU GHRAIB PRISON TORTURE SCANDAL...

"It was Dostoyevsky who said you can judge a society by its prisons." [Ted Gup, "Behind Abu Ghraib, an Even Darker Question", *The Village Voice*, 5/18/04]. "Behind the exotic brutality so paintstakingly recorded in Abu Ghraib... lies a simple truth, well-known but not yet publically admitted in Washington; that since the attacks of 9/11/01, **officials in the United States**, at various locations around the world, from Bagram, Afghanistan to Guantanamo, Cuba to Abu Ghraib, Iraq, **HAVE BEEN TORTURING PRISONERS**." [Mark Danner, "The Logic of Torture", *The NY Review of Books*, Vol. 51 No. 11, 6/24/04, emphasis added].

In his search for contractors to oversee the construction and organization of American prisons in Iraq, John Ashcroft personally selected two discredited corrections administrators; two men who at the time of Ashcroft's selection were actually under investigation by the Justice Department itself for egregious acts of neglect, abuse and torture in the American prisons under their authority. The two men were Lane McCotter (corrections abuses and illegalities in New Mexico and Utah) and John J. Armstrong (former commissioner of corrections in Connecticut). Both men were forced to resign their American positions under duress after lawsuits were found against them. "In Iraq, it was McCotter who first identified Abu Ghraib as the best site for America's main prison and who helped rebuild the prison and train the guards, according to his own account, given to Corrections.com, an online industry magazine." [Butterfield and Lichtblau, "Screening of Prison Officials is Faulted by Lawmakers", *New York Times*, 5/21/04]

During the autumn of 2003 when many of the infamous abuses were taking place, McCotter gave Paul Wolfowitz a personal tour of Abu Ghraib, accompanied by Gen. Janis Karpinski.

At one point early in the Iraq war, America held thousands of undocumented prisoners in widely scattered gulags. Most of them were civilians not charged with any crime other than having the misfortune of being in the wrong place at the wrong time. Frustrated with a rising insurgency and limited amounts of ground-level intelligence, Rumsfeld brought in Undersecretary of Defense for Intelligence Steven Cambone, Cambone's military assistant (notorious) Lt. Gen. William (Jerry) Boykin (the religious fanatic who publically equated Islam with Satanism), and Maj. Gen. Geoffrey Miller (the sadistic commander of Camp X-Ray, Guantanamo Bay, Cuba). Under Rumsfeld's direction, these men greatly expanded a highly secret operation for interrogating alleged Al Qaeda operatives to now include all Iraqi prison inmates, identified under several code words including "Copper Green". Thus began the deliberate and systematic use of physical coercion, sexual humiliation, and brute-force torture of Iraqi prisoners throughout the American gulag system in an effort to generate more intelligence about the growing insurgency. [Seymour Hersh, "The Gray Zone", *The New Yorker*, 5/24/04] Bush himself was kept appraised of this plan, as Rumsfeld regularly "got in [Bush's] head" (Rumsfeld's phrase) during these days.

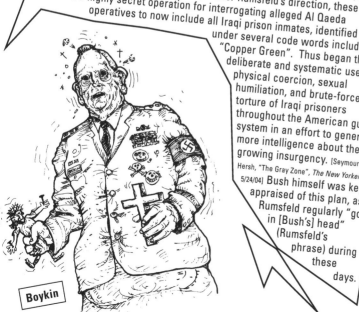

Boykin

Cambone

As a model, they used Miller's torture operations at Camp X-Ray, where (as of this writing) prisoners languish still without formal charges filed, legal representation, or basic human rights.

The astounding extralegal framework for this monstrous strategy was initiated not long after the attacks of 9/11/01. In a series of memos spanning two years, the Junta endorsed secret opinions crafted by their legal flunkies. "The [ultimate] report was compiled by a group appointed by Dept. of Defense General Counsel Wm. J. Haynes Jr... Air Force General Counsel Mary Walker headed the group, which comprised top civilian and uniformed lawyers from each military branch and consulted with the Justice Dept., the Joint Chiefs of Staff, the Defense Intelligence agency, and other intelligence agencies... Among the legal memos that circulated within the Administration in 2002, one was famously declaring the Geneva Convention 'quaint', by White House counsel Alberto Gonzalez, and another from the CIA asking for an explicit understanding that the administration's public pledge to abide by the spirit of the Geneva Convention did not apply to its operatives... In April 2002, Secretary Rumsfeld sent a memo to Gen. James T. Hill outlining 24 permitted interrogation techniques, four of which were considered so stressful as to require Rumsfeld's explicit approval before they were used." [Molly Ivins, "Whatever Happened to the Constitution?", Creators Syndicate, 6/10/04]

Aerial view of Abu Ghraib prison. Built by British contractors for Saddam, infamous as "a square kilometer of Hell"

While the full accounting of American atrocities may not be known for some time, the more extreme cases include doing a "Vietnam" on male prisoners (electrodes to the genitals), ritualized and video-recorded gang-rape of female prisoners, and stripping, beating and rape of children in front of parents or relatives. [www.politrix.org, "Soldiers tortured 12 year old girl in Iraqi prison", 5/8/04, originally posted on ITV.com; "Norway protests child abuse in Iraq", 7/6/04, www.aftenposten.no/english/local/article823183.ece; and many others]
Even Arabic journalists were not spared the sadistic frenzy of the American torturers: Arabic stringers for NBC and Reuters, as well as Al Jazeera reporters, were imprisoned and beaten mercilessly. [Andrew Marshall, "Reuters, NBC Staff Abused by US Troops in Iraq", Reuters.com, 5/18/04]

The gleefull crew of cuddly All-American fiends at Abu Ghraib (many of them poor rural men and women from Virginia and Maryland Army Reserve units) took such a delight in their work that they held photographic "gross-out" contests and posted the winning images as desktop backgrounds on their personal computers. The use of photography, in conjunction with nudity and sexual humiliation (so-called "Israeli" strategies), was a key element in the acute concentration of Arabic inmates' sense of shame. This strategy was subsequently used throughout the American gulag system. At Abu Ghraib, generous amounts of alcohol reportedly fuelled the torturer's debaucheries.

"James Fellner, the director of US programs for Human Rights Watch, said... 'we believe that [these memos] show that at the highest levels of the Pentagon there was an interest in using torture as well as a desire to evade the criminal consequences of doing so.'" [Lewis and Schmitt, "Lawyers Decided Bans on Torture Didn't Bind Bush", The New York Times, 6/8/04]

The International Red Cross and other NGOs knew of some of these abuses for many months and attempted to do something about it. Their protestations fell on deaf ears, while the Army actually moved to constrain Red Cross access to the prisons. These Red Cross reports subsequently generated much mirth and amusement amongst senior Army officers. They knew that they had the direction and approval of the most executive elements possible in the Junta. [Danner, ibid.]

Operating under direct orders from Rumsfeld's Torture Task Force, on 10/13/03 the overall commander in Iraq, Lt. Gen. Ricardo Sanchez, signed a classified memo directing military police to work in conjunction with military intelligence and private interrogation contractors in the systematic

Sanchez

Soon thereafter, Karpinski herself wrote to the Red Cross, insisting that prisoners were NOT entitled to protection under Geneva Conventions, thus putting lie to statements otherwise by Bush.

IN REALITY, AMERICA HAS BEEN FOSTERING TORTURE FOR MANY YEARS.

Two CIA manuals ("KUBARK Counter-intelligence Manual", 1963 and "Human Resource Exploitation Training Manual", 1983) are textbooks for torture. These manuals have been periodically altered to create the illusion that the CIA and DoD knew that torture was illegal and immoral even as they continued torturing. They underwent extensive scrutiny and obfuscation in 1992 under then-Secretary of Defense Dick Cheney. For many years, American sadists, foreign butchers and dictators have been trained at **The School of the Americas**, Fort Benning, GA, now innocuously re-named **The Western Hemisphere Institute for Security Cooperation**

WELCOME TO FORT BENNING U.S. ARMY RESERVATION

~ and the ~

Western Hemisphere Institute *for Security Cooperation*

A New Institute for a New Century!

Libertad, Paz y Fraternidad
Freedom, Peace and Brotherhood,
War is Peace, Freedom is slavery

(WHISC). "It's part of US Army training curricula. The Army's School of the Americas – WHISC runs interrogation courses. During the 1980s and 1990s its students studied 'torture manuals' written by senior Army officers. Drawn from techniques used in Vietnam two decades earlier, the manuals flouted US and international law. Kept classified, they were used for years without a murmur from the Army or Pentagon." [Ed Kinane, "Abu Ghraib: It Goes With the Territory", *School of the Americas Watch*, www.soaw.org, 5/24/04] The difference between then and now, of course, is that whereas the Army once utilized foreign proxy armies and CIA specialists as their official state torturers, the Bush Junta has now codified the practice as normal operating procedure.

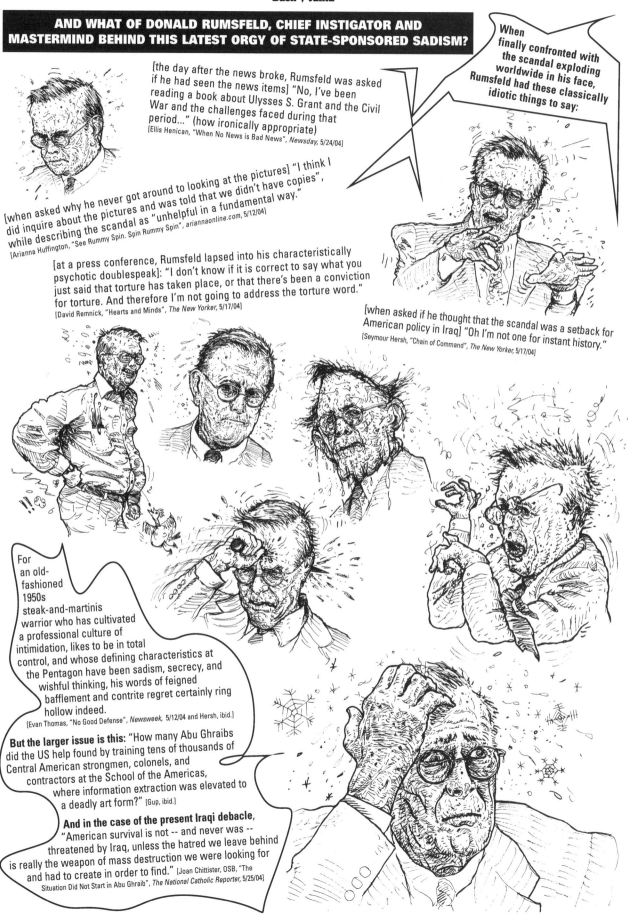

AND WHAT OF DONALD RUMSFELD, CHIEF INSTIGATOR AND MASTERMIND BEHIND THIS LATEST ORGY OF STATE-SPONSORED SADISM?

When finally confronted with the scandal exploding worldwide in his face, Rumsfeld had these classically idiotic things to say:

[the day after the news broke, Rumsfeld was asked if he had seen the news items] "No, I've been reading a book about Ulysses S. Grant and the Civil War and the challenges faced during that period..." (how ironically appropriate)
[Ellis Henican, "When No News is Bad News", *Newsday*, 5/24/04]

[when asked why he never got around to looking at the pictures] "I think I did inquire about the pictures and was told that we didn't have copies", while describing the scandal as "unhelpful in a fundamental way."
[Arianna Huffington, "See Rummy Spin. Spin Rummy Spin", *ariannaonline.com*, 5/12/04]

[at a press conference, Rumsfeld lapsed into his characteristically psychotic doublespeak]: "I don't know if it is correct to say what you just said that torture has taken place, or that there's been a conviction for torture. And therefore I'm not going to address the torture word."
[David Remnick, "Hearts and Minds", *The New Yorker*, 5/17/04]

[when asked if he thought that the scandal was a setback for American policy in Iraq] "Oh I'm not one for instant history."
[Seymour Hersh, "Chain of Command", *The New Yorker*, 5/17/04]

For an old-fashioned 1950s steak-and-martinis warrior who has cultivated a professional culture of intimidation, likes to be in total control, and whose defining characteristics at the Pentagon have been sadism, secrecy, and wishful thinking, his words of feigned bafflement and contrite regret certainly ring hollow indeed.
[Evan Thomas, "No Good Defense", *Newsweek*, 5/12/04 and Hersh, ibid.]

But the larger issue is this: "How many Abu Ghraibs did the US help found by training tens of thousands of Central American strongmen, colonels, and contractors at the School of the Americas, where information extraction was elevated to a deadly art form?" [Gup, ibid.]

And in the case of the present Iraqi debacle, "American survival is not -- and never was -- threatened by Iraq, unless the hatred we leave behind is really the weapon of mass destruction we were looking for and had to create in order to find." [Joan Chittister, OSB, "The Situation Did Not Start in Abu Ghraib", *The National Catholic Reporter*, 5/25/04]

CONCLUSION

In Donald Rumsfeld, the sadistic ultra-right paranoid-delusional Zionist wing of American politics have found their ultimate existential warlord, cheerfully cracking doublespeak jokes en route to some slobbering Xtian fantasy of Armageddon. At the very least, he provides a splendid All-American front for a lot of criminal profiteering through genocidal warmongering, torture, and global terrorization. Though he is drenched in the blood of thousands of murdered innocents, he has even become something of a cultish sex-symbol for post-menopausal neo-fascist females. And just like the dualistic teachings of their patron saint, Leo Strauss, every utterance of the Bush Junta can be reinterpreted as an ironic projection and applied to themselves:

Rumsfeld, less than a month before 11 Sept. 01: "Now, am I against US forces engaging around the world? No. Is the President? No, he's obviously not. He's made the decisions that have **created** the situation that we're currently in."
[Dept. of Defense, *defenselink.mil*, "Pentagon press conference", 8/17/01, Rumsfeld reacting to a question about the US being the world's policemen (emphasis added).]

And **only a day before 11 Sept. 01**, from Brit Hume's prophetic introduction to an interview with Rumsfeld: "Defense Secretary Donald Rumsfeld has issued a dire warning about a security threat to America, but it's not from the sources you might think. He says the danger is not a foreign government or a terrorist, but, as the comic strip character Pogo once said, '**we have met the enemy, and them is us.**'"
[Dept. of Defense, *defenselink.mil*, Brit Hume, "Interview with Donald Rumsfeld", FOXNews, 9/10/01 (emphasis added).]

EPILOGUE: In this piece, I have tried to profile who Donald Rumsfeld is, and the immoral and psychotic role he has played in the criminal enterprises of the illegitimate Bush Junta; but by no means has he acted alone. The story of the neoconservative "movement" (such that it is) and its societal impact is one that involves more individuals, organizations, and publications than is prudent to include here. What I have tried to do is simply highlight Rumsfeld and analyze the murderous trajectory within which he and his co-conspirators have operated.

As of this writing, the next presidential election cycle is in full swing. While the outcome, of course, is unknown, the fact of ANOTHER (and this time, *SUSTAINABLE*) Bush defeat will not mean that these accursed neocon/Zionist fiends will wind up on trial before a war-crimes tribunal or quietly decomposing in a Soylent Green facility. Recent history has shown that these creeps will continue to fester and work their evil on the filth-encrusted rim of the Washington political toilet; indeed, it is within their own paranoid M.O. to consider themselves as marginal "outsiders". **Let this document, then, serve as a chronicle of recent events, as well as a cautionary warning for future generations.**

Note: Thanks to Jake Sexton and his posting of 8/22/02 on *straybulletins.com/Lying Media Bastards*, wherein he observed that Rumsfeld possesses a similarity to the comic book character "Skeletor", thus suggesting the Grim Reaper/corporate axe-man aspect of Rumsfeld's personality. The only difference is that Rumsfeld is not "grim" whatsoever; he is the jocular, friendly face of US fascism. — SM

THE DAY KARL ROVE WAS SENT TO MEET THE ELDEST
SON OF HIS BOSS, GEORGE BUSH SENIOR, WOULD CHANGE
TEXAS AND NATIONAL POLITICS FOREVER. ROVE IS
THE BRILLIANT STRATEGIST WHO TOOK A DRUNKEN,
SLACK-JAWED FRAT BOY AND MADE HIM INTO THE MOST
POWERFUL MAN IN THE WORLD. IN APPRECIATION,
DUBYA AFFECTIONATELY NICKNAMED HIM:

Turd Blossom

THE MARK OF ROVE

by Lloyd Dangle

"I REMEMBER WHAT HE WAS WEARING: AIR NATIONAL GUARD FLIGHT
JACKET, COWBOY BOOTS, JEANS, A WONDERFUL SMILE... HE EXUDED
MORE CHARISMA THAN ONE INDIVIDUAL SHOULD BE ALLOWED TO HAVE."
—KARL ROVE

THE EARLY 70'S WERE FUN AND RAUCOUS TIMES ON COLLEGE CAMPUSES. 1971 FOUND KARL ROVE MOPING AROUND THE UNIVERSITY OF UTAH IN JACKET AND TIE, OPENLY ADMIRING NIXON, AND STAKING OUT HIS TURF WITHIN THE ORGANIZATION OF COLLEGE REPUBLICANS.

COLLEGE REPUBLICANS WERE SO UNPOPULAR, THEY COULDN'T AFFORD TO TAKE THEMSELVES TOO SERIOUSLY, BUT ROVE CERTAINLY DID. RUNNING FOR CHAIRMAN IN 1973, HE STAGED A COUP D'ETAT BY USING ARCANE PROCEDURAL CHICANERY.

HALF OF THE DELEGATES HERE REGISTERED IMPROPERLY, THEREFORE I WIN BY DEFAULT!

STICK BY DICK

COLLEGE REPUBLICANS

IT WOULD BE ROVE'S FIRST BUT NOT HIS LAST QUESTIONABLE ELECTION VICTORY.

ROVE'S OPPONENT APPEALED THE OUTCOME AND HAD A FEW TRICKS OF HIS OWN. A YOUNG REPUBLICAN TRAINING VIDEO THAT FEATURED ROVE BOASTING ABOUT HIS DIRTY CAMPAIGN TRICKS JUST HAPPENED TO FALL INTO THE POSSESSION OF THE WASHINGTON POST.

Washington Post

GOP PROBES OFFICIAL AS TEACHER OF TRICKS

THE ISSUE WENT TO BE SETTLED BY THE CHAIR OF THE REPUBLICAN NATIONAL COMMITTEE, A WASHED UP, PREPPY, PARTY HACK NAMED GEORGE HERBERT WALKER BUSH.

YOU LEAKED A SECRET REPUBLICAN VIDEO! YOU'RE IN DEEP DOO DOO, BUDDY! GET THE HELL OUT OF THE REPUBLICAN PARTY, YOU'RE FINISHED!

WHERE CAN I GET IN TOUCH WITH THIS ROVE KID? I LIKE HIS STYLE!

BUSH SENIOR SENT ROVE TO TEXAS TO RUN A POLITICAL ACTION COMMITTEE, BUT SOME SAY HIS REAL JOB WAS TO KEEP THE PERPETUALLY-WASTED DUBYA OUT OF TROUBLE.

BREATHE DUBYA!

ON THE SIDE, ROVE STARTED A DIRECT MAIL BUSINESS AND DEVELOPED HIS CAMPAIGN CHOPS THROUGH DISTRICT BY DISTRICT GRUNT WORK. HE DISCOVERED THE VULNERABILITES OF THE THEN DEMOCRAT-CONTROLLED STATE GOVERNMENT, AND OVER THE NEXT DECADE USED THEM TO ENGINEER A REPUBLICAN TAKEOVER OF THE STATE!

TEXAS

ROVE MARRIED HIMSELF A RICH TEXAN GAL, VALERIE WAINRIGHT, A HOUSTON DEBUTANTE WHOSE FAMILY RAN IN THE BUSHIE SOCIAL CIRCLE, ALLOWING ROVE TO FURTHER INGRATIATE HIMSELF AMONG THE POWERFUL AND PRIVILEGED. THE MARRIAGE LASTED FOR ABOUT A YEAR.

ROVE BECAME A KING MAKER. DISTRICT AFTER DISTRICT WENT REPUBLICAN. ROVE WOULD START WITH A FAIRLY HANDSOME CANDIDATE WITH A NICE SMILE, AND HE WOULD SUPPLY THE REST.

AS A CANDIDATE, I STAND FOR DEREGULATION, WATER FLUORIDATION, VOUCHERS, AND FISCAL RESPONSIBILITY.

NOBODY CARES WHAT YOU STAND FOR. IF YOU WANT TO WIN, SAY EXACTLY WHAT I TELL YOU.

UH, OKAY, SORRY, KARL.

BUT IT WAS ROVE'S DIRTY CAMPAIGNING THAT EARNED HIM HIS REPUTATION. HIS CANDIDATE FOR GOVERNOR OF TEXAS IN 1985, BILL CLEMENTS, WAS LAGGING BEHIND THE INCUMBENT DEMOCRAT...

I'M GONNA LOSE, KARL, I CAN FEEL IT, IT'S ALL OVER, OH, POOR ME!

SHUT UP, BILL! I'LL THINK OF SOMETHING.

THEN, THE NIGHT BEFORE THE GUBERNATORIAL DEBATE, ROVE CALLED THE MEDIA AND ANNOUNCED THAT HIS OFFICE HAD BEEN BUGGED! OF COURSE HE PLANTED THE DEVICE HIMSELF.

WHAT WILL THEY STOOP TO NEXT?

AS ROVE TRICKS WENT, THIS WAS A LAME ONE, BUT IT WORKED, BILL CLEMENTS WON.

ROVE HAS MASTERMINDED GEORGE DUBYA'S ENTIRE POLITICAL CAREER. FIRST HE HAD TO GET HIM DRIED-OUT, THEN HE PUT BUSH THROUGH RIGOROUS TRAINING, JUST TO MAKE HIM PASSABLY COMPETENT TO RUN FOR GOVERNOR OF TEXAS.

TAKE THESE THREE CARDS, THIS IS WHAT YOU ARE GOING TO SAY OVER AND OVER.

IF YOU GET CONFUSED BY AN ISSUE, JUST GO BACK TO WHAT'S ON THE CARDS.

YOU'LL BE JUST FINE.

DUBYA FOLLOWED DIRECTIONS AND PULLED OFF A STUNNING VICTORY OVER A POPULAR DEMOCRAT, ANN RICHARDS. ONE THING THAT MAY HAVE HELPED WAS THE PHONE CALLS RECEIVED BY VOTERS FROM "POLLSTERS" IN THE DAYS LEADING UP TO THE ELECTION.

WOULD YOU BE MORE LIKELY OR LESS LIKELY TO VOTE FOR ANN RICHARDS IF YOU KNEW THAT HER ENTIRE STAFF WAS MADE UP OF EXTREMELY HAIRY LESBIANS?

ALTHOUGH THERE WAS NO PROOF, POLITICOS SAY IT DEFINITELY HAD "THE MARK OF ROVE."

SIX YEARS LATER, AFTER JOHN MCCAIN BEAT DUBYA IN NEW HAMPSHIRE AND WAS RUNNING NECK AND NECK IN SOUTH CAROLINA FOR THE PRESIDENTIAL NOMINATION, THE PHONES RANG AGAIN.

WOULD YOU STILL VOTE FOR MCCAIN IF YOU KNEW THAT HE BETRAYED HIS COUNTRY WHILE HE WAS A P.O.W. IN VIETNAM?

I'LL TALK! I'LL TALK!

WHAT IF YOU KNEW THAT HIS WIFE, CYNDI, WAS A CRACK WHORE, AND THAT MCCAIN FATHERED A CHILD WITH ANOTHER PROSTITUTE WHO IS BLACK?

I ♥ HOES!

WHEN FORMER AMBASSADOR JOSEPH WILSON BLEW THE WHISTLE ON BUSH'S FAKE EVIDENCE THAT SADDAM HAD TRIED TO BUY URANIUM FROM NIGER, WELL, WE ALL REMEMBER WHAT HAPPENED NEXT...

I HAVE IT FROM A VERY GOOD SOURCE WITHIN THE WHITE HOUSE THAT WILSON'S WIFE IS A COVERT CIA OPERATIVE!

BOB NOVAK

ROVE'S TACTICS ARE SLEAZY, BUT USUALLY NOT ILLEGAL. THIS WAS DIFFERENT. IN 1982 THE STATE OF TEXAS BEGAN PURGING ITS VOTER ROLLS OF FELONS, A PROCESS THAT SUSPICIOUSLY FAVORED GOP CANDIDATES. IT WAS STOPPED IMMEDIATELY WHEN IT WAS DISCOVERED THAT 8000 NON-FELONS HAD BEEN ERRONEOUSLY SCRUBBED.

I'M SORRY, MR. JONES, YOUR NAME DOESN'T APPEAR ON THE VOTER ROLLS.

I'VE BEEN A REGISTERED DEMOCRAT FOR THIRTY NINE YEARS!

SOUND FAMILIAR? EIGHTEEN YEARS LATER THE SAME THING HAPPENED IN FLORIDA WHERE 60,000 "FELONS" WERE PURGED, PAVING THE WAY FOR GEORGE DUBYA'S 537 VOTE "ELECTION VICTORY." THE TEXAS AND FLORIDA SCHEMES HAD ONLY ONE ELEMENT IN COMMON—KARL ROVE RAN THE CAMPAIGNS OF BOTH CANDIDATES THAT STOOD TO BENEFIT DIRECTLY.

THEY CALL HIM TURD BLOSSOM, MEANING A BEAUTIFUL THING WHICH EMANATES FROM SOMETHING NASTY AND DISGUSTING. IT'S AN APT METAPHOR FOR BUSH, WHO WILL NEVER FIND ANOTHER TURD BLOSSOM TO DO HIS BIDDING WHO WILL BE AS LOYAL AND DETERMINED AS HIS ADMIRER, KARL ROVE.

END

With Sweetness

Let us Begin with a confession. I have never Been to the Deep South. If I am to fulfill the Role of Pop Historian in a Pop Culture, it is imperative that I confess in the Beginning. In writing this piece, I am only interested and intrigued By Factual truth. Of course, this includes the use of inductive and deductive logical thought Based upon those facts. To do so, I must also tell the truth about myself. As I said, I have never Been to the Deep South. But during the past decade, the Deep South has Been to me. This is what qualifies me for the job. It has Been to all of us, Like an unknown Third Cousin who shows up on the Doorstep halfway through his family vacation, Looking for Free Lodging and Eats while he takes the Little Lady and the Brood to Disneyland.

Dear Reader, Let us go Down South together. Autumn in Birmingham, Alabama. Let us go Back to the Cold Sunday Morning of November 14, 1954. While the Reverend John Rice Led his Congregation in Prayer, his wife Angelena was at the Hospital giving Birth to a Beautiful Baby Girl whom she would name Condoleezza. Angelena was a musician and the Baby's name came from the Italian Musical term "con dolcezza" which instructs a musician to play "with sweetness".

Condoleezza or "Condi" was the only child of Angelena and the Reverend John W. Rice. Angelena taught Music and Science at Fairfield High, a segregated School. She was also the organist at Westminster Presbyterian Church.

At the time of Condi's Birth, the Reverend John W. Rice was the Pastor at Westminster Presbyterian Church, where he preached for many years. Later, he became the Dean of Stillman College in Tuscaloosa. Eventually he would wind up as the Vice Chancellor of the University of Denver.

The Rice family was a fixture of Birmingham's segregated and isolated Black Middle Class. As you can see, Condoleezza's parents were steeped in a Culture of Achievement. Quite soon they realized that they had given birth to a Gifted Child. She was their precocious wunderkind. As a small child Condi could read fluently. Angelena took a one-year leave of absence from her teaching career in order to home school the child. The Rices desired confirmation of their little smarty pants. So they took Condoleezza to Southern University in Baton Rouge, Louisiana where she underwent psychological testing. Afterwards, Angelena was heard to exclaim to friends and family, "I knew my baby was a genius!"

Condi actually learned to read Music prior to learning how to read Books. Condi's Grandmother, Mattie Ray began teaching her Piano when she was three years old. They immersed her in the world of Classical Music and soon they were in the presence of a child prodigy. They did not have to force it. Amazingly, the child actually wanted it. At the age of four she gave her first recital. As a child she preferred practicing Mozart to playing outdoors. In 1964 when Condoleezza turned ten, she enrolled in the Birmingham Southern Conservatory of Music. She was the first Black Student to attend the newly integrated conservatory.

Prior to the Civil Rights Act of 1964 things were quite different. Jim Crow ruled. Once while shopping at a downtown Department store, Angelena and Condi were looking at Beautiful Dresses. Condi found one she wanted to try on. As she headed towards the Dressing Room, a white saleswoman Blocked the child's path.

The Saleswoman Grabbed the Dress from Condi's hands. She told Angelena that the fitting room was not for them. It was reserved for white customers. She pointed to a dusty storage Room and told them to go in there. Angelena calmly told the clerk that her daughter would try the Dress on in the true Dressing Room or they would take their money along with the woman's commission elsewhere. Shocked, the woman took them to the Dressing Room furthest from view, nervously guarding the Door.

Let's FACE it. THE Deep SouTH HAS NEVER GoTTEN OVER THE CiViL WAR: HiSToRiCALLY SpEAKiNG, it is just too SooN. Coming fRom A GREEK immiGRANT FAMILY giVES ME A BeTTER uNDERStANDiNG of CuLTuRAL Time than THE AVERAGE AMERicAN. IT HAS moRE iN CommoN with GeoLoGiCAL time than with THE LiNEAR MODE iDEALized iN THE WEST. BELiEVE you mE, while sitting AT THE DiNNER TABLE, I HAVE witNESSED many A LAMENT OVER THE FALL of ConStANTiNoplE, AND its NEW MoNiKER IStANBuL. This EVENT took placE oN TuESDAY MAY 29th, 1453. GREEKS ARE still pissED off ABouT it. It is THE rEASoN WHY, FiVE HuNDRED AND FifTy-ONE YEARS LATER, GREEKS believe that TuESDAY is THE uNLucKiEST DAY of THE WEEK. It is why THE TuRKiSH FLAG still DepictS THE WANING MooN, to REMIND THE WoRLD that THE moon WAS iN its fiNAL QuARTER wHEN ConStANTiNoplE FELL. IN CompARiSoN, THE CiViL WAR iN THE UNiTED StATES ENDED LESS than ONE HuNDrED and FifTy YEARS Ago. AMERicANS doN'T uNDERStAND that it is still too SooN to tELL wHAT it mEANT. ThE DEHuMANiZATiON of Jim CRow, iNStitutioNALiZED RAcism AND ApARtHEiD tHRouGH StATES RiGHTS WAS too much foR THE VictimS to BEAR. ThE CiViL RiGHTS MOVEMENT WAS BoRN. BiRMiNGHAM'S PoWER BoSS WAS BuLL CoNNoR. He iNFLAMED RAcism iN THE WHitE WoRKiNG CLASS, VSiNG THE PoLiCE AND FiRE DepARtMENTS' FoRcE to stop DEMONStRATioNS. PeRHAPS THE ONLY DiffERENcE BETWEEN A REDNECK'S flying THE CoNFEDeRATE FLAG AND A TuRK'S Flying THE CRESCENT MooN iS how LoNG tHEy'VE BEEN DoiNG it.

On SuNDAY MoRNiNG SEptEMBER FifTEENTH, NiNETEEN HuNDRED AND SixTy-ThREE, HATRED AND ViolENcE ESCALATED iNTo THE MuRDERS of FouR LiTTLE GiRLS wHEN SixtEENTH StREET BAptist CHuRCH WAS HiT BY A BoMB. ThE FACE of CHRiST WAS BLowN out of THE ONLY SuRViViNG StAiNED GLASS WiNDow.

The little girls' names were Carole Robertson, Cynthia Wesley, Addie Mae Collins, and Denise McNair who was one of Condoleezza's friends from kindergarten. Thus, in childhood Condi had her first real experience with terrorism. With her parents she attended the girls' funeral. The sight of four small coffins was something she would never forget.

Yet she would skate away from the South, psychologically and physically. The Rice family were solidly part of Birmingham's black middle class. So, while her dad was a part of the civil rights movement, he was not marching in the streets. They didn't want to lose the socio-economic standing that they had worked so hard to achieve. So when the opportunity arose to move his family to Denver, he took it and got his family out. In Colorado, Condi would become a competitive figure skater.

In Denver the Rices enrolled Condi in Saint Mary's Academy, an excellent Catholic school. For the first time in her life she attended an integrated school. Yet, while integrated, Denver was overwhelmingly white. With seventy students in her class, Condi was one of three Blacks.

As always, Condi the prodigy excelled in every course. At the start of her senior year she had finished all requirements for graduation. So during her senior year she began attending the University of Denver. She was only fifteen years old.

The very same year she won top prize in a young artists competition and performed Mozart's Piano Concerto in D minor with the Denver Symphony.

Condi was now a piano performance major at the University of Denver's Lamont School of Music. But she wanted to attend Juilliard. Her father forbade it. He was against a conservatory education. Once again, bourgeois values triumphed.

For the first time in her life, she was in the PRESENCE of a group of gifted children. No longer the only gifted child, she met children half her age who could play Rachmaninoff and Shostakovich with transcendental beauty.

For years Condi had dreamt of becoming a concert pianist. The summer between her sophomore and junior years at college she enrolled in the prestigious Aspen Musical Festival. While attending this musical summer camp, she was about to have a revelation of stunning HORROR.

In childhood she had experienced two distinct types of isolation. The isolation of culturally instituted bigotry, along with the isolation imposed by her parents in order to protect her. At that moment, this dualistic naïveté suddenly conspired to smash the FANTASIES of a beautiful PRINCESS.

Condi's identity had just been trashed by little tiny snotnosed kids. She realized that at best she would wind up a music professor. At worst, she would tinkle ivories at NORDSTROM. CARNEGIE HALL was not in her future. DEAR READER, I now ask you to indulge me in a diagnosis based on the aforementioned facts. The thwarted artist is a dangerous personality type. A failed narcissist will either crumble into DEEP DESPAIR, or will find another way to receive the horrible levels of attention and adoration she required. Much like a vampire REQUIRES the BLOOD. THE BLOOD IS THE LIFE.

With her superior intellect, Condoleezza falls into the second camp. She would frantically search for a new major. She explored English literature, only to reject it. She wasn't in the mood for anything else artistic.

Then she took a class that would transform her life. It was taught by Professor Josef Korbel. He was a former European diplomat and the father of Madeline Albright, the first and so far only female Secretary of State. She served in the administration of William Jefferson Clinton.

Condi joined the University's School of International Relations, becoming obsessed with Soviet Studies and Russian language courses. Condi's new career choice was all about power, and Josef Korbel was poised to become her mentor. He would become her "intellectual father". Daddy's little girl had just found a brand new "surrogate daddy." And "surrogate daddy" had just found a brand new little girl whose mind he could mold and influence.

Condi was a fast study. She earned her Bachelor's Degree in political science, cum laude and Phi Beta Kappa from the University of Denver in nineteen hundred and seventy-four. She was nineteen years old.

And now, DEAR READER, PLEASE forgive ME AS I PRESENT FOR your EDIFICATION, the teDious and the tendentious ACADEMIC ACCOMPLISHMENTS of our HEROINE. CONDi went on to RECEIVE her MASTER'S FROM the UNIVERSITY of NOTRE DAME iN 1975. She RECEIVED her Ph.D. FROM the GRADUATE School of INTERNATIONAL STUDIES AT the UNIVERSITY of DENVER iN 1981. She is A FELLOW of the AMERICAN ACADEMY of Arts and SciENCES. She has rECEIVED honoRARY DocToRATES from MOREHOUSE College iN 1991, the UNIVERSITY of ALABAMA iN 1994, the UNIVERSITY of NOTRE DAME iN 1995, And the MISSISSippi COLLEGE SCHOOL of LAW iN 2003. Dr. RICE joiNED the FACULTY of STANFORD University iN 1981 AS A PROFESSOR of POLITICAL Science. She HAS won two of its HIGHEST HONORS, the 1984 WALTER J. GORES AWARD For ExCELLENCE iN TEACHING AND the 1993 School of HUMANITIES and SciENCE'S DEAN'S Award for DISTINGUISHED TEACHING. At STANFORD SHE WAS A MemBer of the CenTER foR INTERNATIONAL Security and ARMS CONTROL, A SeNiOR FELLOW of THE INStituTE for INTERNATIONAL STUDIES, AnD FELLOW (by COURTESY) of the HOOVER INSTITUTION. CoNDi is ALSO the AutHor of NUMEROUS Books and ARTICLES on SOViET AND EAST EVRoPEAN foREign and DEFENSE Policy. She COMPLETED A SiX-YEAR teNURE AS STANFORD'S PROVost iN JUNE 1999, whERE she BALANCED the BUDGET in Her FiRST YEAR, AnD REPORTED BUDGET SURPLUSES thRoughOut the REMAINDER of her tENURE. I can't stand it, I REALLY can't!

CONDI ALSO MOVED ON TO AN ILLUSTRIOUS AND GLAMOUROUS CAREER IN BOARDROOMS ACROSS THE LAND. SHE HAS BEEN ON THE BOARDS OF DIRECTORS FOR THE CHEVRON CORPORATION, THE CHARLES SCHWAB CORPORATION, THE WILLIAM AND FLORA HEWLETT FOUNDATION, THE INTERNATIONAL ADVISORY COUNCIL OF J.P. MORGAN, THE TRANSAMERICA CORPORATION, HEWLETT PACKARD, AND THE RAND CORPORATION. DADDY'S LITTLE GIRL WAS NOW TRULY REPRESENTING THE INTERESTS OF BIG DADDY AGAINST THE TINY MANY.

SHE WAS FIRST CALLED INTO THE SERVICE OF THE BUSH DYNASTY DURING THE FAILED SINGLE TERM OF GEORGE THE FIRST. SHE SERVED AS DIRECTOR, AND THEN SENIOR DIRECTOR, OF SOVIET AND EAST EUROPEAN AFFAIRS IN THE NATIONAL SECURITY COUNCIL, AND AS SPECIAL ASSISTANT TO THE PRESIDENT FOR NATIONAL SECURITY AFFAIRS. OUR LITTLE MARTINET WAS GOING PLACES.

Condoleezza Rice

THE CHEVRON CORPORATION WAS SO PLEASED WITH CONDI'S REPRESENTING THEIR OIL INTERESTS IN KAZAKHSTAN, THAT NOT ONLY DID THEY PAY HER IN RETAINERS, FEES, AND SHARES OF STOCK, THEY NAMED AN OIL TANKER AFTER HER. THE 136,000 TON SS CONDOLEEZZA RICE. CONDI RESIGNED FROM CHEVRON'S BOARD ON JANUARY 15, 2001 AFTER HER APPOINTMENT AS GEORGE THE SECOND'S NATIONAL SECURITY ADVISOR. THREE MONTHS LATER CHEVRON WOULD SNEAKILY AND QUIETLY RENAME THE HUGE OIL TANKER THE ALTAIR VOYAGER.

At one time, the Republican Party was essentially the Party of Capital and Corporate Interests. It was not overtly preoccupied with a backwards social conservative religious agenda. While the party of the Rockefellers, it also had room for progress and the unexpected innovation, such as Nixon's trips to China and the Soviet Union which began Détente and effectively speaking were the beginning of the end of the Cold War. For Christ's Sakes! Nixon started the Environmental Protection Agency with a martini in one hand and a Pall Mall slithering smoke in the other. During the twenty years since Reagan's inauguration, the party had pandered to the Christian Right. A disenfranchised, yet craftily organized, group of angry hillbillies and treacherous cretins. By the time the 2000 Republican National Convention rolled around, these yahoo god bullies had so completely taken control of the party, that you couldn't get a goddamn drink at the convention site! That's right, what they had instead of booze was ice cream socials. Childish and churlish nonsense! I'm not kidding! To help you endure the bile and the horseshit, there was not a drop of sauce to be found. But you could get a great big goopy, drippy, hot fudge banana split courtesy of the Southern Baptists! At the end of each day, journalists from around the world were seen fleeing to the nearest hotel bar, while some began carrying flasks.

"We have, ladies and gentlemen, a presidential nominee who knows what America must do to fulfill the promise of this new century. We have a nominee who knows the power of truth and honor. George W. Bush is a man of his word, friend and foe will know that he keeps his word and tells the truth. George W. Bush will never allow America and our allies to be blackmailed. And make no mistake about it, blackmail is what the outlaw states seeking long-range ballistic missiles have in mind. And I want to assure you, if the time even comes to use military force, President George W. Bush will do so to win, because for him, victory is not a dirty word. He believes that we Americans are at our best when we exercise power without fanfare and arrogance. He speaks plainly...."

So in the year of our Lord 2000, in the City of Brotherly Love, Philadelphia, at the Republican National Convention, Condi was chosen by the Bush family to be a keynote speaker and to thereby nominate their little prince, George W. Bush, to the presidency of the United States.

AFTER THE FRAUD IN FLORIDA, THE GREAT PRETENDER WAS GIVEN THE SCEPTRE AND THRONE TO WHICH HE INDELICATELY ASCENDED. CONDI WAS SWORN IN AS NATIONAL SECURITY ADVISOR ON JANUARY 22, 2001. HER ACADEMIC BACKGROUND AND UNCOMPROMISING SELF-RIGHTEOUS POSITIONS WOULD GIVE HER CONSIDERABLE INFLUENCE OVER THE ADMINISTRATION'S FOREIGN POLICY STRATEGY. PRECISE AND PRISSY, HER RADICAL UNILATERALIST IDEOLOGY WON ON ISSUES SUCH AS THE ANTI-BALLISTIC MISSILE TREATY AND THE KYOTO ACCORD — BOTH OF WHICH, TO THE DISMAY OF OUR ALLIES, WERE TRASHED.

A TRAINED SOVIETOLOGIST, SHE WAS NOT UP TO THE TASK THAT WAS ABOUT TO PRESENT ITSELF. ESSENTIALLY IGNORANT OF THE CULTURAL HISTORY OF THE MIDDLE EAST, THE MEAGER UNDERSTANDING SHE DID POSSESS STEMMED MORE FROM THE BIBLE STORIES SHE HEARD AS A CHILD IN HER FATHER'S CHURCH, THAN FROM HISTORICAL CONFLICTS. SEPTEMBER 11, 2001 WAS A TUESDAY, THE UNLUCKIEST DAY OF THE WEEK. THE WANING MOON WAS IN ITS FINAL QUARTER, IN THE SHAPE OF A CRESCENT. THESE FACTS MEANT NOTHING TO CONDOLEEZZA RICE THAT SUNNY MORNING. THEY MUST HAVE MEANT SOMETHING TO THE NINETEEN YOUNG MEN WHO HIJACKED AIRPLANES THAT DAY. FIVE HUNDRED AND FORTY-EIGHT YEARS HAD PASSED SINCE CONSTANTINOPLE FELL TO ISLAM. IN OUR TIME, WHAT IS NEW YORK, IF NOT CONSTANTINOPLE?

FOR the Second time in hER LiFe, ConDi haD come into DiRect Contact witH TeRRoRiSm. FoR the first EighT monTHs of His tErm, "W"'s AdmiNiStRaTion haD Done its veny BeST to AngER and ALiEnaTE the BeTTer PaRt of the WoRLD, incLudiNG most of Our ALLies. TREAty AfTeR TReAty HaD BeeN BRokEn. ConcEpts of EngAgEMEnt witH the WoRLD that EvEry PRESidEnt SinCe F.D.R. had upHELd wERE piSSed upon witH uTtER conTEmpt. Yet, whEn ouR BetRAyED ALLies saw the WRECkAge of the Twin ToWERs, thE AbsoLvte WanTon AtRocity of it all, they immEdiatELy FoRgAve THE Bush AdmiNiStRATion and the VniTEd States. Even the PaRis DaiLy "Le MondE" StaTED in A LARGE HeADLinE "WE aRe ALL AMeRiCANs Now". HoWevER, making shoRt woRk of it, the ARRoGAnce of tHE ToXiC TexAn TRoGLodyTE And HiS GanG of NEo-Cons would take this FoRGiVEnESS and GooDWiLL and vTteRly SAVANdER it.

> I DoN't tHiNk anyBoDy couLD haVe pREDiCTed that these peopLe wouLD take an AiRpLane and sLam it into the WoRLD TRade CentER, take AnotheR one and sLam it into the PenTAGon. No one PREDiCTed that tHey wouLD tRy to use an AiRpLanE as a MiSSiLe, A hijACkEd AiRpLane as a miSSiLe.

Why did ConDoLEEZZA and the AdminiStRation cHoose to iGnoRe iNTelLiGEnce? It is now known that the inTeLLigEnce AgEncies of ELeven CouNtRiEs PRoViDED aDvANce WaRNiNg to the VNiTED States of the "09-11 AtTacks. On JvNe 28, 2001, ConDi wAs given An intElLigEnce SvmmARy that StaTED "it is hiGhLy LikELy tHat a SigNifiCAnt AL QAiDA atTack is in the nEAR futuRE, withIn sEVERAL WEEKs". On JuLy 5, 2001, RichARd ClaRke, the GoVERnment's top CounTeRTERRoRism OFFiCiAL, waRnEd that "SoMETHing SPECtACULaR is going to HaPpeN HERE, and it's going to haPpEN SooN". Two SEniOR MoSSAD ExPeRts WERE Sent to WashiNgton on AuGust 6, 2001 'to ALert the CIA and FBI to a CeLL of 200 teRRoRiSts Said to Be pREPaRing a Big OpERAtion that would invoLve the hijackinG of CoMMeRciAL AiRLinERs. The LiST they pRoViDED incLuDED the naMes of FouR of the 9-11 hijACkERs, nonE of whom was ARResTED. ❦ "W" was inFoRmED of tHis RePoRt whiLe ON A "WoRkinG vACaTion" AT HiS RANCH iN TeXAS.

THE DESTRUCTION of THE TWIN TOWERS SHATTERED MORE than GLASS and STEEL. A BELIEF SYStEM FIRMLY HELD By PROTEStANT AMERICANS, ESPECIALLY EVANGELICALS, WAS DASHED to NOTHING. THE IDEA that the UNITED States is GOD'S FAVORITE COUNTRY, INVINCIBLE, IMMUNE, And INVULNERABLE, HAD BEEN SORELY put to the tEST. MANIFEST DESTINY WAS FOUND WANTING in the RUINS. THE NAUSEA, FEAR, AND DREAD of DISCOVERING that WE WERE ONLY human, just ANOTHER TRANSITORY CULTURE iN HISTORY, WAS UNBEARABLE to A CULTURE WITH NO SENSE of HISTORY. THE BORN-AGAIN DRY DRUNK AND the PREACHERMAN'S DAUGHTER WERE EXACTLY the TONIC FOR THE PETTY DESPERATION of the BODY POLITIC.

At that MOMENT iN HISTORY, THE UNITED States HAD EVERY RIGHT to DEFEND itSELF. I pose no QUARREL with +HE DECISION to iNVADE AfgHANISTAN or to GO AFTER AL QAIDA. But, with +HE iNTELLIGENCE tHEY HAD befoREHAND, why didn't tHEY TRY to PREVENT it? DOES the ANSWER LiE with the PROJECT FOR the NEW AMERICAN CENTURY? CHENEY, RUMSFELD, WOLFOWITZ, AND OTHER MEMBERS of the ADMINISTRATION BELONG to this NEO-CON THINK TANK, which sHARES +HE VALUES of CONDOLEEZZA RICE. FOR the PAST DECADE tHIS ORGANIZATION HAS BEEN ADVOCATING the GOAL of U.S. WORLD HEGEMONY AND SECURING By FORCE COMMAND OVER WORLD OIL SUPPLIES, AND NINETY-FIVE PERCENT of REMAINING GLOBAL OIL CAPACITY iS iN +HE CONTROL of tHE MUSLIM WORLD.

So ENORMOUS LIES WERE SPUN to the WORLD ABOUT SECRET EVIL STASHES of WEAPONS of MASS Destruction. MAKING SADDAM HUSSEIN SEEM LIKE A BATMAN VILLAIN, A DESERT PENGUIN, the RIDDLER of BABYLON WAS de RIGUEUR IN D.C. ONE of the MOST OFFENSIVE PUBLICITY STUNTS WAS ON FEBRUARY 6, 2003. CONDI AND "W" APPEARED TOGETHER AT the NATIONAL PRAYER BREAKFAST. SHILLING FOR DEATH, WHILE PANDERING to THEIR BASE CONSTITUENCY of RADICAL FUNDAMENTALIST CHRISTIANS, THEY OPENLY PRAYED FOR VICTORY IN WAR. That SAME WEEK, POPE JOHN PAUL II and ECUMENICAL PATRIARCH BARTHOLOMEW, ARCH BISHOP of CONSTANTINOPLE, ISSUED STATEMENTS DENOUNCING ANY WAR of AGGRESSION AGAINST IRAQ. Then ON MARCH 20, 2003 it BEGAN. It has YET to END. Who KNOWS WHEN it WILL?

In consummate childishness, ugliness, and flippancy they deemed to call it "Shock and Awe." As if the death and maiming of innocent civilians, many of them children, were merely an afternoon pastime on a playstation or gameboy. Or is it that Condi and "W" believe they are fulfilling a divine mandate? The born again dyslexic dry drunk imbecile taking his cues from the brainy resentful self-righteous daughter of a preacherman. Lately they are both making references to a theology that implies that god is intervening in events, is on America's side, and has chosen Bush as president. Whether they actually believe this or are just pandering to the Christian Right is a moot point. Simply put, either way it is a terrifying ideology. Don't listen to what they say. Watch what they do. All of them have conflicts of interest due to their ties to big oil. They did nothing with the intelligence they had before September Eleventh. They lied to the world about Iraq's weapons of mass destruction. Because of these lies, thousands are dead or maimed, many of them children. Thousands more will be. They have awarded all of the reconstruction contracts to their former employers, Halliburton, Bechtel, The Carlyle Group. Draft dodgers themselves, they misuse our military to further enrich their own class, at our expense and peril. All of this horror from the same party that moralised, ranted, raved, and impeached a president for having a girlfriend. They see themselves as the untouchable class. No matter what they say about god, god does not want us to act like this. This year we have a chance to "reach out and touch" the untouchable class. Since taking office, this administration's tax policy has destroyed three million jobs. This November, let's make it three million and one.

A good speech always begins with a good joke, and a speech by John Ashcroft is no exception:

CLAP! CLAP! CLAP! CLAP! CLAP! CLAP! CLAP! CLAP! CLAP! CLAP! CLAP!CLAP! CLAP! CLAP! CLAP! CLAP! CLAP!

Hi Everybody

HI JOHN!

You know, a funny thing happened on the way into work this morning ...

I ran into a peace-loving Muslim ...

but I didn't like the look of him

So I made up some story about him being a terrorist - and then I stuck him in a windowless 4x4 jail cell for the rest of his natural *GOD-FEARING LIFE!*

HA! HAA!!

snicker!

oh that's good! that's good!

heh, that bit always _kills_ 'em

heh.

It's funny BECAUSE IT'S TRUE!

HA! Been goin on for years!

HAHAHAHAHAHAHAHAHAHAHAHAHAHAHAHAHAHAHAHAHAHAHAHAHAHAHAHAHAHAHAHAHA!

The number one rule of comedy? Timing!

No, but seriously folks.

I'm really happy to be speaking with you this evening.

I'm guessing most of you know me first and foremost as the prosecuting _fist_ behind George W. Bush's highly televised 'Holy War on Terror'

Yes! and we love you for it, John!

good good.

Well, as you know, this "Crisis of War" has allowed me to redefine my job as U.S. Attorney General from one of **a public defender of your civil rights** — into a complete opposite of that role: One of unprecedented, threatening powers. Able to meddle with and snoop on all, and truly **terrorize** all Americans. Able to prosecute with lawless abandon ...

why, I'm the new J. Edgar Hoover!

Oh yes you are! And Thank you for keeping America free, John!

Thank you, and you're welcome. But did you know that this is not my first job in a publicly-held office? Did you know this is not the first job I have successfully **hijacked** and re-purposed into being a cruel tool for my own baffling and hateful agendas? Did you know that all these jobs add up to years of harm done to all of America?

Huh? No. Tell us. *WHAT OTHER JOBS HAVE YOU HAD ? WHAT OTHER HARM HAVE YOU DONE ?*

Well, cue the title:

Blacks, Babies, and Battered Women: John Ashcroft's Missouri Years discussed

by Ethan Persoff, http://www.ep.tc/

Part One:
The Job Positions.
To fully understand the nature of my political behavior, you must first get the facts on the jobs I have held, and during what times I held them. It spans decades and is a lot of political power.

To begin: Fresh out of Yale, and then University of Chicago Law School, I began my climb up the Republican ladder in two minor Missouri positions: First, as an Auditor for the state from **1973 to 1975**, and then as an — *Assistant* — Attorney General from **1975 to 1976**.

Then there are the three jobs that matter, and are the focus of this comics piece:

First, Attorney General of Missouri, from **1976 to 1985**

Second, Governor of Missouri from **1985 to 1993**

and Third: United States Senator

I only served Missouri as a U.S. Senator for one term, from **1995 to 2001**. From that point on I have been United States Attorney General

heheh

Excuse me, are you laughing at me?

Yes I am. Isn't it true the only reason you're not a Senator anymore is because you *lost to a dead guy?*

well ...

That you lost the 2000 reelection because the people of Missouri voted in a dead person, instead of reelect you? That all of this is available on the Internet for a good laugh? That you were a humiliated political laughing stock and George W. Bush bailed out your career with the Attorney General appointment? Isn't it also true that you are a coward who **dodged the Vietnam draft for six years**, using family influence to avoid service?

yes, that's all true.

OH! *So that's the way a patriot acts !?!* Ha! You loser <u>coward</u> idiot!

Charles, can you do something about this heckler, please?

Go ahead and try! It's a free country. I can talk! I've got Ri --

Well, now that you know my career, let's get into the specifics.

BLACKS

Back when I controlled Missouri, two things were important to me when it came to black people:

I wanted them kept from any political power.

And I wanted them kept from a good education.

In other words: stupid and powerless.

Here I'll explain

— see notes on losing the Senate reelection and draft-dodging at the end of this piece —

(continued next page)

ADDITIONAL BIOGRAPHIC INFORMATION – Born: 1942. Father — a deeply religious man. The family belongs to the Assembly of God – the largest Pentecostal denomination in America. Ashcroft's father, an Assembly minister grew to great political and religious influence in Missouri, creating a number of Bible colleges throughout the state, all this influence would later benefit young John's career. Assembly of God followers shun dancing, drinking and other forms of 'reckless sinful behavior.' A.O.G. has extremely narrow and unaccepting views on other cultures and faiths, and rigidly condemns much of modern society. Other notable and holy Assembly ministers/preachers include: Jim Bakker and Jimmy Swaggart.

John Ashcroft is the first Assemblies worshipper to ever be elected as a state Governor or a Senator, or U.S. Attorney General, leading some Assembly followers to compare him to JFK and his political achievements for Catholics.

Making them stupid:

Let's begin by discussing my strong opposition to desegregation. It might sound out-dated to even mention that word, since so many of you probably think desegregation isn't even an existing civil rights issue any more. But I made it one during the eighties.

Here's the story: in 1980, a number of federal courts found St. Louis public schools liable for continuing to segregate white and black students — still operating under racist state provisions from as far back as 1865, which mandated, in writing, separate schools for blacks and whites.

We all know that separate-but-equal never actually means equality in any way. Schools for black kids are always underfunded and in disrepair when compared to schools for white kids. The courts ordered this to stop immediately.

oddly ...

St. Louis public schools completely agreed with the courts ... but I didn't.

There was a feeling of healing from the court decision. Changes were to begin the upcoming fall, with a bussing program bringing black students into white neighborhoods and into white schools.

Bussing *them* in? Can you imagine?

I was outraged, and the people who got me into government were outraged. So, as Missouri's Attorney General, I appealed the whole thing. I couldn't allow it to happen. My first appeal was turned down, and the local newspapers <u>attacked</u> me for destroying all the 'goodwill' that had been created through finally addressing all of this racial inequality through the courts. Didn't bother me, I kept fighting. Upon denial, I appealed again. And again. All appeals were denied, even ones to the Supreme Court! By then, as the state's legal representative, I had delayed things for a full school year. A District Court judge almost found the entire state in contempt!

An abuse of power? Of course it was! Bother me? Not one bit.

Eventually, of course, I lost and St. Louis desegregated. But it took years.

At the time, my behavior was so blatantly racist that it was likened to "massive-resistance" a tactic that Southern lawmen used in the fifties during the *Brown vs. Education* times, in which you just ignore the actual rule of law for as long as possible, making change very difficult and intimidating. The only difference being that this was, well, the eighties.

But hey, if the hood fits, right?

an explanation

it's true!

So why did I do this? Racism? Economics? Both are a possibility. But it's more simple than that. Two words: Criminal Development. It's a money and power game I'm in. And I need criminals.

Brown vs. Board of Education (1954) — Historic Supreme Court decision outlawing segregation in U.S. Public Schools.
Many southern school districts chose to close all schools instead of comply and allow blacks to attend school with their white children.

Criminals are great. They can't vote, and you get a lot of money for them once you build a prison to store them in. And later, if you're really lucky, you can kill a few of them. A lot of people fear them too, which justifies heavy laws and other spooky nonsense. And — more than any one thing, criminals keep people like me in power.

Criminals! They're the second best thing to owning slaves!

So ... As anyone who's ever watched the evening news knows, blacks make the perfect criminals. But here's the catch: They aren't dumb or naturally crime-minded. You have to *make* them stupid! This all has to do with schooling. You have to start young. And you need to limit their exposure to ideas. Later you limit their income, then frustrate them into a sad hopelessness and then, finally, into a life of crime! Really, it's an old game.

Now, I fought this desegregation thing for years, partly because I'm an arrogant bigot — but also because separate schools for blacks and whites means you can just *neglect* blacks, which is the easiest way to make criminals out of them. But put them in the same school *together* and things get very difficult to manage, see?

This is what matters. Neglect is easy, and crime pays.

Why mess with such a great thing?

— NOTE: By 'BLACKS' we mean minorities of all colors and faiths, naturally. But Ashcroft only sees things in two colors: White (him!) and <u>Fill-In-The-Black</u> (you!) —

What's truly amazing, is the longer the court appeals went on, the more it really became just me against everyone. Local churches, suburbs, shit, even the legislature began to urge me to give up the battle. This entire desegregation battle is <u>thoroughly</u> <u>upsetting</u>, and I encourage you to do research on it yourself

But I had my own agendas. This was early in my career. I saw resisting desegregation as the perfect opportunity to get noticed on the national stage, and for all the right reasons.

And the right people *did* notice, trust me. Just look at me now, right?

So, curiously:

Despite politics being so heavily dependant on public image, this blatant racism issue somehow didn't harm my career at all ... in fact ...

... soon ... I even got to become a governor

QUOTE: "Here is a man who has no compunction whatsoever to standing on the necks of our young [black] people merely for the sake of winning political favor" – St. Louis American, 1984

Well, let's begin with their voting privileges.

If the last presidential election proved any one thing, it was the power that one single vote can truly carry.

As you'll recall, this entire presidency was decided by a mere handful of separately cast votes in Florida.

Of course, that's really not true. Thousands of black voters complained of being kept from the polls. And other votes were tampered with.

Then there's those senior citizens who accidentally got tricked into voting for the wrong candidate.

... blah blah blah. Old news, right?

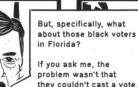

But, specifically, what about those black voters in Florida?

If you ask me, the problem wasn't that they couldn't cast a vote, *The problem was that they were ever given the right to vote in the first place!*

Here, Let me tell you a story:

When I was Governor of Missouri, I used my right to veto legislation in a number of very biased, odd, mean and insensitive ways. (which i'll go into more detail on in a minute)

And when it came to voter registration, I used my veto to keep blacks and other minorities from registering to vote as easily as whites.

See, if you lived in a Missouri suburb, it was pretty easy to register. There were private groups who conducted voter registration-drives often, and to great success. This never bothered me because suburban voters are often white and wealthy.

This all worked out fine until a bill appeared on my desk that aimed to bring the same sort of registration into the inner-cities of Missouri. I was furious. Black votes have no value to me, so I vetoed it, and quick. I was happy with how difficult it was for minorities to register to vote. The idea of a voter-bus coming through some ghetto like it's an ice cream truck bugged me to no end. Does this make sense? Are you beginning to see a trend? This, like desegregation, is a weird story, and I suggest you do your own research on it!

Note – this was before federal "motor voter" laws, so registering to vote was much more difficult, especially if you lived in a part of the city far from a State building, or worked during the week.

Now, we have discussed how I affect the lives of the poorest minorities by keeping them in crappy schools and keeping them from becoming active empowered voters, but what about minorities that are making a success of themselves? Educated ones, with ambition? Can I harm those ones? Yes I can.

Especially those minorities working in Law, or looking to work for Missouri or for the government.

As a Senator I developed a wild record of stalling judicial appointments and other jobs going to blacks and other minorities; here's a very partial list:

1) **Ronnie White** — the first black man to ever be appointed to the Missouri Supreme Court. Clinton gave him a District Court Judge position. I fought this appointment for over two years, for a number of bullshit reasons. I claimed he was soft on crime, but even I couldn't hide the fact that his being black was really all it came down to.

Lots of people consider Ashcroft's battle against Ronnie White to be his clumsiest show of racism. It is full of contradictions and bigotry, all carried out on the Senate floor and in the public record. For someone interested in Ashcroft, and how he will ruin his own integrity to assault and distort the credibility of someone else, this is a good topic to begin with. Ashcroft lost, and White became a federal Judge, but it took two years, and is worth your time to read up about. Ashcroft's big complaint on Ronnie White was that, as a judge, he didn't kill enough prisoners. (e.g. the death penalty)

→ the irony being, White actually sent a ton of convicts off to be executed!
Further exposing Ashcroft as indefensibly racist, just grabbing for excuses

All these names are worth researching on your own (Google in their name with "Ashcroft")

moving on..

2) **Dr. David Satcher** and 3) **Dr. Henry Foster**
Both of these men tried to become Surgeon General for Clinton. Not only were they black, but they were both pro-choice, a topic I'll soon discuss. Dr. Satcher managed to get the job but I helped to block Foster out, thank you very much.

Actually, the more I talk about this, the harder it is to shut me up. This list is long and redundant. And a lot of my harm goes on behind the scenes, too. Anyway, you get the point. So, to keep this short, here's just one more:

(a woman)

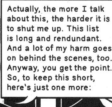

4) **Margaret Morrow** — She was the first woman to head the California Bar Association. Another two year battle for a federal court appointment. I complained that she was a threatening liberal activist of all things. But the point was that she was not a man.

If you do the digging you'll find I have a long record of keeping **tons** of women from becoming judges and from many other powerful jobs.

Well, this is all depressing, isn't it? Here's some brevity, but then we've gotta jump right back into the facts!

To acknowledge the first mention of a woman in this piece, here are three panels of me reaching sexual climax

mmm hrm mmhrmm. hrmmm

I'm sorry! I'm sorry! I'm sorry! I'm sorry! i'msorryi'msorryi'm sorryi'msorry!i'msor-

BABIES

Oh! Babies! My favorite topic. But before we jump into that one, I need to clean up a little bit. So I'll be right back ...But hey, why don't you take this time to review what a United States Attorney General is? Since you've just learned about my problems with minorities, and you're just about to learn about my problems with women and reproduction – it might interest you to see how completely wrong I am for U.S. Attorney General. In fact, it should really disturb, trouble and worry all of you, now that I have that job!

Well now I'm all a mess. Anyway, where were we?

LEARNING SECTION

A UNITED STATES ATTORNEY GENERAL

1) Heads the Department of Justice, which is responsible for enforcement of all federal laws (including enforcement of all civil rights legislation)
☒ True ☐ False

2) Is the chief law enforcer for the United States. Makes decisions that determine how justice is defined and pursued by the Executive Branch.
☒ True ☐ False

3) Is the chief lawyer and prosecutor for the government — representing the government in Supreme Court cases. But the Attorney General is also the assumed lawyer for -every- citizen of the country, to keep the government from unlawfully harming you.
☒ True ☐ False

4) Is sworn, by oath, to protect and enforce the civil rights of all American citizens. Meaning our Bill of Rights, the entire Constitution, etc. It is the Attorney General's job to defend our rights from being maliciously or accidentally tampered with by government officials or from new legislation. Is also responsible for the enforcement of all federal laws (especially those defending American citizens, i.e. immigration, reproductive rights, gun laws, the environment, federal hate crimes, corporate banking laws, etc)
☒ True ☐ False

5) Helps to screen and recommend nominees to the federal courts. A highly powerful position. Can effectively alter the political landscape if he or she decides to nominate only conservative judges, or only liberal ones, etc. A respect for fairness and lack of agendas is crucial with this power.
☒ True ☐ False

6) Reviews proposed legislation and renders advice as to whether particular proposals violate the Constitution as interpreted by the Supreme Court.
☒ True ☐ False

7) Above all, must show an unwavering respect for the Constitution and the fundamental equality of law for all of this country's citizens — of any sex, race, faith, or lifestyle; no matter how different, poor or wealthy.
☒ True ☐ False — yes! all true!

OPTIONAL ESSAY QUESTION: Should a person with a proven record of hostile insensitivity to civil rights be given the authority to protect and/or alter them? What damage can be done?

WHY DOES THIS JOB REQUIRE SO MUCH INTEGRITY AND WHAT IS THE RISK IF THE POSITION IS ABUSED?

Think of the job of Attorney General as a position in the government designed to purposefully keep the laws and freedoms of our government in good shape. It is crucially important that this person respects this power and not abuse it for self-gain. If the Attorney General is not critical of a government's behavior or is, him or herself, a willing participant in the corruption of government (or a sponsor of corrupt legislation or corrupt judge appointments,) then a necessary check-and-balance of the Democratic system becomes threatened. In short, the risks involved with an Attorney General who abuses their job through arrogance and/or corruption is a high risk to the rights, safety and prosperity of all Americans. Therefore, only people of the highest proven fair-minded record, both political, legal and personal, should ever be entrusted with this powerful job.

So ...Was that review helpful? The point of that whole large block of text is this:

The Attorney General is not someone who is supposed to have any agendas, and yet my entire career is about agendas. And I have brought these agendas to that job. Really if we had more time to talk I could tell you about how I'm getting away with Constitutional murder, and I'm letting this administration get away with murder, as well. It should really frighten you. ... Or at least seriously piss you off.

Okay I'm back. I'm all cleaned up, too. Or as clean as I can get, anyway. Heh.

but we all let it happen

The thing that is so troubling about me getting to be U.S. Attorney General is that my past political record is so absent of any respect for the Constitution or civil rights at all. It makes no sense. I developed a huge public record like we're discussing. And then I'm given this job?

Of the entire political landscape, I was really the worst qualified for the job. That I was given the delicate job of U.S. Attorney General raises more questions than it answers. Do you want more examples of how bizarre my previous public record was? Of course you do, so let's continue.

all 50 Republican U.S. Senators voted unanimously en-masse for the confirmation of Ashcroft as U.S. Attorney General, with the support of only eight Democrats, making the final vote 58–42

um. where were we?

BABIES

Oh yes, babies. Well ...

Buckle in, folks, for some of the strangest shit you'll ever hear!

The eight Democrats who voted to support the nomination were: Sens. John Breaux of Louisiana, Zell Miller of Georgia, Russ Feingold of Wisconsin, Christopher Dodd of Connecticut, Robert Byrd of West Virginia, Benjamin Nelson of Nebraska, and Kent Conrad and Byron Dorgan of North Dakota.

— Babies —

Now, when I say Babies, I am really referring to reproduction and a woman's right to medically-safe abortions.

Prior to this war on Terrorism, if I was known for any one thing it was for my extremely radical and a hostile views against abortion, and women.

Naturally, abortion is a controversial subject. I'm not trying to suggest that someone who is for or against abortion rights is a bad person. But if you look at my public record you'll find a disturbing extremism to laws I try to pass on abortion, and of the ways I go about trying to pass these laws.

It's also important to note: These views are not just a religious and/or moral oppositions to a woman's right to choose. They are much more disturbing. To anyone worried about how much damage I might do to the civil rights of every American citizen, it is invaluable to see how bizarre and insensitively cruel I behave on abortion. I am a zealot. I threaten.

But let's start off with something mild ...

Ashcroft's views on abortion weigh in on the most extreme and troubling in the political, social and religious spectrum.

Check out this this crazy bumper sticker of a court case title, "Planned Parenthood vs. Ashcroft"

In 1983, I defended a Missouri law of my own design, requiring ALL second-trimester abortions to be held in hospitals and never to be allowed in clinics. Here's the thought:

Most abortions occur in the second trimester. And most poor women can't afford a real hospital. My attempts at outlawing clinic-based second-trimester abortions in Missouri would have put in motion a plan to end medically-safe abortions for good in the state.

Also, bear in mind how many Missouri hospitals are church-owned and don't offer abortion as a procedure ... And let's not forget the potential shame of a woman having to get an abortion, and how important discretion is. Especially poor women, or ones who can't speak english. It's simple, they'd never go to a hospital.

This is only the beginning of my examples. But it's a funny one to start off with, I think. Especially the court case title of Planned Parenthood versus ME! It's still a real shocker, even with twenty years having passed.

Google in court case titles for more information.

Just think. Had I won this case, Planned Parenthood would have become as useful as a neighborhood pharmacy. Women without access to pricey hospitals would be back to coat hangers and other terrifying procedures to deal with unanticipated pregnancy — Like having their boyfriends punch them in the gut, or drinking the baby away. You know, back from when America was innocent.

I don't mean to be so immediately graphic, but that is, after all, what I am fighting for a return to. So let me remind you of that before I go into any more specifics on my battle against this reproductive issue.

Unfortunately, though, I lost. But the fight would not be over. Not by a long shot. I would only become more ridiculous.

(Much more ridiculous, in fact. To be fair, this example is almost explainable, from a conservative anti-abortion standpoint. The rest gets much more extreme and difficult to defend, however.)

Case in point: that same year (1983) ...

Still as Missouri's Attorney General, and bitterly reeling from losing that Planned Parenthood case, I chose to aggressively defend a state agency's attempt at blocking nurses from administering gynecological services. This included breast and pelvic exams, PAP smears and other things that women need annually to keep from dying.

Do I have your attention?

That same court case also sought to keep nurses from handing out information about contraceptives. Why would I defend this? Because I only wanted doctors to have this right. Why? .... oh wait a second. You know, that's actually a very good question. So I'll stop for a second to explain.

... Do you recall my tangent on developing criminals?

This might be tough to wrap your head around, but my battle against abortion is the same exact battle I fought against educating minorities.

It's all much easier explained if you consider the people I'm fighting to keep abortion rights from:

the poor.

Sermchief v. Gonzales and State of Missouri , 660 S.W2d 683 (Mo. 1983)

Listen, I could talk a lot more (and I will) about all the hard work I do to outlaw abortion, but if I do that without explaining how it ties into creating criminals, you might accidentally think I do this out of a fanatic, almost religious love for families. But that is false. (Read the note, to my left) The fact is I have no record of showing love or sympathy for families. I'm a cold brick when it comes to loving anything. So there is a troubling <u>inconsistency</u> with me being such a staunch advocate against abortion, don't you think? So what else could my fight suggest?

The facts are, if you are poor, once you are born, I do a lot of things to neglect you so you turn to crime and become a criminal. I did this for minorities by limiting education, and I'll explain in a minute how I encourage broken homes to become full of abuse and neglect. Why? Remember: I need criminals. They keep me in power. So, who is at risk to become criminals? THE POOR. If I'm looking to make criminals, who do I need to guarantee will continue making unwanted children? THE POOR. Who do I get to execute and earn tax dollars off of once the system has turned them to crime? THE POOR!

So please keep making your babies.

This is all that matters to me.

elaborating on that topic ....

For the record, the Missouri Supreme Court proved to be completely unreliable to me, throwing the nurses/contraception case out of court. They called it "overtly-extreme" and stated that, at the time, over 40 states had been drastically expanding a nurse's capacity to help in hospitals, so why would I even think to limit them? I didn't really have a reply.

Again, all this from me, the man who would one day become the nation's top law enforcer and the guardian of your civil rights. Your friend in the White House. Unless you need a condom. or a breast exam. Or a nurse.

As Missouri's governor this all would only become more threatening.

Okay, here we go.

In 1990 I proposed a restriction on abortion in the state of Missouri that would, get this, limit women to ONLY ONE ABORTION EVER, outlawing subsequent abortions, except for cases that threatened a woman's health.

Doctors would lose their licenses if they performed a second abortion on a woman. And, in a remarkable foreshadowing of my U.S. Attorney General interest in snooping on your personal privacy, consider this:

With each abortion, doctors would be forced, by law, to ask women to disclose their reasons for getting an abortion, and report these to the state. WHY? I'm not sure why. But it was in the bill, and so you better tell me why you're aborting that baby. I like to call this my "Baby's First Patriot Act". Certainly a chilling bit of history for anyone not trusting me with recent terrorist legislation, isn't it?

The newspapers had a joyride calling me an idiot over this proposed legislation. The best name they gave it was the *"One To A Customer Plan"* - and the law died quietly in the Missouri State Assembly. But like all the laws I suggest, it isn't that they are passed, it's that I even conceive them. Isn't that troubling enough for you?

And let's remember why I do this. Who would I be affecting the most with this legislation? Terrified women, is who. Those who are unfortunately unable to give a good home to their babies. Why would I make this so intimidating for them? Because I need these children later on, as criminals. Or at the very least, as contributors to the lower class. Please, try to keep that in mind as we continue on with this. I get a lot of political power by operating this way.

Wealthy people have never been kept from abortions, even when they've been outlawed. It's the poor I'm targeting with these laws.

At this point in my career the laws I try to pass suddenly begin to resemble science fiction:

In 1986, still as a governor, I tried to declare fetuses as "state citizens" — giving unborn babies the same rights as already born citizens. This would make abortion 'murder', and immediately illegal. I lost, but my mind was just -starting- to fill up with ideas on this one.

There are a lot of other things I did on this front as State Attorney General and Governor, but those are the big ones. Nothing, however, could predict how strange I would get as a Senator.

Once I got to Washington, things really started to pick up steam.

And what's beautiful about my Senate years is how focused my assault on abortion had become by that point. In fact, you only need to know about one bill. Just Google this title:

"Human Life Amendment"

Let's discuss it, okay?

The "Human Life Amendment" is a proposed amendment to the Constitution that I introduced, and co-wrote with the help of Jesse Helms and Bob Smith. If it had been passed it would have outlawed ALL abortions, including those from rape or incest. Easy enough to consider.

But here's more science fiction: The "Human Life Amendment" _also_ defined Human Life at the point of "fertilization" — which, if passed, would have potentially outlawed contraception. I'm not shitting you. The pill, IUD, Depo-Vera and other widely used contraception that interrupts (blocks, 'aborts') "fertilization" could have become illegal.

So, considering that this bill makes contraception potentially illegal, what's next? Well, if this bill had passed, many claim I would go on to seek a ban on 'abortifacients' - or devices that aid in blocking fertilization. In other words:

condoms

Seriously. google in ashcroft (and) abortifacients

The only exceptions to this ban on abortions would be pregnancies where a mother's life was threatened, but that can sometimes be very difficult to predict or prove before the act of childbirth.

This bill didn't get passed. But still, how alarming is this? The Constitution has only been amended twenty-seven times. Ten of those are our Bill of Rights. It was my attempt to permanently alter the Constitution to include this bill, with this kind of talk on the dawn of life and bans on the pill.

And now, I am the single voice that DEFENDS the Constitution for you.

Man, Bush knew what he was doing when he picked me. Talk about a wolf in the kitchen

He knew I'd let him get away with anything!

Anyway

So that summarizes my opinions on abortion.

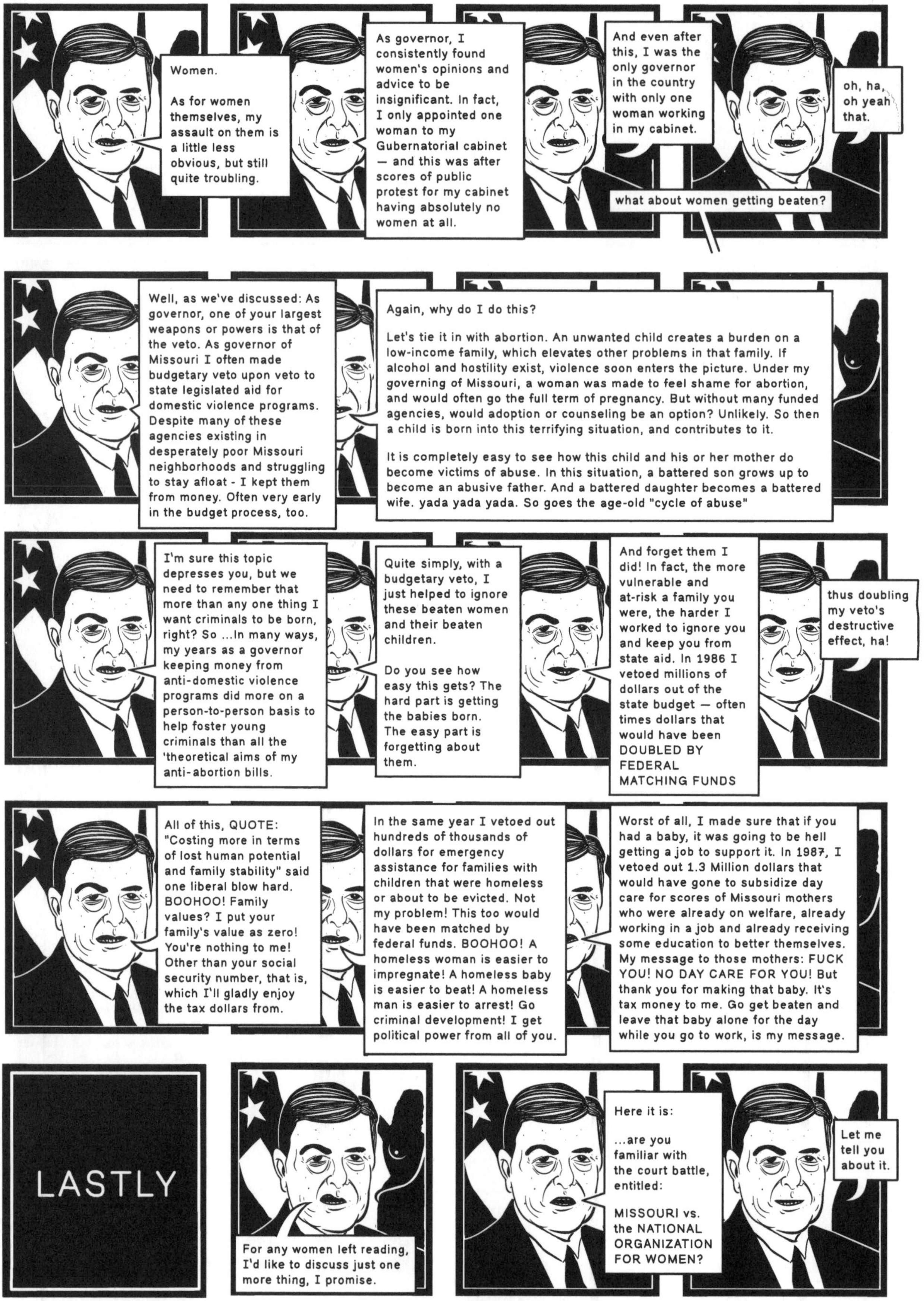
Women.
As for women themselves, my assault on them is a little less obvious, but still quite troubling.
As governor, I consistently found women's opinions and advice to be insignificant. In fact, I only appointed one woman to my Gubernatorial cabinet — and this was after scores of public protest for my cabinet having absolutely no women at all.
And even after this, I was the only governor in the country with only one woman working in my cabinet.
oh, ha, oh yeah that.
what about women getting beaten?
Well, as we've discussed: As governor, one of your largest weapons or powers is that of the veto. As governor of Missouri I often made budgetary veto upon veto to state legislated aid for domestic violence programs. Despite many of these agencies existing in desperately poor Missouri neighborhoods and struggling to stay afloat - I kept them from money. Often very early in the budget process, too.
Again, why do I do this?
Let's tie it in with abortion. An unwanted child creates a burden on a low-income family, which elevates other problems in that family. If alcohol and hostility exist, violence soon enters the picture. Under my governing of Missouri, a woman was made to feel shame for abortion, and would often go the full term of pregnancy. But without many funded agencies, would adoption or counseling be an option? Unlikely. So then a child is born into this terrifying situation, and contributes to it.
It is completely easy to see how this child and his or her mother do become victims of abuse. In this situation, a battered son grows up to become an abusive father. And a battered daughter becomes a battered wife. yada yada yada. So goes the age-old "cycle of abuse"
I'm sure this topic depresses you, but we need to remember that more than any one thing I want criminals to be born, right? So ...In many ways, my years as a governor keeping money from anti-domestic violence programs did more on a person-to-person basis to help foster young criminals than all the 'theoretical aims of my anti-abortion bills.
Quite simply, with a budgetary veto, I just helped to ignore these beaten women and their beaten children.
Do you see how easy this gets? The hard part is getting the babies born. The easy part is forgetting about them.
And forget them I did! In fact, the more vulnerable and at-risk a family you were, the harder I worked to ignore you and keep you from state aid. In 1986 I vetoed millions of dollars out of the state budget — often times dollars that would have been DOUBLED BY FEDERAL MATCHING FUNDS
thus doubling my veto's destructive effect, ha!
All of this, QUOTE: "Costing more in terms of lost human potential and family stability" said one liberal blow hard. BOOHOO! Family values? I put your family's value as zero! You're nothing to me! Other than your social security number, that is, which I'll gladly enjoy the tax dollars from.
In the same year I vetoed out hundreds of thousands of dollars for emergency assistance for families with children that were homeless or about to be evicted. Not my problem! This too would have been matched by federal funds. BOOHOO! A homeless woman is easier to impregnate! A homeless baby is easier to beat! A homeless man is easier to arrest! Go criminal development! I get political power from all of you.
Worst of all, I made sure that if you had a baby, it was going to be hell getting a job to support it. In 1987, I vetoed out 1.3 Million dollars that would have gone to subsidize day care for scores of Missouri mothers who were already on welfare, already working in a job and already receiving some education to better themselves. My message to those mothers: FUCK YOU! NO DAY CARE FOR YOU! But thank you for making that baby. It's tax money to me. Go get beaten and leave that baby alone for the day while you go to work, is my message.
LASTLY
For any women left reading, I'd like to discuss just one more thing, I promise.
Here it is:
...are you familiar with the court battle, entitled:
MISSOURI vs. the NATIONAL ORGANIZATION FOR WOMEN?
Let me tell you about it.

In 1972, Congress passed the Equal Rights Amendment (E.R.A.), which is a simple Constitutional Amendment declaring equal rights for all American citizens. It was originally written in 1923 during the women's rights movement. It has been a political hot potato for civil rights ever since, due to its basic wording of equality for all. But getting the bill through Congress did not mean it was now an Amendment.

See, for the bill to become a Constitutional Amendment it needed to be ratified by a set number of States. By 1977, three States, one of those being Missouri, had not ratified (or approved passage of) this document. The bill would expire if it was not recognized by these States. Civil rights advocates and Women's groups began to worry.

And they had good reason to be concerned. It took almost fifty years to get the bill through Congress. For it to get through Congress, and then die in ratification would mean the Amendment would have to go back to being a bill presented to Congress, trying annually to get approved.
So ... back in 1977, if you'll recall, I was the Attorney General for the State of Missouri.

talk about being in the right place at the right time.

The E.R.A. is still very controversial, given debate over how labor and social groups interpret the word 'equal' — but it is also something fiercely resisted by others for its mere message of equality

Like desegregation, this was early in my career and I needed to let the right people know I was someone they could count on. At this same time, The National Organization for Women (N.O.W.) was helping to organize a boycott of the three remaining states who hadn't ratified the E.R.A. — encouraging groups they had relationships with to not hold conventions in these three states until these states ratified the Amendment

Well I saw that as a threat, and no one threatens me! I dug into my law books to find something, anything to attack N.O.W. with for suggesting these boycotts. In some old dusty book I found an 1890 law – the Sherman Anti-trade Act (look it up in Google), which was created to protect commercial trade between states. And I accused N.O.W. of violating it!

Makes no sense. But it's a serious charge and has to be taken seriously, so N.O.W. had to go to court. What would have happened if I had won? Serious inability for the National Organization <u>for Women</u> to function as a political organization is what. Including their ability to sponsor other organizations. (can you imagine what a kill this would be for me?)
But the boycott was not commercially driven. It was free speech, the first amendment I was trying to squash. The U.S. District Court solidly shot me down, saying "anti-trust laws do not apply to a non-commercial, politically motivated boycott". Do I respect this opinion? No.

What do I do next? I file an appeal with the U.S. Court of Appeals. What do they say? "The right to petition is of such importance that it is not an improper interference even when exercised by way of the boycott" hm. Sounds like harsh language, doesn't it? Do I take the point? Do I respect the courts? No. I take it all the way to U.S. Supreme Court. They end up turning me down, but what did I accomplish? Two and a half years of NOW's time and money, is what — as well as threatening a gigantic political organization's livelihood. And why? Because they had the audacity to try and bring Equal Rights to my state. (This also sent quite a threatening message to others who might want to get in my way in the future, don't you think?)

My use of bending the Sherman Act to attack N.O.W. should trouble all of you. If a law doesn't exist, I'll change one to fit the charge.

What precedent does this suggest to anyone trying to change any of the Terrorist Laws I've helped to create? Ha. Try, seriously. I don't respect the courts and I don't respect you.

I'll have you in a box heading off to Cuba in a New York 9-11 minute. Or at least in court for some bogus charge of my choosing if you get in my way. (get my drift?)

What was I attacking in this lawsuit against NOW? Practically everything Democracy is based upon. And women. And the Equal Rights Amendment. And the First Amendment ...and the freedom to protest
And in less than thirty years, what have I become?

Who am I now?

black hating, women hating, poor hating,

Ladies and Gentlemen

I am your United States Attorney General.

THANKS AND APOLOGIES - *Ethan Persoff* 2004

closing comments: Even if Bush is voted out of office, the story of John Ashcroft is certainly far from over. He has ambitions to become President. He conducted an exploratory committee to see if enough people were ready to vote for him as a candidate in the 2000 presidential election. (The support was not there at the time.) However, his job as Attorney General has proven so successful to his public image of a protector of this country and of its values that it is likely he will, in fact, run for president within the coming decade. → e.g. http://www.cnn.com/ALLPOLITICS/stories/1998/12/04/ashcroft/

Postscripts: 1) Due, in part to John Ashcroft's court delay and harassment against the National Organization for Women, the 1972 Equal Rights Amendment failed to be ratified in time, and expired. Many blame Ashcroft personally for the bill's death. It remains, to this day, an unpassed bill, annually-introduced to Congress ... 2) For a flip-side, if you look around on the Internet you'll find a huge amount of Right-wing support for reintroduction of the Human Life Amendment to the Senate floor ... 3) From the heckler's comment at the beginning of this piece: Technically Ashcroft did not lose the Senate reelection to a dead man. The man he was running against, Mel Carnahan, DID die weeks before the election — and the ballots did show Mel Carnahan beating Ashcroft in votes. But many considered a vote for Mel Carnahan to be a vote for his wife, who did go onto Washington to serve as a Senator in her husband's honor. But Ashcroft losing to a dead man is still a funny joke everyone can enjoy. Excuses aside, it is still the only time in history a dead man has been on a ballot and won a Senate Seat and that's funny as hell ... 4) Ashcroft's draft-dodging is real, however. For information on that, Google in: Ashcroft+Business+Law+Vietnam+Draft

And finally, a dictionary definition. **Ter-ror-ism** - n (1795) : **The systematic use of fear and threats** (can include legal harassment) **as a means of coercion** (meaning to give up fighting against) – See also: Ashcroft vs. Women, Ashcroft vs. Minorities, Ashcroft vs. Reproductive Rights, Ashcroft vs. Pornography, Ashcroft vs. Civil Rights. Ashcroft vs. Muslims. Ashcroft vs. Drinking. and Ashcroft vs. Dancing.

FREE FROM THE ILLUMINATION OF LIGHT, SAFELY RECLUSED IN HIS SECURE UNDISCLOSED LOCATION, DICK CHENEY HIDES IN THE SHADOWS LIKE SOME GIANT PALE SPIDER. HE LIKES IT THAT WAY...

THE MAN IN THE SHADOWS

"AM I THE EVIL GENIUS IN THE CORNER THAT NOBODY EVER SEES COME OUT OF HIS HOLE? IT'S A NICE WAY TO OPERATE, ACTUALLY."
USA TODAY-1/18/2001

RICHARD BRUCE CHENEY IS ALMOST INVISIBLE...

RARELY SEEN, HE IS SELDOM ACCESSIBLE TO THE PRESS EXCEPT ON HIS TERMS.

ALL THIS IS IN DIRECT OPPOSITION TO THE INFLUENCE HE WIELDS AS *THE MOST POWERFUL VICE-PRESIDENT IN AMERICAN HISTORY-*

WEAPONS OF MASS DESTRUCTION!!!
CHEEP-CHEEP!

BUT EVEN THE MOST CRAFTY OF SPIDERS GETS CAUGHT IN THE OPEN SOMETIMES. LET'S LOOK AT WHAT *IS* KNOWN ABOUT DICK CHENEY...

IN 1962 CHENEY'S LOW GRADES FORCED HIM TO ABANDON HIS YALE SCHOLARSHIP CHENEY RETURNED TO WYOMING TO WORK AS A LINEMAN WHERE HE MANAGED TO GET ARRESTED TWICE FOR DRIVING UNDER THE INFLUENCE...

HIS FUTURE WIFE, LYNNE, WHO HE HAD DATED SINCE HIGH SCHOOL, "MADE IT CLEAR SHE WASN'T INTERESTED IN MARRYING A LINEMAN FOR THE COUNTY." *WASHINGTON TIMES 5/4/01 "CHENEY'S TURNING POINT" BY GREG PIERCE*

THIS MADE CHENEY "BUCKLE DOWN" AND RETURN TO THE UNIVERSITY OF WYOMING TO "MAKE SOMETHING OF MYSELF." *WASHINGTON TIMES 5/4/01 "CHENEY'S TURNING POINT" BY GREG PIERCE*

BY 1968 THE NOW HUSTLING CHENEY WON A CONGRESSIONAL FELLOWSHIP TO WORK IN THE OFFICE OF WYOMING REPUBLICAN CONGRESSMAN BILL STEIGLER.

IN 1969 CHENEY JOINED RICHARD NIXON'S ADMINISTRATION.

IN 1974 HE MOVED FROM THE SINKING NIXON ADMINISTRATION TO GERALD FORD'S ADMINISTRATION...

OUT OF A JOB WHEN THE "ACCIDENTAL PRESIDENT" LOST HIS RE-ELECTION BID, CHENEY RAN FOR CONGRESS IN 1977 WYOMING, WINNING AND BEING RE-ELECTED 5 TIMES.

IN 1978, CHENEY HAD HIS FIRST HEART ATTACK–

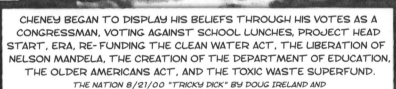

CHENEY BEGAN TO DISPLAY HIS BELIEFS THROUGH HIS VOTES AS A CONGRESSMAN, VOTING AGAINST SCHOOL LUNCHES, PROJECT HEAD START, ERA, RE-FUNDING THE CLEAN WATER ACT, THE LIBERATION OF NELSON MANDELA, THE CREATION OF THE DEPARTMENT OF EDUCATION, THE OLDER AMERICANS ACT, AND THE TOXIC WASTE SUPERFUND. *THE NATION 8/21/00 "TRICKY DICK" BY DOUG IRELAND AND CNN 7/27/2000 "DICK CHENEY IS THE PERFECT CHOICE-FOR DEMOCRATS" BY BILL PRESS*

CHENEY COMPLETED A BUSY DECADE WITH TWO MORE HEART ATTACKS IN 1984 AND 1988...

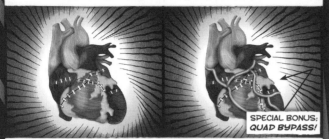

SPECIAL BONUS; QUAD BYPASS!

IN 1989 CHENEY BECAME SECRETARY OF DEFENSE FOR THE FIRST PRESIDENT BUSH...

IN 1991, JAMES BAKER'S AND DICK CHENEY'S CONFUSED SIGNALS GAVE IRAQ THE GREEN LIGHT TO INVADE KUWAIT. HTTP://DIR.SALON.COM/POLITICS/FEATURE/2000/11/22 CHENEY/INDEX.HTML

THE CONFLICT ALLOWED CHENEY TO LAUNCH ONE OF THE LARGEST PRIVATIZATION EFFORTS IN THE HISTORY OF THE PENTAGON, STEERING HUGE MILITARY LOGISTICS CONTRACTS TO PRIVATE CONTRACTORS. 2 1/2 YEARS AFTER HE LEAVES HIS FEDERAL JOB, CHENEY WILL CASH IN ON THE VERY CONTRACTS HE HELPED CREATE. *THE TEXAS OBSERVER 10/6/2000 "THE CANDIDATE FROM ROOT AND BROWN" BY ROBERT BRYCE*

DESPITE THE EVIDENT THAWING OF THE COLD WAR, CHENEY REMAINED A STAUNCH ALARMIST. CHENEY AND PAUL WOLFOWITZ WERE CONVINCED THAT MIKHAIL GORBACHEV, TIME MAGAZINE MAN OF THE YEAR IN 1987 AND WINNER OF THE 1990 NOBEL PEACE PRIZE, WAS A COMMUNIST NO DIFFERENT THAN HIS PREDECESSORS, WITH DESIGNS FOR *GLOBAL CONQUEST!* CHENEY AND WOLFOWITZ REPEATED THEIR MESSAGE OF FEAR RIGHT UP TO THE COLLAPSE OF THE SOVIET UNION IN LATE 1991... *WWW.AITIMES.COM FRONT PAGE 12/16/03 "BAKER'S RETURN SPELLS CHENEY'S HEARTBURN" BY JIM LOBE*

IN 1992 CHENEY'S SUBORDI- NATES WOLFOWITZ AND LIB- BY WROTE THEIR DEFENSE PLANNING GUIDANCE DRAFT, A *RADICAL* RETHINKING OF AMERICAN FOREIGN POLICY THAT CALLED FOR A STRAT- EGY OF UNILATERALIST GLO- BAL DOMINATION AGAINST ROGUE STATES AND EMERG- ING RIVALS, *BY NUCLEAR MEANS IF NECESSARY!* THIS DRAFT ALSO INCLUDED RECOMMENDATIONS FOR *MILITARY INTERVENTION IN IRAQ* TO "SAFEGUARD" PER- SIAN GULF OIL... *WWW.AITIMES.COM FRONT PAGE 10/1/03 "CHENEY'S MASK IS SLIPPING" BY JIM LOBE, AND WWW.BUSH-PRESIDENT2004.COM/PNAC*

THE PLAN SO HORRIFIES BUSH SR., JAMES BAKER, BRENT SCOWCROFT, ARMED FORCES CHIEF OF STAFF COLIN POWELL, AND EUROPEAN ALLIES THAT CHENEY IS ORDERED TO HAVE HIS PEOPLE RE-WRITE IT.
WWW.AITIMES.COM FRONT PAGE 10/1/03 "CHENEY'S MASK IS SLIPPING" BY JIM LOBE

IN LATE 1992 BILL CLINTON IS ELECTED AND BY 1993 CHENEY IS ONCE AGAIN OUT OF WORK.

CHENEY SPENDS THE NEXT TWO YEARS MULLING RUNNING FOR PRESIDENT...

CONTRIBUTORS TO HIS ELECTION PAC INCLUDE EXECUTIVES AT COMPANIES THAT WENT ON TO WIN LARGE GOVERNMENT CONTRACTS IN IRAQ RECONSTRUCTION INCLUDING HALLIBURTON, BECHTEL (CONTRACT WORTH $2.8 BILLION) AND SCIENCE APPLICATION INTERNATIONAL (7 CONTRACTS)...

NEWT GINGRICH'S ASCENDANCY MADE CHENEY FEEL COMFORT-ABLE IN DROPPING HIS PRESIDEN-TIAL RUN, AS THINGS WERE NOW IN GOOD HANDS. THAT AND THE FACT HIS PAC HADN'T RAISED ENOUGH MONEY ANYWAY...
THE NEW YORKER, 2004, 2/16 THRU 23, "CONTRACT SPORT" BY JANE MAYER

IN 1995, DESPITE HAVING NO BACKGROUND IN THE OIL BUSINESS, CHENEY IS MADE *CEO OF HALLIBURTON*, CASHING IN ON THE WEALTH OF GOVERNMENT AND GULF WAR CONNECTIONS HE HAS MADE. "DICK WAS GOOD AT OPENING DOORS... HE HAD CONTACTS FROM HIS FORMER LIFE AND HE USED THEM EFFECTIVELY." *LAWRENCE EAGLEBURGER, SEC. OF STATE, BUSH SR. ADMINISTRATION.* CHENEY BECOMES VERY *RICH*, EARNING *$44 MILLION* DURING HIS TENURE, PLUS DEFERRED COMPENSATION WORTH APPROXIMATELY *$150 THOUSAND A YEAR* AND STOCK OPTIONS WORTH OVER *$18 MILLION!* *THE NEW YORKER, 2004, 2/16 THRU 23, "CONTRACT SPORT" BY JANE MAYER*

THANKS FOR YOUR PATRONAGE! PLEASE MAKE THE CIRCUIT AGAIN SOON! *Sincerely, The Management*

IN: FED. GOVT. JOBS

OUT: PRIVATE SECTOR JOBS

PRE-CHENEY HALLIBURTON DOES APPROX 33% OF ITS BUSINESS ABROAD, DURING CHENEY'S TENURE THIS RISES TO OVER 70% OF ITS $14.9 BILLION BUSINESS, BOOSTING STOCK VALUE NEARLY 100%. CHENEY'S HALLIBURTON NEARLY TRIPLES ITS SPENDING ON FEDERAL LOBBYING, WITH A RESULT OF DOUBLING ITS GOVT. CONTRACTS. CHENEY'S HALLIBURTON ALSO GETS $1.5 BILLION IN US GOVT. LOANS FROM THE EXPORT-IMPORT BANK & OVERSEAS PRIVATE INVESTMENT CORPORATION, SIGNIFICANTLY UP FROM THE PALTRY PRE-CHENEY SUM OF $100 MILLION.

LATER, DURING THE VICE-PRESIDENTIAL DEBATE WITH JOE LIEBERMAN, CHENEY WOULD SAY OF HIS HALLIBURTON RICHES;

I CAN TELL YOU THE GOVERNMENT HAD *ABSOLUTELY NOTHING TO DO WITH IT!*

THE NATION 8/21/00 "TRICKY DICK" BY DOUG IRELAND, AND THE NEW YORKER, 2/16 THRU 23 2004, "CONTRACT SPORT" BY JANE MAYER

CHENEY DIDN'T LET MISPLACED PATRIOTISM STAND IN THE WAY OF PROFITS. DESPITE STRICT U.S. SANCTIONS HALLIBURTON DID BUSINESS WITH LIBYA, IRAN AND IRAQ, USING THE LEGAL LOOPHOLE OF SUBSIDIARY COMPANIES. CHENEY'S HALLIBURTON TRADED WITH THE IRAQI REGIME FOR OVER A YEAR...

ABC "THIS WEEK", JULY 30 2000

I HAD A FIRM POLICY THAT WE WOULDN'T DO ANYTHING IN IRAQ, EVEN ARRANGE-MENTS THAT WERE SUPPOSEDLY LEGAL...

ABC "THIS WEEK", JULY 30 2000

...WE'VE NOT DONE ANY BUSINESS IN IRAQ SINCE U.N. SANCTIONS WERE IMPOSED ON IRAQ IN 1990, AND I HAD A STANDING POLICY THAT I WOULDN'T DO THAT!

ABC "THIS WEEK" 3 WEEKS LATER:

I DIDN'T KNOW WE WERE DOING BUSINESS WITH IRAQ!

A FORMER CHAIRMAN OF ONE OF THE SUBSIDIARY COMPANIES, JAMES E. PARRELLA, SAID, BASED ON HIS KNOWLEDGE OF COMPANY POLICY AND PROCEDURE...

OH DEFINITELY, HE WAS AWARE OF THE BUSINESS...

ABC "THIS WEEK" PROGRAM, JULY THRU AUGUST 2000, WASH-INGTON POST JUNE 23 2001, AND THE NEW YORKER, 2004, 2/16 THRU 23, "CONTRACT SPORT" BY JANE MAYER

IN THE SPRING OF 2000 CHENEY DID DOUBLE DUTY AS CEO OF HALLIBURTON AND HEAD OF THE G. W. BUSH VICE-PRESIDENT SEARCH COMMITTEE, AFTER MUCH SOUL SEARCHING AND DUE DILIGENCE HE PICKED HIMSELF...

SURPRISE IT'S ME!

HOORAY FOR US!

"THE MOST MACHIAVELLIAN FUCKING THING I'VE EVER SEEN!" WAS HOW LONG-TIME CHENEY FRIEND STUART SPENCER DESCRIBED THE MOVE...
THE NEW YORKER, 2004, 2/16 THRU 23, "CONTRACT SPORT" BY JANE MAYER

NOVEMBER 22, 2000, FOURTH HEART ATTACK...

AFTER "WINNING" THE ELECTION, CHENEY IS PUT IN CHARGE OF THE TRANSITION TEAM, ALLOW-ING HIM TO PLACE THE OLD NEOCON TEAM OF RUMSFELD, WOLFOWITZ AND LIBBY BACK IN POSITIONS OF AUTHORITY...

SYDNEY MORNING HERALD, OCT. 5 2003, "WORLD DOMINATION WITH A PLASTIC-METAL TICKER"

CHENEY'S FIRST ASSIGNMENT AS VICE-PRESIDENT IS AS CHAIRMAN OF THE NATIONAL ENERGY POLICY DEVELOPMENT GROUP...

NEW GUARD AT HEN HOUSE!

DESPITE LAWSUITS AND FREEDOM OF INFORMATION ACT REQUESTS, CHENEY STILL HASN'T DISCLOSED WHO WAS ON THE ENERGY TASK FORCE. HOWEVER, ONE ECONOMIC ANALYST DESCRIBED IT AS "...SO FAVORABLE IT ALMOST SEEMED LIKE THE POWER COMPANIES GOT EVERYTHING THEY ... ASKED FOR," QUOTE FROM BARRY ABRAMSON "POWER COMPANY STOCKS FALL" ASS. PRESS 5/31/01

THE RESULTS WERE INDEED EVIDENT, PROMOTING OPENING OF PROTECTED LANDS FOR OIL AND GAS DRILLING, BUILDING OF MORE THAN 1,300 ELECTRICAL PLANTS, WEAKENING ENVIRONMENTAL STANDARDS, LIMITING OF STATES' POWERS, BOOSTING THE USE OF COAL AND NUCLEAR POWER, AND REMOVING OTHER "REGULATORY OBSTACLES"...

MANY OF THESE PROPOSALS BENEFITED COMPANIES WHO WERE MAJOR CAMPAIGN CONTRIBUTORS TO THE BUSH/CHENEY TEAM, INCLUDING ENRON, RELIANT ENERGY, DYNERGY, AND DUKE ENERGY. NATIONAL RESOURCES DEFENSE COUNCIL, "THE BUSH-CHENEY ENERGY PLAN, PLAYERS, PROFITS AND PAYBACKS"

WHEN CHALLENGED THAT HIS PRIVATE MEETINGS WITH INDUSTRY OFFICIALS WHO GAVE MONEY TO THE REPUBLICAN CAMPAIGN HAD THE APPEARANCE OF IMPROPRIETY, CHENEY REPLIED;

JUST BECAUSE SOMEBODY MAKES A CAMPAIGN CONTRIBUTION DOESN'T MEAN THAT THEY SHOULD BE DENIED THE OPPORTUNITY TO EXPRESS THEIR VIEWS TO GOVERNMENT OFFICIALS! WASHINGTON POST 5/17/01

CHENEY ATTEMPTED TO USE THE CALIFORNIA "ENERGY CRISIS" AS A WAY TO BOLSTER HIS PLANS, BEING PROMINENTLY QUOTED AS SAYING "CALIFORNIA HAS A PROBLEM BECAUSE THEY HAVEN'T BUILT ANY NEW POWER PLANTS" AND "ONE OF THE PROBLEMS IN CALIFORNIA IS AN INADEQUATE TRANSMISSION LINE GOING FROM SOUTHERN CA TO NORTHERN CA, OTHER PLACES ITS PIPELINE CAPACITY." WWW.PBS.ORG AND INTERVIEW WITH CNN'S JOHN KING CHENEY MADE NO MENTION OF THE BLATANT AND RUINOUS GAMING OF CALIFORNIA'S ENERGY RULES BY HIS PALS IN THE ENERGY INDUSTRY...

YEE-HAW!

CHARDONNAY!

RON SUSKIND'S BOOK "THE PRICE OF LOYALTY" QUOTED FORMER TREASURE SECRETARY PAUL O'NEILL'S WHITE HOUSE EXPERIENCES, CLAIMING THAT CHENEY ACTIVELY FOMENTED INTERVENTION IN IRAQ *BEFORE 9/11...*

A PREVIOUSLY UNDISCLOSED NATIONAL SECURITY COUNCIL DOCUMENT FROM FEB. 2001, *MONTHS BEFORE 9/11*, DIRECTED NSC STAFF TO COOPERATE FULLY WITH CHENEY'S ENERGY TASK FORCE IN THE "MELDING" OF TWO SEPARATE AREAS OF POLICY; "*THE REVIEW OF OPERATIONAL POLICIES TOWARDS ROGUE STATES*" AND "*ACTIONS REGARDING THE CAPTURE OF NEW AND EXISTING OIL AND GAS FIELDS.*"

SADDAM'S *LAUGHING AT YA* KID!

I THINK HE MUST BE *CHEATIFICATING!*

KID U.S.A. VS. THE SWARTHY HEATHEN

THIS STORY IS CALLED "*HOW TO MAKE MONEY WITH OTHER PEOPLE'S OIL*"!

I WUV MY UNCA DICK...

THE NEW YORKER, 2004, 2/16 THRU 23, "CONTRACT SPORT" BY JANE MAYER

JUNE 2001, CHENEY RECEIVES A PACEMAKER FOR HIS HEART—

1) THE U.S. HAD A MUCH LARGER MILITARY PRESENCE IN THE OIL-RICH PERSIAN GULF, AND 2) HALLIBURTON WAS AGAIN MAKING HUGE PROFITS PROVIDING SERVICES AND SUPPORT, INCLUDING A *NO-BID* $7 BILLION CONTRACT TO REBUILD IRAQ'S OIL INFRASTRUCTURE.

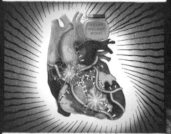

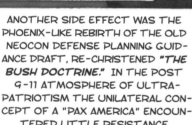

SEPTEMBER 11, 2001, THE U.S. WAS DEVASTATED BY A TERRORIST ATTACK. THE TRAGEDY ULTIMATELY LED TO TWO WARS, WITH TWO CLEAR RESULTS;

ANOTHER SIDE EFFECT WAS THE PHOENIX-LIKE REBIRTH OF THE OLD NEOCON DEFENSE PLANNING GUIDANCE DRAFT, RE-CHRISTENED "*THE BUSH DOCTRINE.*" IN THE POST 9-11 ATMOSPHERE OF ULTRA-PATRIOTISM THE UNILATERAL CONCEPT OF A "PAX AMERICA" ENCOUNTERED LITTLE RESISTANCE.

"*THE BUSH DOCTRINE*" WAS SOON EXERCISED IN IRAQ, FUELED BY ALARMIST STATEMENTS OF IRAQI WMD CAPABILITIES AND INNUENDO SUGGESTING IRAQI INVOLVEMENT IN 9-11. IN MAKING HIS CASE FOR WAR, CHENEY *IGNORED* DATA THAT DIDN'T SUPPORT THE WAR, AND "POUNDED ON" CIA ANALYSTS TO PROVIDE *WORST-CASE* SCENARIO ASSESSMENTS. CHENEY SENT THIS CHERRY-PICKED INFORMATION TO TOP LEADERSHIP, *BYPASSING THE NORMAL FILTERING SYSTEM USED TO AVOID BAD INTELLIGENCE...*

TO SATISFY CHENEY'S INTEREST IN ITALIAN INTELLIGENCE REPORTS OF URANIUM SALES TO IRAQ, THE CIA SENT RETIRED AMBASSADOR JOSEPH WILSON TO NIGER TO INVESTIGATE IN FEBRUARY OF 2002. HIS CONCLUSION WAS THERE WAS NO VALIDITY TO THE STORY. WILSON RETURNED AND FILED HIS REPORT.

DESPITE WILSON'S REPORT, THE ADMINISTRATION AND CHENEY CONTINUED TO CLAIM IRAQ WAS PROCURING EQUIPMENT FOR NUCLEAR WEAPONS FOR OVER A YEAR, UNTIL AN ANGRY WILSON PUBLICLY CORRECTED THE RECORD IN THE JULY 6TH NEW YORK TIMES.

BOO!

THE WHITE HOUSE RESPONDED BY BLAMING GEORGE TENET'S CIA FOR GIVING THEM BAD INFORMATION...
THE NEW YORKER, 2003 10-27, "THE STOVEPIPE" BY SEYMOUR M. HERSCH

SHORTLY AFTER WILSON'S REVELATION, LEAKED INFORMATION IN A COLUMN REVEALED THE IDENTITY OF WILSON'S WIFE VALERIE PLAME AS A CIA OFFICER. WILSON FELT THIS "OUTING" WAS RETRIBUTION FOR HIS PUBLIC STATEMENTS.

ON FEBRUARY 5, 2004 UPI'S RICHARD SALE CLAIMED THAT THE FBI HAD UNCOVERED "HARD EVIDENCE" OF MISCONDUCT IN THE VALERIE PLAME CASE BY TWO PEOPLE IN DICK CHENEY'S OFFICE...

ACCORDING TO THESE SOURCES, JOHN HANNAH AND CHENEY'S CHIEF OF STAFF, LEWIS "SCOOTER" LIBBY, WERE THE TWO CHENEY EMPLOYEES. "WE BELIEVE THAT HANNAH WAS THE MAJOR PLAYER IN THIS," ONE FEDERAL LAW-ENFORCEMENT OFFICER SAID. CALLS TO THE VICE PRESIDENT'S OFFICE WERE NOT RETURNED, NOR DID HANNAH AND LIBBY RETURN CALLS.

HERE'S IS A SHORT TIMELINE OF CHENEY'S EVOLVING COMMENTS REGARDING THE FABLED IRAQI WMD...

"SIMPLY STATED, THERE IS NO DOUBT THAT SADDAM HUSSEIN NOW HAS WEAPONS OF MASS DESTRUCTION." *SPEECH TO VFW NATIONAL CONVENTION, AUG. 26, 2002 FROM PBS FRONTLINE*

"WE DO KNOW, WITH ABSOLUTE CERTAINTY, THAT HE IS USING HIS PROCUREMENT SYSTEM TO ACQUIRE THE EQUIPMENT HE NEEDS IN ORDER TO ENRICH URANIUM FOR A NUCLEAR WEAPON" *MEET THE PRESS SEPT. 8, 2002*

"WE KNOW THAT HE HAS A LONG-STANDING RELATIONSHIP WITH VARIOUS TERRORIST GROUPS, INCLUDING THE AL-QAEDA ORGANIZATION." *MEET THE PRESS, MARCH 14, 2003*

"...HIS DEVELOPMENT AND USE OF CHEMICAL WEAPONS, HIS DEVELOPMENT OF BIOLOGICAL WEAPONS, HIS PURSUIT OF NUCLEAR WEAPONS. ... IT'S ONLY A MATTER OF TIME UNTIL HE ACQUIRES NUCLEAR WEAPONS." *MEET THE PRESS, MARCH 14, 2003*

"WE LEARNED MORE AND MORE THAT THERE WAS A RELATIONSHIP BETWEEN IRAQ AND AL-QAEDA THAT STRETCHED BACK THROUGH MOST OF THE DECADE OF THE '90S... WITH RESPECT TO 9/11 ... WE JUST DON'T KNOW." *MEET THE PRESS, SEPT. 14 2003*

"THERE'S NO DOUBT IN MY MIND BUT THAT SADDAM HUSSEIN HAD THESE CAPABILITIES. ... I'M NOT WILLING AT ALL AT THIS POINT TO BUY THE PROPOSITION THAT SOMEHOW SADDAM HUSSEIN WAS INNOCENT AND HE HAD NO WMD AND SOME GUY OUT AT THE CIA, BECAUSE I CALLED HIM, COOKED UP A REPORT SAYING HE DID. THAT'S CRAZY...." *MEET THE PRESS, SEPT. 14, 2003*

AS OF THIS DATE THERE IS NO CREDIBLE REPORT OF ANY WMD IN IRAQ OR PREVIOUS CONNECTIONS BETWEEN AL QUAEDA AND SADDAM...

BESIDES FIGHTING FOR THE IRAQ WAR, CHENEY HAS CONTINUED TO FIGHT INQUIRIES INTO THE MEMBERSHIP OF HIS SELECT ENERGY TASK FORCE...

DESPITE CHENEY'S BEST EFFORTS, LOWER COURT RULINGS HAVE GONE AGAINST HIM AND THE CASE WILL GO TO THE SUPREME COURT...

WORLD'S HEAVYWEIGHT
★ CHAMPIONSHIP ★
ALL STAR PROFESSIONAL BOXING!

15 EXCITING HEAVYWEIGHT ROUNDS!

DICK "THE SPIDER" CHENEY

VS.

SIERRA "TREE HUGGERS" CLUB

TICKETS ON SALE AT ALL MEDIA OUTLETS NOW!

THIS FACT CALLED INTO QUESTION THE PROPRIETY OF CHENEY AND SUPREME COURT JUSTICE SCALIA'S RECENT DUCK HUNTING TRIP TOGETHER, JUST 3 WEEKS AFTER THE COURT AGREED TO HEAR THE CASE. JUSTICE SCALIA WAS REPORTEDLY CONFIDENT THEIR LONG FRIENDSHIP WOULD NOT INFLUENCE HIS JUDGMENT AND REFUSED REQUESTS TO RECUSE HIMSELF...
WWW.USATODAY.COM/NEWS/WASHINGTON/2004-02-11-SCALIA-CHENEY_X.HTM

"...IT'S ACCEPTABLE PRACTICE TO SOCIALIZE WITH EXECUTIVE BRANCH OFFICIALS WHEN THERE ARE NOT PERSONAL CLAIMS AGAINST THEM! THAT'S ALL I'M GOING TO SAY FOR NOW! *QUACK, QUACK!*"
WASHINGTON POST 2/12/2004

CHENEY'S FORMER COMPANY HALLIBURTON HAS CONTINUED TO PROFIT FROM THE WAR, BUT HAS BECOME EMBROILED IN NUMEROUS SCANDALS INCLUDING OVERCHARGES OF $61 MILLION ON FUEL, INVOLVEMENT OF EMPLOYEES IN A KICKBACK SCHEME RESULTING IN OVERCHARGES OF $6.3 MILLION, AND OVERCHARGES OF $16 MILLION ON FEEDING TROOPS... *THE NEW YORKER, 2004, 2/16 THRU 23, "CONTRACT SPORT" BY JANE MAYER*

BETWEEN SCANDALS, WARS AND INCREASINGLY NEGATIVE POLL NUMBERS, CHENEY HAS BEGUN TO BE VIEWED BY MANY AS A *"DRAG"* ON THE PARTY. NEVERTHELESS, AT THIS WRITING, HE IS *STILL* SLATED TO CONTINUE TO BE THE REPUBLICAN VICE PRESIDENTIAL CANDIDATE...

POSITIVE APPROVAL RATINGS

3/8/04 - 5/20/04

Ceci n'est pas une comic

This is not... a pipe.

This is not... an invasion.

This is not... pollution.

This is not... unemployment.

This is not... necessary.

This is not... dangerous.

This is not... your concern.

This is not... a problem.

So... do I have your vote?

with apologies to Magritte

The End

by Adam Gorightly

Hitler Was A Good American:
The Bush Crime Family and a Kindler, Gentler Fascism

When Prescott Bush dug up Geronimo's skull as part of an initiatory frat-boy ritual, this ghoulish graveyard grab set in motion the first in a series of Bush Family crimes that culminated in its monstrous magnum opus, the WTC tragedy of 9/11, Dubya's very own Reichstag, where amidst the lingering smoke and ash-strewn wreckage he emerged triumphant, issuing forth a call to arms directed at an unseen menace that may be staring back at you from the mirror. But we're getting ahead of ourselves...

Pappy Prescott–after his desecration of this aforementioned sacred Indian burial site–decided his next course of action would be to align himself with the Nazi party of the 1930s, as deftly chronicled earlier in this collection by Marcel Ruijters in the "Bush Nazi-Connection." (As a side note, I've always based my selection in Presidential elections by *not* voting for the candidate who would look most comfortable in Nazi regalia. Needless to say, I voted against Reagan and Bush amidst these troubled visions of Gentle George and affable Uncle Ronnie dressed to the nines in SS uniforms and sporting toothbrush moustaches.) With a thousand points of light in his kinder, gentler crosshairs, Herr Bush—during his administration—brought the New World Order out of the shadows and into the Beltway, throwing it full-force into the face of America. But once again I'm getting ahead of myself... ▬▬▬▬

In the late 1980s, an FBI document surfaced demonstrating that George Bush was part of the CIA management team behind the Bay of Pigs invasion, code named "Operation Zapata." Zapata, as it so happens, was the name of Bush's oil drilling company. At the time of the Bay of Pigs invasion, Bush had oil rigs located a mere thirty miles off the coast of Cuba near Cay Sal, a CIA operations base. In this regard, former CIA members have alleged that Bush allowed the CIA to use Zapata as a front for their Cuban operation, working in cahoots with several legendary spooks, including E. Howard Hunt, Frank Sturgis and Felix Rodriguez. Vice Pres Tricky Dick Nixon was also knee-deep in these covert operations directed against Castro's Cuba. These very same spooky alliances that conspired against Castro appear to have been the same players cast in leading roles in some of the most popular conspiracies that have colored our generation's imagination, from the Bay of Pigs/JFK assassination to Watergate, The October Surprise, Iran-Contra, Votescam and ultimately 9/11. And the Bush Junta can be traced back to all of the above. But shit, I got ahead of myself once more...

A CIA agent named "George Bush" just happened to be in Dallas on the day that JFK got blown away, as was former Vice President Nixon whose purported reason for being there was to deliver a speech at a Pepsi-Cola convention. *I'd like to teach the world to sing in perfect harmony*...It should be noted that Prescott Bush is credited with creating the winning Eisenhower-Nixon ticket of 1952, and in fact had cultivated a relationship with young Tricky Dicky dating back to 1941, at the same time he was courting darling Dolphie (Hitler).

In the late 1980s–when these revelations of George Bush in Dealey Plaza first came to light–CIA officials claimed that the "George Bush" in question was just some simple clerk shuffling papers, and not the very same George Herbert Walker Bush we have all come to know and love. The CIA has never been able to clearly identify this other George Bush, which only causes the

★ AFTERWORD ★

plot to thicken and sicken. Of course, Bush has claimed he can't exactly remember where he was when Kennedy got his cranium catapulted across Dealey Plaza and into the history books. Go figure...

Some have suggested that Nixon's ascendancy to the Presidency was through the barrel of a gun and that the same gang of goons behind the Bay of Pigs operation were also the ones who took JFK down in one bright shining moment. During the Watergate period, George Bush was Nixon's Director of Central Intelligence (DCI). Although it has been claimed that Bush had no relationship with the CIA prior to his appointment to this post, it's hard to take this assertion seriously. With his DCI appointment, Bush ostensibly became The Company's "keeper of secrets," the biggest of which was the knowledge of the Dealey Plaza death squad. And the conspiracies keep on coming...

As the 1980s rolled around, The October Surprise featured George Sr. on a secret mission to Paris on the weekend of Oct. 18-19, 1980 to negotiate the release of the hostages in Iran, this according to former Israeli intelligence official Ari Ben-Menashe in testimony before Congress in the early 1990's. At this time, Ben-Menashe claimed that he saw Bush and William Casey at a downtown Paris hotel as they headed into a meeting with a representative of Iran's ruling faction, although Bush denied that this meeting ever took place. Whatever the case, this arms-for-hostages deal–according to the popular conspiracy theory–helped usher in the reign of Uncle Ronnie and the face of friendly fascism.

It has also been conjectured—by other "conspiracy theorists"—that Reagan was just a Howdy Doody type front man for the Bush Junta pajama party. Curiously enough, sonny-boy Neil Bush had dinner with Scott Hinckley, brother of John Hinckley Jr., shortly before Hinckley took pot shots at Uncle Ronnie.

So was the Bush crime family responsible for Uncle Ronnie's "attempted assassination"? (Insert creepy organ music here.) Was this, in effect, a coup d'etat that put Bush at the helm of the Secret Government, leaving Reagan in place as the friendly fascist front-man ("Great Communicator") while behind the scenes Bush was calling the shots for Iran-Contra and other assorted shenanigans including the whole S&L mess co-starring sons Neil and Jeb. And while it may appear that George Bush was ousted from power by the Slick Willie revolution, this transition was in reality a seamless continuation of Bush's foreign policy, a Bush/Clinton partnership that got rolling back in the early 1980s on a Mena, Arkansas airstrip used for drug running.

And now once again we've transitioned into another Bush Presidency that some say was won by a rigged election engineered by brother Jeb. I guess I could also talk about the cozy relationship between the bin Laden and Bush families that dates back to the mid 1970s, and its possible relation to 9/11, but I think I'll save that for another time, as I'd hate to upset your dinner.

Anyway, I hope you've enjoyed this thumbnail sketch/retrospective of the Bush Family Crime Syndicate.

Sieg Heil!
Support family values!

Sources

MARCEL RUIJTERS THE BUSH-NAZI CONNECTION

Buchanan, John. "Bush-Nazi Link Confirmed," The New Hampshire Gazette, Vol. 248, No. 1, October 10, 2003.

Sutton, Antony. *Wall Street and the Rise of Hitler*. Seal Beach: '76 Press, 1976.

Tarpley, Webster G.; Chaitkin, Anton; Wertz, Mariana. *George Bush: The Unauthorized Biography*. Washington, DC: Executive Intelligence Review, 1992.

JAIME CRESPO BAD TO THE BONE

Chaitkin, Anton. *Treason in America: From Aaron Burr to Averell Harriman*. Executive Intelligence Review, 1998.

Millegan, Kris (ed.). *Fleshing out Skull & Bones: Investigations into America's Most Powerful Secret Society*. Trine Day, 2003.

Robbins, Alexandra. *Secrets of the Tomb: Skull and Bones, The Ivy League, and the Hidden Paths of Power*. Little, Brown, 2003.

Woodward, Bob, and Pincus, Walter. "Bush Opened Up to Secret Yale Society," Washington Post, August 7, 1988.

ALBO HELM SUPER SPOOK

Tarpley, Webster G.; Chaitkin, Anton; Wertz, Mariana. *George Bush: The Unauthorized Biography*. *Executive Intelligence Review*, 1992.

Bowen, Russell. *The Immaculate Deception: The Bush Crime Family Exposed*. America West, 1992.

LARRY RODMAN IRAN-CONTRA

Ball, Rick and NBC News. *Meet the Press: 50 Years of History in the Making*. McGraw-Hill, 1998.

Hewitt, Gavin. *Terry Waite and Ollie North*. Little, Brown, 1991.

Jinks, Harold. *Ronald Reagan: Smile, Style and Guile*. Vantage Press, Inc., 1986.

Bowling For Columbine (film). Directed by Michael Moore. United Artists, Alliance Atlantis, and Dog Eat Dog Films, 2002.

Noonan, Peggy. *What I Saw at the Revolution*. Random House, 1990.

Tarpley, Webster Griffin and Chaitkin, Anton. *George Bush: The Unauthorized Biography*. *Executive Intelligence Review*, 1992.

Virga, Vincent. *The Eighties*. Edward Burlingame Books, 1992.

Wallison, Peter J. *Ronald Reagan*. Westview Press, 2003.

Walsh, Lawrence E. *Firewall: The Iran-Contra Conspiracy and Cover-up*. W.W. Norton & Co., 1997.

DAVID PALEO & MACK WHITE THE BUSH-HINCKLEY CONNECTION

"Bush Son Had Dinner Plans with Hinckley Brother before Shooting," Associated Press, March 31, 1981.

"Government Retaliating against Hinckley's Father?" United Press International, July 13, 1982.

"Previous Houston Report Links Suspect with Bushes," United Press International, March 31, 1981.

Brussel, Mae. "The Bush Family Ties to John Hinckley, Jr., the Shooter of President of Ronald Reagan," World Watchers International, Tape 487, April 5, 1981.

Cook, Frank. "Clements Criticizes Shooting Coverage," United Press International, March 31, 1981.

Gorightly, Adam. "Masters of Deceit," MindControlForums.com.

Judge, John. November 2000 Interview, Part II, Ratical.org.

Mossman, John. "Family 'Destroyed' by Assassination Attempt," Associated Press, April 1, 1981.

Tarpley, Webster G.; Chaitkin, Anton; Wertz, Mariana. *George Bush: The Unauthorized Biography*. Executive Intelligence Review, 1992.

ALEKSANDER ZOGRAF & MACK WHITE OPERATION JUST CAUSE

"Bush: Daddy Was a Killer Too," *Socialist Worker*, December 15, 2001.

Cohen, Hillel. "Invasion's Real Goal: Break Canal Treaty," *Workers World*, September 28, 1995.

The Panama Deception (film). Produced and directed by Barbara Trent. The Empowerment Project, 1992.

JEM EATON & HACK SMITH POPPY THE PRESIDENT

1. All of the Bush family biographical information in this first strip can be found in the following: "Bush Family Values: War, Wealth, Oil" by Kevin Phillips, *Los Angeles Times*, February 8, 2004 and "Bush-Law in the Land of Mannon" by Alfred Mendes, *Spectre Magazine*, December 7, 2002.

2. "Bush Battles the 'Wimp Factor,'" by G. Margaret Warner, *Newsweek*, October 1987, p. 28.

3. Quote of State Department Spokesperson Margaret Tutwiler, *Washington Post*, July 19, 1990.

4. Actual quote (unattributed), *Time*, January 7, 1991, p. 20.

5. "The Thirty-Year Itch" by Robert Dreyfuss, *Mother Jones*, April 2003.

6. "Threats and Responses: The Bioterror Threat" by Philip Shenon, *New York Times*, March 16, 2003.

7. A reference to Iraqi soldiers calmly visiting barber shops and other merchants directly after invasion of Kuwait. *Washington Post*, August 3, 1990.

8. *New York Times*, August 3, 1990.

9. "How PR Sold the War in the Gulf" by John Stauber, December 7, 2002, Counterpunch.Org.

10. *Time*, January 17, 1991.

11. Actual quote of Margaret Thatcher, as included in George Will's column of August 21, 2003.

12. Another Thatcher quote, as reported in *Newsweek*, January 28, 1991, p. 58.

13. Not actual quote, but attributed to Bush, *Newsweek*, January 28, 1991, p. 64.

14. *Atlanta Constitution*, February 17, 1991.

15. A reference to Bush witnessing a fellow Navyman's accidental and gruesome death aboard an aircraft carrier during World War II, recounted in "What Bodies?" by Patrick J. Sloyan, DigitalJournalist.org, November 2002.

16. *George Bush's War* by Jean Edward Smith, p. 78.

17. A reference to Saudi Arabia's claim that Iraq's army was weak. *The Washington Post*, September 7, 1990.

18. A reference to General Powell regularly playing squash with Prince Bandar. *George Bush's War* by Jean Edward Smith, p. 78.

19. CBC's Emmy-Award Winning TV Documentary *To Sell A War*.

20. A reference to Lauri Fitz-Pegado, Vice President, Hill & Knowlton, coaching young Kuwaiti girl, Nayirah, for false "baby incubator" testimony before Congress. *Second Front, Censorship and Propaganda in the Gulf War* by John R. MacArthur, p. 64.

21. A reference to Hill & Knowlton Washington office CEO Craig Fuller being Bush's good friend (and ex-Chief of Staff). "Packaging the Emir," *PR Watch*, Disinfopedia.org.

22. *George Bush's War*, p. 134.

23. From Saddam Hussein's *Open Letter to President Bush*, *New York Times*, August 17, 1990.

24. Actual Bush quote, *New York Times*, August 16, 1990.

25. *George Bush: The Unauthorized Biography* by Webster G. Tarpley and Anton Chaitkin.

26. Actual Congressional testimony quote of Nayirah al-Sabah, from "Nayirah's Testimony," EmperorsClothes.com.

27. Ibid.

28. "Suffer the Little Children," PR Watch, Disinfopedia.org.

29. A reference to the "Free Kuwait" t-shirts made and distributed by the "Citizens for a Free Kuwait" PR front. *Second Front* by John R. MacArthur, p. 50.

30. *Toxic Sludge is Good for You*, Chapter 10, by John Stauber and Sheldon Rampton.

31. Reference to *The Rape of Kuwait* by Jean Sasson.

32. A passage from *The Rape of Kuwait.*

33. *New York Times*, August 29, 1990.

34. Actual quote of President Bush, *New York Times*, August 31, 1990.

35. Actual quote of President Bush from 1988. *A Man of Integrity* by George Bush and Doug Wead.

36. "Flacking for the Emir" by Arthur E. Rowse, *The Progressive*, May 1991, pp. 21-22.

37. *New York Times*, December 20, 1990.

38. Actual Hussein quote, *Washington Post*, October 14, 1990.

39. Actual quote of Bush from presidential documents. Weekly Compilation of Presidential Documents, Administration of George Bush, October 5, 1990, p. 2047.

40. Actual Bush quote. *Washington Post*, December 21, 1990.

41. A reference to Bush purposefully mispronouncing Saddam as "SAD-dam," a CIA-inspired strategy. *George Bush's War*, p. 232.

42. Ibid., p. 216.

43. *Washington Post*, December 2, 1990.

44. A reference to Bush's taking thyroid medication. *George Bush's War*, p. 90.

45. Ibid., p. 222.

46. Ibid., p. 219.

47. Actual Bush quote. David Frost PBS Interview, January 2, 1991.

48. Actual General Powell quote. *Washington Post*, January 31, 1991.

49. *George Bush's War*, p. 220.

50. Actual Bush quote. President's Address to the Nation, January 16, 1991.

51. A reference to Honeywell employees watching bombing at their desks and celebrating. Associated Press, January 1991.

52. "Amiriyah Shelter Revisited," ActivistReader.com, February 2004.

53. "'Smarter' Bombs Still Hit Civilians" by Scott Peterson, CommonDreams.org, October 22, 2002.

54. A reference to Cheney actually adding his inscription "To Saddam, with fond regards" to bombs to be dropped on Iraq. CASI.org.uk, September 12, 2002.

55. Actual newscaster quote. "Preface," Unreliable Sources by Martin Lee and Norman Solomon.

56. Actual Bush quote. "Presidential Quotes," InfoPlease.com.

57. A reference to McDonald's issuing terrorist alerts to all employees, having them search dumpsters for suspicious packages. "War Slows the Pace at Businesses while Americans Watch TV," Associated Press, mid-January 1991.

58. "The Gulf War: Secret History" by William M. Arkin, TheMemoryHole.org.

59. Actual General Schwarzkopf quote. *Washington Post*, September 1, 1990.

60. A reference to thousands of Iraqi soldiers being buried alive in their trenches by U.S. Ace bulldozer earth-movers. "What Bodies?" by Patrick J. Sloyan, DigitalJournalist.org, November 2002.

61. Actual Cheney quote from "The Lost Forum," AsylumNation.com, February 27, 1991.

62. A reference to U.S. pilots dropping bombs on Iraqi soldiers and their families retreating from Kuwait on the "Highway of Death." For an extraordinary documentation of this atrocity, see "The Unseen Gulf War: A Harrowing Photo Essay" by Peter Turnley, DigitalJournalist.org.

63. Actual Cheney quote. "What Bodies?" by Patrick J. Sloyan, DigitalJournalist.org, November 2002.

64. Paraphrase of General Powell quote. News conference, January 23, 1991.

65. A reference to the U.S. use of fuel-air bombs on Iraq. "Ordnance: High Tech's Gory Side," *Los Angeles Times*, February 24, 1991.

66. A reference to 73% of U.S. public (supposedly) wanting Saddam dead or captured during Gulf War. *Wall Street Journal*/NBC News Poll.

67. A reference to ABC Sunday Night Movie, *Heroes of Desert Storm*. In "Seven TV Appearances, Wealth of Exposure for Bush," New York Times, October 6, 1991, p. 26.

68. *TV Guide*, October 5, 1991, p. 34.

69. Quote of U.S. soldier, Sgt. Wess Schultze, in reference to the Persian Gulf War, *Army Magazine*, August 1991, p. 35.

70. Actual Bush quote. Interview with David Frost, January 1996.

KENNETH R. SMITH BUSH FAMILY VALUES

Dallas Morning News, February 26, 1997.

Houston Chronicle, March 9, 1995.

Brewton, Peter. *The Mafia, CIA and George Bush: The Untold Story of America's Greatest Financial Debacle*. SPI Books, 1992.

Chossudovsky, Michel. "Bush Family Links to the Mexican Drug Cartel," *Global Outlook*, No. 5, Summer/Fall 2003.

Friedman, Alan. *Spider's Web: The Secret History of How the White House Illegally Armed Iraq*. Bantam, 1993.

Oppenheimer, Carl. *The Miami Herald*, February 17, 1997.

Timmerman, Kenneth R. *The Death Lobby: How the West Armed Iraq*. Houghton Mifflin, 1991.

Wilmsen, Steven. *Silverado: Neil Bush and the Savings and Loan Scandal*. National Press Books, 1991.

SCOTT GILBERT THE SKIES OF TEXAS

Hatfield, J. H. *Fortunate Son: George W. Bush and the Making of an American President*, 3rd edition. Soft Skull Press, 2001.

Phillips, Kevin. *American Dynasty: Aristocracy, Fortune, and the Politics of Deceit in the House of Bush*. Viking Press, 2004.

PENNY VAN HORN & MACK WHITE THE COMPASSIONATE CONSERVATIVE

Bradach, James. "Bush's Ecocide," BushKills.com.

Carlson, Tucker. "Devil May Care," *Talk Magazine*, September 1999.

Cockburn, Alexander. "George W. Bush: The Death Penalty Governor," CommonDreams.org.

Ivins, Molly, and Dubose, Louis. *Shrub: The Short but Happy Political Life of George W. Bush*. Random House, 2000.

CAROL SWAIN 11/7/00

Financial Times, November 16, 2000.

Daily News, November 11, 2000.

St. Petersburg Times, December 7, 2000.

Inter Press, November 14, 2000.

SETH TOBOCMAN THE CARLYLE GROUP

The main source of information for Seth Tobocman's piece on the Carlyle Group was Dan Briody's excellent book *The Iron Triangle* (John Wiley & Sons, 2003). Tobocman also drew on his experience last year at a protest in front of the Carlyle Group's New York offices where he, along with more than a hundred other protesters and bystanders, was illegally arrested and detained for the better part of a day. After several months in court, all charges were dropped.

TED RALL CHECKLIST FOR THE NEO-FASCISTS

Johnson, Chalmers. *The Sorrows of Empire: Militarism, Secrecy and the End of the Republic*. Metropolitan Books, 2004. Disinfopedia Website: www.disinfopedia.org

PNAC Website: www.NewAmericanCentury.org

Pitt, William Rivers. "The Project for the New American Century," InformationClearingHouse.info, Feb. 25, 2003

MACK WHITE 9/11

9/11: The Road to Tyranny (film). Produced and directed by Alex Jones. 2002.

9/11Review.org.

Agence France-Press, August 28, 2001.

Ahmad, Ishtiaq. "How Enron Courted the Taliban," *Pakistan Observer*, October 20, 2001.

"Alleged Hijackers May Have Trained at U.S. Bases," *Newsweek*, 9/15/01.

Allen, Mike. "Bush Reacts to Attacks, Moves to Nebraska," *Washington Post*, September 11, 2001.

Arnie, Catherine. "The Secret Saudi Flight on 9/13 Could Be the Key to the Bush-Saudi-Al Qaeda Connection," Democrats.com.

"Ashcroft Flying High," CBS.com, July 26, 2001.

Associated Press, September 13, 2001; May 21, 2002.

"Bin Laden Family Evacuated," CBS.com, September 30, 2001.

Brisard, Jean-Charles, and Dasquie, Guillaume. *Forbidden Truth: Taliban Secret Oil Diplomacy and the Failed Hunt for Bin Laden*. Thunder's Mouth Press, 2002.

Brzezinski, Zbigniew. *The Grand Chessboard: American Primacy and Its Geostrategic Imperatives*, 1997.

Bunch, William. "We Know It Crashed, But Not Why," *Philadelphia Daily News*, November 15, 2001.

Bunch, William. "Three-Minute Discrepancy in Tape: Cockpit Voice Recording Ends before Flight 93's Official Time of Impact," *Philadelphia Daily News*, September 16, 2002.

Chossudovsky, Michel. "Who is Osama bin Laden? ," GlobalResearch.ca, September 12, 2001.

Chossudovsky, Michel. "Mysterious September 11 Breakfast Meeting on Capitol Hill," GlobalResearch.ca, August 4, 2003.

Coleen Rowley's Memo to FBI Director Robert Mueller (edited version), *Time*, May 21, 2002.

"Conspiracy Theories: The Saudi Connection," *The Fifth Estate*, CBC, October 29, 2003.

Crichton, Torcuil. "Britain Warned US to Expect September 11 Al-Qaeda Hijackings," *Sunday Herald*, undated.

"Dark Heart of the American Dream," *The Observer*, June 16, 2002.

Davis, Douglas. "Mossad Warned CIA of Attacks," *Jerusalem Post*, September 17, 2001.

Doran, James. "Rushdie's Air Ban," *The Times of London*, September 27, 2001.

Eggen, Dan. "Hijack Plot Suspicions Raised with FBI in August," *Washington Post*, January 2, 2002.

Escobar, Pepe. "Pipelineistan" (Parts 1 and 2), *Asia Times*, January 26, 2002.

Thompson, Paul. "Complete 9/11 Timeline," CooperativeResearch.org.

Fahrenheit 9/11 (film). Produced and directed by Michael Moore. 2004.

Flight93Crash.com.

"FBI Ignored Warnings of Fanatical Student Pilot," NewsMax.com, September 14, 2001.

"Former German Defense Minister Confirms CIA Involvement in 9/11: Alex Jones Interviews Andreas Von Buelow," PrisonPlanet.com, February 11, 2004.

Frankfurter Allgemeine Zeitung, Sept. 14, 2001

"German Police Confirm Iranian Deportee Phoned Warnings," Ananova.com, September 14, 2001.

Gibb, Tom; O'Toole, James; and Lash, Cindi. "Investigators Locate 'Black Box' from Flight 93; Widen Search Area in Somerset Crash," *Pittsburgh Post-Gazette*, September 13, 2001.

Gibson, Charles. "Terror Hits the Towers: How Government Officials Reacted to Sept. 11 Attacks," ABCNews.com, 9/14/02.

Golden, Daniel; Bandler, James; and Walker, Marcus. "Bin Laden Family Could Profit from a Jump in Defense Spending Due to Ties to U.S. Bank," *Wall Street Journal*, September 27, 2001.

Gomez, Jim, and Solomon, John. "Authorities Warned of Hijack Risks," Associated Press, March 5, 2002.

Gugliotta, Guy. "Reconstructing the Hijackers' Last Days," *Washington Post*, September 16, 2001.

Harnden, Toby. "How Flight 93 Revolt Nearly Succeeded," *The Telegraph*, August 6, 2002.

"Heroes of Flight 93," MSNBC.com, July 30, 2002.

Hersh, Seymour. "The Price of Oil," *The New Yorker*, July 9, 2001.

Hirsh, Michael. "We've Hit the Targets," *Newsweek*, September 13, 2001 issue.

Hopsicker, Daniel. "Did Terrorist Pilots Train at U.S. Military Schools?," MadCowMorningNews.com.

Hopsicker, Daniel. "Terror Flight School Owner's Plane Seized for Heroin Trafficking," MadCowMorningNews.com.

Hopsicker, Daniel. *Welcome to Terrorland: Mohammed Atta and the 9/11 Cover-up in Florida.* Trine Day, 2004

Johnson, David. "Pre-Attack Memo Cited Bin Laden," *The New York Times*, May 14, 2002

Johnson, Jeff. "Tearful FBI Agent Apologizes to Sept. 11 Families and Victims," CNSNews.com, May 30, 2002.

Jones, Alex. *9/11: Descent into Tyranny*. AEJ Productions, 2002.

Joshi, Manoj. "India Helped FBI Trace ISI-Terrorist Links," *The Times of India*, October 9, 2001.

Judis, John B., and Ackerman, Spencer. Report, *The New Republic*, August 1, 2003.

Kim, Won-Young, and Baum, Gerald R. "Seismic Observations during September 11, 2001, Terrorist Attack," U.S. Army Authorized Study.

Knight Ridder/Tribune News Service, 9/16/2002.

"La CIA aurait rencontré Ben Laden en juillet," *Le Figaro*, 11/2/01

Leyne, John. "U.S. Right Questions Saudi Ties," BBC.co.uk, May 31, 2002.

Lines, Andy. "Pentagon Chiefs Planned for Jet Attack," *The Mirror*, 5/24/02.

Martin, Patrick. "The Strange Case of Zacarias Moussaoui: FBI Refused to Investigate Man Charged in September 11 Attacks," World Socialist Web Site/WWWS.org, January 5, 2002.

Matier, Phillip, and Ross, Andrew. "Willie Brown Got Low-Key Early Warning about Air Travel," *San Francisco Chronicle*, September 12, 2001:

Mineta, Norman, Secretary of Transportation, Congressional Testimony, May 21, 2003.

Meyssan, Theirry. *9/11: The Big Lie*, Carnot USA Books, 2002.

Moran, Michael. "Bin Laden Comes Home to Roost," MSNBC.com, August 24, 1998.

Nashua Telegraph, September 13, 2001.

New York Times, October 29, 2003.

Newsweek, November 25, 2001.

"Officials: Government Failed to React to FAA Warning," CNN.com, 9/17/01.

Pacenti, John. "Intelligence Panel Hears from Glass," *The Palm Beach Post*, October 17, 2002.

Palast, Greg. "Has Someone Been Sitting on the FBI?." *BBC Newsnight*, 11/6/01.

Ridgeway, James. "U.S. Ignored Warnings from French," *Village Voice*, May 28, 2002.

Panossian, Joe. "Egypt Leader Says He Warned America," Associated Press, December 7, 2001.

Papers of the Project for the New American Century (PNAC), September 2000.

"Rebuilding America's Defenses," Project for the New American Century (PNAC), September 2000.

Rotella, Sebastian, and Meyer, Josh. "Wiretaps May Have Foretold Terror Attacks," *Los Angeles Times*, May 29, 2002.

Ruppert, Michael. "A Timeline Surrounding September 11th: If CIA and the Government Weren't Involved in the September 11 Attacks What Where They Doing?," FromTheWilderness.com, 2002.

"Rushdie Claims US Authorities Knew of Attack," *Hindustan Times*, September 27, 2001,

"Rushdie Given US Air Ban Week before Terrorist Attacks," Ananova.com, September 27, 2001:

Seal, Cheryl. "John O'Neill: Was He a Casualty of the Bush Administration?," Democrats.com.

Serrano, Richard A., and Dahlburg, John-Thor. "Feds: Evidence Suggests Hijackers' Support in U.S.," *Los Angeles*, September 20, 2001.

Sorensen, Harley. "Heads-Up to Ashcroft Proves Threat Was Known before 9/11," *SF Gate*, June 3, 2002.

Silver, Jonathan D. "Day of Terror: Outside Tiny Shanksville, a Fourth Deadly Stroke," *Pittsburgh Post-Gazette*, September 12, 2001.

Stafford, Ned. "Echelon Gave Authorities Warning of Attacks," *Washington Post*, September 13, 2001.

"Taliban in Texas for Talks on Gas Pipeline," BBC.co.uk, December 4, 1997.

Tyler, Patrick E., and MacFarquhar, Neil. "Egypt Warned U.S. of Al-Qaeda Plot, Mubarak Asserts," *New York Times*, June 4, 2002.

Unger, Craig. "The Great Escape," *New York Times*, June 1, 2004.

Vero Beach Press Journal, September 12, 2001.

Vidal, Gore. "The Enemy Within," *The Observer*, October 27, 2002.

Vuilliamy, Ed. "Let's Roll," *The Observer*, December 2, 2001.

Washington Post, January 12, 2002; May 18, 2002.

Wastell, David, and Jacobson, Philip, "Israeli Security Issued Urgent Warning to CIA of Large-Scale Terror Attacks," *Daily Telegraph of London*, September 16, 2001.

Weiss, Murray. *The Man Who Warned America*. Harper-Collins, 2004.

"Why Was Russia's Intelligence on Al-Qaeda Ignored?," *Jane's*, October 5, 2001.

Woodward, Bob, and Eggen, Dan. "August Memo Focused on Attacks in U.S.," *Washington Post*, May 18, 2002.

Wright, Robert G. Wright, Jr. Press Conference, Broadcast on CSPAN, May 31, 2002.

STEVE BRODNER Environmental Plunder Administration

"The Bush Record," National Resources Defense Council Website/www.nrdc.org.

Kennedy, Robert F., Jr. "Crimes Against Nature," *Rolling Stone*, December 11, 2004.

Kennedy, Robert F., Jr. Speech at Wilmington at the 13th Annual Westheimer Peace Symposium at Wilmington College, October 29, 2003.

ALEJANDRO ALVAREZ Camp X-Ray Guantanamo

"A Light Falls on Camp X-Ray," *The Guardian*, January 20, 2004.

Call to Prayer, http://website.lineone.net/~jlancs/adhan.htm.

"Guantanamo Bay—Camp X-Ray," Global Security.org.

"Chronology of Cuba in the Spanish-American War," loc.gov.

"Five Guantanamo Britons to Return to U.K.," *The Guardian*, February 19, 2004.

"History of Cuba Independence," Historyof Cuba.com.

The Spanish American War Centennial Website, SpanAmWar.com:
    Austin, Hather W. "Valeriano Weyler y Nicolau."
    Giessel, Jess. "Black, White and Yellow."
    Daley, Larry. "The Taking of Guantanamo."
    Van Houten, Amy. "Frederic Remington."

"Terror of Torture in Cuba Camp," *London Mirror*, March 12, 2004.

"U.S. Drops Camp X-Ray Turban Ban," *The Guardian*, March 1, 2002.

White House Website (WhiteHouse.gov):
    Address to a Joint Session of Congress and the American People, United States Capitol, Washington, DC, September 20, 2001.

President Meets with Afghan Interim Authority Chairman, January 28, 2002.

President Calls on World Leaders to Condemn Terrorism, March 30, 2002.

Borger, Julian. "Camp X-Ray Hunger Strikers to be Force Fed, *The Guardian*, Monday, April 1, 2002.

Branigan, Tania. "Camp Delta Briton Claims Racial Abuse," *The Guardian*, January 12, 2004.

Christian, Louise. "Guantanamo Bay: A Global Experiment in Inhumanity," *The Guardian*, January 10, 2004.

Cohen, Richard. "Lawless in Guantanamo," Washington Post, January 20, 2004.

Rose, David. "How We Survived Jail Hell (Parts 1 and 2)," *The Guardian*, March 14, 2004.

Engel, Matthew. "Amnesty Sends U.S. Dossier of Complaints over Afghanistan Detainees," *The Guardian*, April 15, 2002.

Left, Sarah. "Guantanamo Bay," *The Guardian*, August 4, 2003.

Meek, James. "People the Law Forgot (Parts 1and 2), The Guardian. Wednesday December 3, 2003.

Rashid, Haroon, "Pakistani Relives Guantanamo Ordeal," BBC News, May 22, 2003.

Rashid, Haroon. "Guantanamo Prisoners Speak Out,"BBC News, November 24, 2003.

Teather, David. "U.S. Plans for Executions at Guantanamo,"The Guardian, June 12, 2003.

SPAIN RODRIGUEZ The War

"Civilians Shot Dead at Checkpoint," CNN.com, April 1, 2003.

"Eyewitness Report: The Toppling of the Statue of Saddam Was a Staged Media Event," SBS Australia/SBS.com.au, April 17, 2003.

"Questions Linger about Hillah Battle that Left Hundreds of Civilian Casualties," Associated Press, May 15, 2003.

Edwards, Rob. "Who 'Suppressed' Scientific Study into Depleted Uranium Cancer Fears in Iraq," *Sunday Herald*, February 22, 2004.

Johnson, Larry. "Iraqi Cancers, Birth Defects Blamed on U.S. Depleted Uranium," *Seattle Post-Intelligencer*, November 12, 2002.

Mackey, Neil. "US Forces Use of Depletion Uranium is Illegal," *Sunday Herald*, March 30, 2003.

Mackey, Neil. "US: 'Saddam Had No Weapons of Mass Destruction,'" *Sunday Herald*, May 4, 2003.

ETHAN PERSOFF & JASUN HUERTA Your Very Own Information Campaign

American Civil Liberties Union Website:
http://www.aclu.org/SafeandFree/SafeandFree.cfm?ID=12126&c=207
http://www.aclu.org/SafeandFree/SafeandFree.cfm?ID=11835&c=206

Center for Democracy and Technology Website:
http://www.cdt.org/security/usapatriot/analysis.shtml

"EFF Analysis of the Provisions of the USA PATRIOT Act that Relate to On-Line Activities," Electronic Frontier Foundation/EFF.org, October 31, 2001.

Jones, Alex. "A Brief Analysis of the Domestic Security Enhancement Act 2003, Also Known as Patriot Act II," Infowars.com.

"PATRIOT Act," Wikipedia.org.

PATRIOT Act On-Line:
http://www.epic.org/privacy/terrorism/hr3162.html
http://www.epic.org/privacy/terrorism/usapatriot/

"PATRIOT Act: A Legal Analysis," Congressional Research Service Report, Library of Congress, April 15, 2002.

SCOTT MARSHALL Snowflake

Alterman, Eric. Salon.com (quoted in englishdaralhayat.com, June 2003).

Brokaw, Tom, quoted in Rotten.com, August 13, 1996.

Butterfield and Lichtblau. "Screening of Prison Officials is Faulted by Lawmakers," *New York Times*, 5/21/04.

Chittister, Joan, OSB. "The Situation Did Not Start in Abu Ghraib," *The National Catholic Reporter*, 5/25/04

Danner, Mark. "The Logic of Torture," *The New York Review of Books*, Vol. 51 No. 11, July 24, 2004.

Decter, Midge. *Rumsfeld: A Personal Portrait*. Random House, 2003.

Dowd, Maureen. "A Neoconservative's Love Ode to Rumsfeld," *New York Times*, September 29, 2003.

Gup, Ted. "Behind Abu Ghraib, an Even Darker Question," *The Village Voice*, May 18, 2004.

Henican, Ellis. "When No News is Bad News," *Newsday*, May 24, 2004.

Hersh, Seymour. "Selective Intelligence," *The New Yorker*, April 6, 2003.

Hersh, Seymour. "Offense and Defense," *The New Yorker*, April 7, 2003.

Hersh, Seymour. "Chain of Command," *The New Yorker*, May 17, 2004.

Hersh, Seymour. "The Gray Zone," *The New Yorker*, May 24, 2004.

Huffington, Arianna. "See Rummy Spin. Spin Rummy Spin," AriannaOnline.com, May 12, 2004.

Ivins, Molly. "Whatever Happened to the Constitution?," Creators Syndicate, June 10, 2004.

Kakutani, Michiko. "How Bush's Advisers Confront the World" (Review of *Rise of the Vulcans: The History of Bush's War Cabinet* by James Mann (Viking), *New York Times*, March 4, 2004.

Kinane, Ed. "Abu Ghraib: It Goes With the Territory," School of the Americas Watch, SOAW.org, May 20, 2004.

Lewis and Schmitt. "Lawyers Decided Bans on Torture Didn't Bind Bush," *New York Times*, June 8, 2004.

Lobe, Jim. "Family Ties Connect US Right, Zionists," Disinfopedia.org, Mach 9, 2003.

Mayer, Jane. "Contract Sport," *The New Yorker*, February 16-23, 2004.

Remnick, David. "Hearts and Minds," *The New Yorker*, May 17, 2004.

Rumsfeld, Donald (interview). Larry King, CNN, December 5, 2001.

Rumsfeld, Donald (interview). Jim Lehrer, PBS, September 11, 2003.

Rumsfeld, Donald. Department of Defense Press Briefings, DefenseLink.mil, September 10, 2001; November 18, 2001; February 12, 2002; April 3, 2002; February 20, 2003; July 9, 2003; September 11, 2003.

Rumsfeld, Donald. Pentagon Press Conference, DefenseLink.mil, August 17, 2001.

"Soldiers Tortured 12-Year-Old Girl in Iraqi Prison," May 8, 2004, Politrix.org (originally posted on ITV.com).

Thill, Scott, interview with Mark Crispin Miller, author of *The Bush Dyslexicon*, in Morphizm.com, January 7, 2003.

Thomas, Evan. "No Good Defense," *Newsweek*, May 12, 2004.

Vest, Jason. "The Men from JINSA and CSP," archives.econ.utah.edu, September 2, 2002.

LLOYD DANGLE Turd Blossom

"The Brains," *The Guardian*, March 9, 2004.

Knutson, Charles. "The Texas Blueprint for the Stolen Election," Democrats.com, November 2002.

Lemann, Nicholas. "The Controller: Karl Rove is Working to Get George Bush Reelected, But He Has Bigger Plans,"*New Yorker*, May 12, 2003.

Madsen, Wayne. "Exposing Karl Rove," CounterPunch.org, November 1, 2002.

Palast, Greg. "The Real Reasons for Blackout 2003, Elections Past and Present and Disenfranchised Voters, "transcript of speech given June 19, 2003, InformationClearing House.info.

Reaves, Jessica. "Person of the Week: Karl Rove," *Time*, November 7, 2002.

Waas, Murray S. "Plugging Leaks, "The American Prospect/Prospect.org, February, 2004.

TED JOUFLAS With Sweetness

Adams, John H. "Condi Rice: Presbyterian with Faith, Political Mettle," *The Presbyterian Layman*, Vol. 33, No. 6, November 22, 2000.

Address of His Holiness Pope John Paul II to the Diplomatic Corps, Vatican.va, January 13, 2003.

Al Batal, Hassan. "Condi Rice: Beware the Woman of Steel," *Palestinian Authority Daily Al-Ayyam*, June 22, 2003.

BBC News, November 6, 2001.

Benjamin, Daniel. "Condi's Phony History," Slate.MSN.com, August 29, 2003.

Burger, Timothy J. "Condi and the 9/11 Commission," CNN.com, December 23, 2003.

Biography of Dr. Condoleezza Rice, National Security Advisor, WhiteHouse.gov.

Biography of Condoleezza Rice, U.S. Department of State.

Caldwell, Deborah. The Pew Forum on Religion and Public Life: "George Bush's Theology: Does President Believe He Has Divine Mandate?," *Religion News Service*, February 12, 2003.

CBS News, May 17, 2002.

"Chevron Redubs Ship Named for Bush Aide," *San Francisco Chronicle*, May 5, 2001.

"Condoleezza Rice," CNN Late Edition, September 8, 2002.

"Condoleezza Rice," *Foreign Affairs*, January/February 2000.

"Condoleezza Rice: Smart, Savvy, Strong-Willed Rice Charts Her Own Course," CNN.com, 2003.

Cheney, Richard (Vice President). Speech to VFW National Convention, August 26, 2002.

Cheney, Richard (Vice President). Address to Air National Guard, Denver, December 1, 2002.

Crew, Adrienne. "BAP Like Me," Salon.com, November 26, 2002.

Daily Telegraph, September 16, 2001.

Dracula (film), Directed by Tod Browning, Screenplay by Garrett Fort, Based on the Novel by Bram Stoker and on the Play by Hamilton Deane and Jon L. Balderston. Universal Studios, 1931.

Felix, Antonia. *Condi: The Condoleezza Rice Story*. Newmarket Press, 2002.

Gee, Marcus. "U.S.-British Campaign Falters," GlobeandMail.com, February 17, 2003.

Hawkins, B. Denise. "Condoleezza Rice's Secret Weapon,"ChristianityToday.com, 2002.

Haygood, Wil. "Honored to Have the Chance: Failure in Life Was Never An Option for 'Condi'," *The Boston Globe*, December 21, 2000.

Heath, Allister. "Recent Developments in U.S. Foreign Policy," *The European Foundation Working Paper 3*, November 1, 2000.

Holy Synod of the Greek Orthodox Church, February 4, 2003.

Jackson, Derrick Z. "A Lesson from Condoleezza Rice," *The Boston Globe*, November 20, 2002.

Keim, Brandon. "Lifting the Star-Spangled Shroud of Silence," CommonDreams.org, May 19, 2002.

Kesler, Glenn, and Slevin, Peter. "Rice under Fire: Security Adviser Blamed for Muddles in Foreign Policy by Bush Administration," *Washington Post*, October 13, 2003.

Knepler, Mike. "Aunt G.'s Favorite Niece: Condoleezza," *Knight Ridder-Tribune*, 2003.

Meacher, Michael, MP. "British MP Attacks U.S. on 9/11 and War," *The Guardian*, September 6, 2003.

Merrill, Warren. "John W. Rice," *Palo Alto Weekly*, May 6, 1998.

Milbank, Dana, and Allen, Mike. "Iraq Flap Shakes Rice's Image," *Washington Post*, July 27, 2003.

Nordlinger, Jay. "Star-in-Waiting: Meet George W.'s Foreign Policy Czarina," *National Review*, August 30, 1999.

Norwich, John Julius. *A Short History of Byzantium*. Knopf Publishing Group, 1998.

Powell, Colin (Secretary of State). Address to the United Nations Security Council, February 5, 2003.

"President Prays at Testing Time," Associated Press, February 6, 2003.

"Press Gaggle with Ari Fleischer and Dr. Condoleezza Rice—Aboard Air Force One—En Route Entebbe, Uganda," The White House, July 11, 2003.

"Rebuilding America's Defenses," Project for the New American Century (PNAC), September 2000.

"Rice on Iraq, War and Politics," PBS.org, September 25, 2002.

Rice, Condoleezza. "A Mission to Build on Common Challenges," *Washington Times* Op-Ed, June 11, 2001.

Rice, Condoleeza. Speech at the Republican National Convention (transcript), *Washington Post*, August 1, 2000.

Rice, Condoleezza. "Walk of Faith," *Washington Times*, August 27, 2002.

Rice, Condoleezza (interview). *Al Jazeera*, March 17, 2003.

Rice, Condoleezza (interview). ZDF German Television, July 31, 2003.

Rice, Condoleezza (interview). *The O'Reilly Factor*, Fox News, September 25, 2003.

Robinson, James. "Velvet Glove Forcefulness: Six Years of Provostial Challenges and Achievements," Stanford Online Report/Stanford.edu, June 9, 1999.

Rumsfeld, Donald (interview). ABC News, March 30, 2003.

Schneider, William. "Marketing Iraq: Why Now?," CNN.com, September 12, 2002.

"Security Adviser Rejects New Probe of Iraq Intelligence," Reuters, January 29, 2004.

Thomas, Evan, and Lipper, Tamara. "Condi in the Hot Seat,"*Newsweek*, August 4, 2003.

"Vanilla Replaces Wine at Convention," Associated Press, Thursday, August 3, 2000.

Vidal, Gore. "Richard Nixon: Not the Best Man's Best Man," *Esquire*, December 1983.

Willam Waldo Cameron Forum on Public Affairs, The George Bush Presidential Library Foundation, 2001.

World Skyscrapers, IkonBoard.com.

Wright, Ben. "Profile: Condoleezza Rice: Mr. Bush's Right-Hand Woman, U.S. Affairs Analyst," BBC.co.uk, September 25, 2001.

ETHAN PERSOFF BLACKS, BABIES, AND BATTERED WOMEN

Recordings

Ashcroft, John and Bacon, Max. *Ashcroft and Bacon: The New Gospel Sound*, 12 songs, 1975, 33-1/3 rpm LP, TRUTH Records. (Recorded when Ashcroft was a Missouri State Auditor and Bacon a Missouri State Representative.)

Johnson, Robert. "Me and the Devil Blues,"78 rpm, Vocalion.

Eno, Brian and Byrne, David. "America is Waiting" from *My Life in the Bush of Ghosts*, 1981, 33-1/3 rpm LP, Sire.

Books

Ashcroft, John. *On My Honor: The Beliefs That Shape My Life*. Thomas Nelson Publishers, 2001.

Ashcroft, John. *Lessons from a Father to His Son*. Thomas Nelson Publishers, 1998.

Veerman, David R. and Barton, Bruce B. *When Your Father Dies: How a Man Deals with the Loss of His Father*. Nelson Books, 2003.

Dash, Samuel. *The Intruders: Unreasonable Searches and Seizures from King John to John Ashcroft*. Rutgers University Press, 2004.

Supplemental Reading

Ashcroft, John and Strauss, Annette. *Families First: Report on the National Commission on America's Urban Families*. G.P.O. Superintendent of Documents, 1993.

Ashcroft, John. *Racial Profiling Within Law Enforcement Agencies: Hearing Before the Committee on the Judiciary, U.S. Senate*, Diane Publishing Company.

On-Line Information

People For The American Way (absolutely necessary and biting one-stop summary of Ashcroft's entire Missouri record, heavily researched and footnoted): http://www.pfaw.org/pfaw/general/default.aspx?oid=2355

National Organization for Women Website (type Ashcroft into search box for many documents): http://www.now.org/

People v. Ashcroft Website: http://www.peoplevashcroft.com/bio/bio.asp

The Dossiers on Ashcroft (growing archive of abuse and threats): http://dossiers.genfoods.net/ashcroft.html

Rotten on Ashcroft: http://www.rotten.com/library/bio/usa/john-ashcroft/

AUTHOR'S NOTE: All information found in this piece can be found true by looking up grouped phrases, for example: ashcroft+planned+parenthood, and ashcroft+missouri+bio etc.

MARK LANDMAN THE MAN IN THE SHADOWS

Abramson, Barry. "Power Company Stocks Fall," Associated Press, May 31, 2001.

Bryce, Robert. "The Candidate from Root and Brown," *Texas Observer*, October 6, 2000.

"The Bush-Cheney Energy Plan, Players, Profits and Paybacks," National Resources Defense Council.

Cheney, Richard (interview). John King, CNN.

Cheney, Richard (interview). *Meet the Press*, NBC, September 8, 2002; March 14, 2003; September 14, 2003.

Cheney, Richard (interview). *This Week*, ABC, July-August 2004.

Cheney, Richard. Speech to VFW National Convention, August 26, 2003 (broadcast on *PBS Front Line*).

Hersh, Seymour. "The Stovepipe," *The New Yorker*, October 27, 2003.

Ireland, Doug. "Tricky Dick," *The Nation*, August 21, 2000.

"Justice Scalia Defends Hunting Trip with Cheney," Associated Press (*USA Today*/USAToday.com) February 11, 2004.

Lobe, Jim. "Cheney's Mask is Slipping," Inter Press Service, October 1, 2003.

Lobe, Jim. "Baker's Return Spells Cheney's Heartburn," Inter Press Service, December 16, 2003.

Mayer, Jane. "Contract Sport," *The New Yorker*, February 16-23, 2004.

Pierce, Greg. "Cheney's Turning Point," *Washington Times*, May 4, 2001.

Press, Bill. "Dick Cheney is the Perfect Choice—for Democrats," CNN.com, July 27, 2000.

Shapiro, Bruce. "The Republicans' Type-A Politics," Salon.com, November 22, 2000.

USA Today, January 18, 2001.

Washington Post, February 12, 2004.

Washington Post, June 23, 2001.

"World Domination with a Plastic-Metal Ticker," *Sydney Morning Herald*, October 5, 2003.

RECOMMENDED READING

Dowbenko, Uri. Bushwhacked: *Inside True Stories of True Conspiracy*. Conspiracy Digest, 2003.

Martin, Al. *The Conspiratores: Secrets of an Iran-Contra Insider*. National Liberty Press, 2002.

Palast, Greg. *The Best Democracy Money Can Buy*. Pluto Press, 2002.

Reed, Terry, and Cummings, John. *Compromised: Clinton, Bush and the CIA*. Shapolsky Publishers, 1994.

Sick, Gary. *October Surprise: America's Hostages in Iran and the Election of Reagan*. Random House, 1992.

Thomas, Kenn, and Keith, Jim. *The Octopus: Secret Government and the Death of Danny Casolaro*. Feral House, 1996.

Contributors

✶✶✭✶✶

ALEJANDRO ALVAREZ This is the second publication of this Argentine cartoonist. The first was in *Stripburger* #37. You can spot some of his comics and illustrations at http://mx.geocities.com/illoton.

STEVE BRODNER was born in Brooklyn, New York, in 1954. He has been a satirical illustrator for 27 years. His caricatures of pop and political culture have appeared in *The New York Times Book Review, Harper's, The National Lampoon, Sports Illustrated, Playboy, Spy, Esquire,* and many more publications. In visual essays, he has covered seven national political conventions for *Esquire, The Progressive, The Village Voice,* and others. His article, "Plowed Under," a series of portraits and interviews with beleaguered farm families in the Midwest, ran in *The Progressive.* "Shot From Guns," an art documentary about the Colt Firearms strike in Hartford, Connecticut appeared in *Northeast Magazine* in 1989. For *The New Yorker* he covered Oliver North and the 1994 Virginia Senate race, the Patrick Buchanan presidential campaign, the Million Man March, and an advance story on the Democratic Convention in Chicago. His eight-page profile of George W. Bush appeared in *Esquire* in October 1998. His first book, *Fold 'N Tuck,* was published in 1990 by Doubleday. His animated film and book *Davy Crockett* was produced by Rabbit Ears Productions in 1992. From 1992-97, his weekly feature "Tomorrow's News Tonight" was syndicated nationally and his cartoons are a regular feature in *The Nation.* In 1998 he designed and painted the movie poster for Warren Beatty's "Bulworth." He has won awards from the Society of Illustrators, American Illustration, Communication Arts, the Society of Newspaper Design and the Society of Publication Design, and in 2000 the Aronson Award for Social Justice Journalism. He lives in New York City with his wife, writer and actress Anne Pasquale and their 15-year-old daughter, Terry. *Freedom Fries* is a lush, coffee table retrospective of 30 years of Steve Brodner's political cartooning (Fantagraphics Books). His website is www.stevebrodner.com.

JAIME CRESPO is a native Californian and Chicano artist/musician who has had many comic strips ("Tales form the Edge of Hell") and comic book titles (*La Casa Loca, Narcolepsy Dreams*) published over the past 25 years. He currently contributes the comic strip "No Fun" to the *North Bay Bohemian* in Santa Rosa, California. Also, for more than four years, he has hosted a radio program on KWMR in Pt. Reyes Station, California, which focuses on musical genres and the artists who create them. He has had many group, as well as solo, art shows throughout the U.S. and abroad, and plays several musical instruments, torturing the local masses on occasion with public musical appearances.

LLOYD DANGLE is an illustrator, writer, and cartoonist whose works have appeared in over 100 publications of every type, from the crusty mainstream to the sub-sub alternative. His weekly comic strip, "Troubletown," has been a self-syndicated feature in alternative newsweeklies since the late 1980s and is currently appearing in 25 publications. He has exhibited in the United States and abroad and published numerous collections of his cartoons. An artists' activist, Lloyd recently finished serving as the national president of the Graphic Artists Guild. He lives with wife, Hae Yuon Kim, and son, Oscar, in Oakland, California.

URI DOWBENKO (www.uridowbenko.com) is an artist, writer and publisher. His recent books include *Bushwhacked: Inside Stories of True Conspiracy* (2002) and *Hoodwinked: Watching Movies with Eyes Wide Open* (2004). He is also the founder of Alternative Media websites: *Al Martin Raw* (www.almartinraw. com), *Conspiracy Planet* (www.conspiracyplanet.com), *Steamshovel Press* (www.steamshovelpress.com) and *Conspiracy Digest* (www.conspiracydigest.com). He can be reached at virtualagency@yahoo.com or by snail mail at P.O. Box 43, Pray, Montana 59065.

JEM EATON, who contributes and writes the introduction to Hack Smith's "Poppy the President," lives in

Seattle, where he is currently a self-employed artist, working for such clients as *The Village Voice*, Walt Disney Productions, and Sub Pop Records. His comics have been published by Fantagraphics Books and other alternative imprints. He previously managed an Arthur Treacher's Fish and Chip Restaurant in Breezewood, Pennsylvania.

SCOTT GILBERT drew the weekly comic strip "True Artist Tales" for more than ten years, won a Xeric Grant in 1995, and collaborated with Harvey Pekar in 1996. He has a portrait of Charles Bukowski tattooed on his right eyelid and one of Philip Guston on his left. He believes that someday a real rain will come and wash all the scum off the streets.

ADAM GORIGHTLY is the author of *Kerry Thornley: The Prankster and the Conspiracy* (a biography of the enigmatic counter-cultural figure who was a Marine buddy of Lee Harvey Oswald) and *The Shadow over Santa Susana: Black Magic, Mind Control, and the Manson Family Mythos* (widely recognized as the definitive book on the Manson family). His articles have appeared in magazines such as *The Excluded Middle, Crash Collusion, UFO Magazine, Paranoia, Steamshovel Press, Pills-a-go-go, Dagobert's Revenge, Elf Infested Spaces*, and *Saucer Smear*.

GARY GROTH is the co-founder of Fantagraphics Books and the company's flagship magazine, *The Comics Journal*, and continues to be an ebullient and beloved presence in the comics profession. He has published many interviews, essays, and commentaries in the *Journal* since its inception in 1976. His interviews are currently being collected in book form (*Jack Kirby*, 2001; *R. Crumb*, 2003; *Drawing the Line: Jules Feiffer, Ralph Steadman, David Levine, Edward Sorel*, 2004).

ALBO HELM has been active in comix and cartooning since the 1970s, publishing both in Dutch alternative and mainstream media. In the past year he was the editor of the anthologies *Bulkboek Strip Special* and *Lowlands Comic 2003*, and founder/editor of the Utrecht-based comics quarterly *De Inktpot*. *Soloproject* were the collection of comic shorts 'WoordOp!' and a full color children's SF-comic called *Trashball 4*. Several of his longer stories were part of educational projects. He is the founder and former chairman of the Dutch/ Flemish NuKomix-organisation (www.nukomix.nl).

JASUN HUERTA created alternative comic art for publications in the late 1980s and early 1990s. Some of these publications were Dennis Worden's *Cruel and Unusual Punishment*, Stephen Beaupre's *Buzzard*, and Mark Landman's *Buzz*. Since then, he has concentrated on generating fine art pieces for group art shows and a two-man show with Mack White, known as "Two Zombie Hands for Sister Sarah," a show of surreal western comic art. Jasun currently creates art for various printed products and publications in his own neck of the woods (Austin, Texas) for bands, film festivals, and newspaper and magazine articles. *The Bush Junta* marks his return to comics.

ALEX JONES is a documentary filmmaker, syndicated radio talk show host, and an outspoken enemy of the dark forces of global government. *The Wall Street Journal, USA Today*, and *The Washington Post* are just a few of the publications that have featured him. He has been a guest on hundreds of radio and television shows around the world. His explosive documentaries (which include *9/11: The Road to Tyranny, Police State 2000*, and *Dark Secrets Inside Bohemian Grove*) have sent shockwaves throughout the United States by exposing the evil plans of the criminal elite to turn earth into a prison planet. In 2003, he won the Project Censored Award for his analysis of the PATRIOT Act. He is the author of the book *9/11: Descent into Tyranny*. His websites are www.infowars.com and www.prisonplanet.com.

TED JOUFLAS was born in Utah and raised in Los Angeles, California. He has published two graphic novels, *Scary!* and *Filthy*. His most recent work is *APE, Son of Vision Thing*, a 32-page comic that fuses the Bush Administration with the horror films of the 1930s.

PETER KUPER is a comic artist and illustrator whose work has appeared in *Time, Newsweek, The New York Times, Washington Post, The Village Voice*, and *MAD*, where he illustrates "SPY vs. SPY." His "Eye of the Beholder" was the first comic strip to regularly appear in *The New York Times* and is now syndicated nationally to alternative papers. *Rolling Stone* named him Comic Book Artist of the Year in 1995 and he has won awards from *American Illustration*, *Print*, Society of Illustrators, and *Communication Arts*, among others. His comics have been translated into German, Italian, Portuguese, Swedish, Spanish and Greek and his artwork has been exhibited around the world. He has written and illustrated many books, including *ComicsTrips*, a journal of the artist's eight-month journey through Africa and Southeast Asia. Other graphic works include *Stripped– An Unauthorized Autobiography* and *The System*, a wordless graphic novel. He has also done adaptations of Upton Sinclair's *The Jungle* and *GIVE IT UP!*, adapting nine Franz Kafka short stories. His most recent books include *Topsy Turvy*, a collection of political comic strips, *Mind's Eye*, an "Eye of the Beholder" collection, and *SPEECHLESS*, a coffee table art book covering his career to date. In 1979, he co-founded the political comix magazine *World War 3 Illustrated* with Seth Tobocman and remains on its editorial board.

MARK LANDMAN was born in San Francisco in 1953, and grew up influenced by the comic book art of Kirby, Wood, Ditko, Swan, and Eisner, great paperback reprints of EC horror comics and *MAD* (Elder and Kurtzman!), Warren's *Creepy* and *Eerie*, underground comix (Crumb!), and the psychedelic poster art of the 1960s. Mark was among the first cartoonists to utilize the computer to create comics, with work appearing in *BLAB!*, *Blue Loco*, *Buzz*, *Snarf*, *RAW's The Narrative Corpse*, *Weirdo*, *Heavy Metal*, *Suburban High Life*, *Centrifugal Bumble-Puppy*, and the *Republicans Attack!* card set with Jim Vance. His graphic work has also been seen in *Mondo 2000*, *Europeo*, *Audio Video Interiors*, *Wired*, *Hypno*, and *Time Magazine*. His "Fetal Elvis" character appears semi-regularly in *BLAB!* and was selected for inclusion in *American Illustration* 21. Recently retiring after 28 years from the Novato Fire District, "The Man in the Shadows" is the first strip done with his newfound spare time and marks a departure from the style of his previous work.

SCOTT MARSHALL is an artist and musician living and working in New York City. He has composed original dance scores for choreographers Lar Lubovitch, Scott Rink, and others. He contributed a commissioned audio collage to a scene in Woody Allen's film *Small Time Crooks*. His video work has received two Brooklyn Arts Council grants. He has had essays and artwork published by Autonomedia, Brooklyn. His website is http://subliminal.org/paniculture.

DAVID PALEO is a cartoonist and illustrator. You can see more of his work in various publications, such as *The Comics Journal Special*, Kristine McKenna's *Talk to Her*, *Legal Action Comics #2*, *House of Twelve #3* and toothpaste tubes all over his native Argentina.

ETHAN PERSOFF is a 29-year-old cartoonist, writer, and sound designer who previously lived in Chicago and Denver and currently lives in Austin, Texas. His work has appeared in *Zero Zero*, *Comix 2000* and on the alternative comics subscription site, Serializer.net. The first two issues of *The Pogostick*, a Harvey-nominated comics collaboration with Al Columbia, are available from Fantagraphics Books. Persoff's website (www.ep.tc) has been awarded "best weird/extreme" two years in a row at the SXSW Interactive festival—and contains numerous comics and sound projects, including the *Teddy* and *A Dog* and *His Elephant* stories, and the *SNAP!* mp3. He can be contacted at P.O. Box 7254, Austin, TX 78713 or by email at epersoff@yahoo.com.

SASA RAKEZIC (a.k.a. Aleksandar Zograf) was born in 1963 and started publishing comics in various Serbian magazines in 1986. Starting in the 1990s, most of his work has been published abroad, in magazines such as *Weirdo*, *The Comics Journal*, *Zero Zero*, *Rare Bit Fiends*, *Buzzard*, *The Stranger*, *New City*, *Cow* (U.S.), *Lapin* (France), *Mano*, *Il Manifesto*, *Linus*, *Kerosene*, *Mondo Naif*, *Black* (Italy), *Babel* (Greece), *Galago* (Sweden), *Stripburger* (Slovenia), *Das Magazin*, *Zur Zeit*, *Strapazin* (Switzerland), *Fidus* (Norway), *Nostros somos los muertos* (Spain), *ZONE5300* (Holland), *Sturgein White Moss* (U.K.). His solo books include *Life Under Sanctions* (Fantagraphics), *Psychonaut #1-2* (Fantagraphics), *Psychonaut #3* (Monster Pants Comics/ Freight Films, 1999), *Flock of Dreamers* (Kitchen Sink Press), and *Dream Watcher* (Slab-O-Concrete). During the NATO bombing campaign in Serbia, he wrote e-mail messages that were posted on the Internet in many countries and later collected in the book *Bulletins from Serbia*.

TED RALL At age 41, Rall is one of America's most prolific and controversial syndicated cartoonists. Notorious recently for his portrayal of George W. Bush as the tin-pot dictator "Generalissimo El Busho," the two-time RFK Award winner and Pulitzer Prize finalist is also the author of more than a dozen books, including the graphic novels *My War with Brian* and *To Afghanistan and Back* and the new collection *Generalissimo El Busho: Essays and Cartoons on the Bush Years* (NBM) and an all-prose political manifesto, *Wake Up, You're Liberal!: How We Can Take America Back from the Right* (Soft Skull Press). A liberal talk radio pioneer and Central Asia addict, Rall is currently working on a new book about that region.

LARRY RODMAN is an artist and teacher, and has been a contributing writer to *The Comics Journal*, and other fine publications, since the Reagan administration.

SPAIN RODRIGUEZ was born in 1940 in Buffalo, New York. He first gained fame as one of the founders of the underground comix movement of the 1960s. After drawing comics in New York for the *East Village Other*, he moved to San Francisco where he joined Robert Crumb and other artists on *Zap Comix*. Spain's early years with the Road Vultures Motorcycle Club and his coverage of the 1968 Democratic Convention in Chicago as a reporter for the *East Village Other* are chronicled in his collection *My True Story* (Fantagraphics). Spain's recent work includes the online comic *The Dark Hotel* at www.salon.com, *Sherlock Holmes' Strangest Cases*, and *Nightmare Alley*, his adaptation of William Linday Gresham's 1930s novel.

MARCEL RUIJTERS (pronounced 'writers'). Born 1966 in Holland. Draws comics since age seven. A typical art school dropout, he starts self-publishing his work in 1988, with *Thank God It's Ugly* as his most notable anthology series. Paints and does three-dimensional work, writes comic criticism and is an editor for the Dutch magazine *ZONE5300*. Contributes to numerous international underground publications, like *Hopital Brut*, *Malefact* and *Stripburger*. Four *Troglodytes* books with Oog&Blik and Top Shelf. Currently working on a new book, based on medieval imagery. Inspired by Forteana of all ages.

KENNETH R. SMITH was born in Austin, Texas, and got a BA from the University of Texas at Austin, then an MA and Ph.D. from Yale University. He taught philosophy at LSU/BR from 1972-83 and at the University of Dallas and University of North Texas from 1990 to 1995. His *Phantasmagoria* was well received from 1971 to 1977, for its five-issue run. He has published over 20 portfolios of his fantasy art, as well as *Succubus*, a collection from Eros and *Phantasmagoria II* from Fantagraphics. He contributed stories and art to *Heavy Metal*, *Prime Cuts*, and *Taboo* in the early 1990s. He has been interviewed three times in *The Comics Journal* and wrote a philosophy column, "Dramas of the Mind," and then another, "End Times," and is currently initiating a new column, "Time Out of Joint," all for *The Comics Journal*. He publishes his philosophy books under the imprint Memnon Press, and after *Otherwise* and *Webs* he is currently working on the third book in that series, *Minotaur*. He produces email-criticism and commentaries for subscribers from kensmith@texas.net.

RALPH STEADMAN was born in 1936. He started as a cartoonist and through the years diversified into many fields of creativity. He has illustrated such classics as *Alice in Wonderland*, *Treasure Island*, and *Animal Farm*. His own books include the lives of Sigmund Freud and Leonardo da Vinci and *The Big I Am*, the story of God. With American writer Hunter S. Thompson, he collaborated in the birth of GONZO journalism, the definitive book in the genre being *Fear and Loathing in Las Vegas*, which was made into a feature film. He is also a printmaker. His prints include a series of etchings on writers from William Shakespeare to William Burroughs. In 1989 he wrote the libretto for an eco-oratorio called *Plague and the Moonflower* which has been performed in five cathedrals in the UK and was the subject of a BBC 2 film in 1994. He has traveled the world's vineyards and distilleries for Oddbins, which culminated in his two prize-winning books, *The Grapes of Ralph* and *Still Life With Bottle*. He has an Honorary D. Litt from the University of Kent.

CAROL SWAIN Born London (Cuban Missile Crisis). First comic work: *Way Out Strips* (Cold War, Mutually Assured Destruction). Most recent work: *Foodboy*, a graphic novel from Fantagraphics (War on Terror).

SETH TOBOCMAN is a comic book artist who has been speaking truth to power for over 25 years. In 1980 he founded the radical comic book *World War 3 Illustrated* with Peter Kuper. They continue to publish that magazine today. Tobocman has worked for *The New York Times*, *The Village Voice*, *Heavy Metal*, *Real Girl*, *Real Stuff*, and many other publications. He has three books in print: *You Don't Have To Fuck People Over To Survive* (Soft Skull Press), *War in the Neighborhood* (Autonomedia), and *Portraits of Israelis and Palestinians* (Soft Skull Press). His next book, *No Blood 4 Oil*, will be out in 2005.

PENNY VAN HORN Originally from Rye, New York, she has lived in Austin, Texas, since 1984. She is a cartoonist, illustrator and animator. Although in the past she has predominantly worked in black-and-white, using scratchboard or linoleum/woodblock, she has recently been branching out with some color work in a looser style which draws upon her printing and drawing experience and her work with cartooning, using silk screen and mixed media. Currently she is screen-printing t-shirts with various designs and making reversible Bush/Cheney voodoo doll/dog toys, and screen-printed baby quilts. Her recent work can be found at the store Moxie and the Compound. Her illustrations have appeared regularly in *The Austin Chronicle*, *The Austin American-Statesman* (XLent) and *The Texas Observer*. She is the author of *Recipe for Disaster and Other Stories*, *The Librarian*, and her comics have also been featured in *Wimmen's Comix*, *Twisted Sisters #1 & 2*, *Snake Eyes*, *Weirdo*, *Zero Zero*, *The Comics Journal*, and many more publications. She began animating in 2000, working on the movie *Waking Life* by Rick Linklater and animation director Bob Sabiston. She has also worked on additional animated features by Bob Sabiston such as *Yard* and *Grasshopper*, and an animated segment for the PBS series *Life 360*. Her website is www.pennyvanhorn.com.

MACK WHITE was born in 1952 in Mineral Wells, Texas. His comics and illustrations have appeared in *The Comics Journal Specials*, *Details*, *PULSE!*, *Heavy Metal*, *True West*, *Old West Journal*, *The Austin American-Statesman* (XLnt), *Zero Zero*, *Snake Eyes*, *Buzz*, *Zone5300*, *El Vibora*, *Strapazin*, *Stripburger*, and many more publications in the U.S., Japan, and Europe. He also wrote and illustrated the comic books *The Mutant Book of the Dead* (Starhead) and *Villa of the Mysteries* #1, 2, and 3 (Fantagraphics) and in 1998 illustrated Ken Smith's book *Raw Deal: Horrible and Ironic Stories of Forgotten Americans* (Blast Books). Recently his artwork was included in the highly acclaimed touring art show *Raw, Boiled, and Cooked: Comics on the Verge*. A conspiracy researcher for many years, his articles have appeared in such publications as *The Nose*, *FringeWare Review*, *Austin ParaTimes*, and *The Universal Seduction Vol. 3*. In addition, he has lectured on conspiracy research at the University of Texas at Austin, was interviewed in the documentary *Day 51: The True Story of Waco*, and is frequently a guest on radio and television talk shows. He is currently writing and illustrating a western novel, *Border Roll*. His websites are www.mackwhite.com and www.bisonbill.com.